THE BANTAM
CONCISE HANDBOOK OF ENGLISH
Is Designed to Offer Help

If you find it hard to begin work on a
writing assignment

If you are not always certain about whether
your sentences are grammatically correct

If you need help in punctuation

If your writing lacks strength or polish

In short, **THE BANTAM CONCISE HAND-
BOOK OF ENGLISH** is a textbook and ready
reference for all writers—from high school to
college and beyond.

THE BANTAM CONCISE HANDBOOK OF ENGLISH

Eugene Ehrlich

BANTAM BOOKS
TORONTO · NEW YORK · LONDON · SYDNEY · AUCKLAND

THE BANTAM CONCISE HANDBOOK OF ENGLISH

A Bantam Book / August 1986

Grateful acknowledgment is made for permission to reprint the following:

Thomas Wolfe, excerpted from Look Homeward, Angel. *Copyright 1929 Charles Scribner's Sons; copyright renewed © 1957 Edward C. Aswell, as Administrator, C.T.A. of the Estate of Thomas Wolfe, and/or Fred W. Wolfe. Reprinted with the permission of Charles Scribner's Sons.*

Paragraph from TRB in The New Republic, *June 17, 1978. Excerpted by permission of* The New Republic, *copyright © 1978.*

"The Mightiest Power Plant" by Waldemar Kaempffert, April 2, 1950, The New York Times Magazine. *Copyright 1950 by The New York Times Company. Reprinted by permission.*

Excerpt from the article "English Traits" by Henry Steele Commager. First printed in The Atlantic Monthly, *August 1948. Reprinted by the permission of the author.*

Excerpt from "The Sealed Treasure" by Saul Bellow. Copyright © 1960 by Saul Bellow. Reprinted by permission of the author.

ISBN 0-553-25552-5

Published simultaneously in the United States and Canada

PRINTED IN THE UNITED STATES OF AMERICA

0   0 9 8 7 6 5 4 3 2 1

Contents

This book is dedicated to
Samuel Alexander Ehrlich
and Michael Oliver Ehrlich

Preface

You do not have to be a professional writer to understand the importance of good writing. Everyone experienced in business and the professions knows that skill in writing can further careers and advance personal recognition. Most engineers, for example, do more writing than many novelists, and the engineers selected for promotion are usually those with a proven ability to write clearly and convincingly. Scientists spend much of their time detailing their findings in professional reports and published articles, and it is by this work that they establish their reputations. Scholars in every field consider publication part of their career responsibility. People in business frequently write letters, memorandums, and proposals, and a successful business career often depends on the ability to write well.

Oddly enough, we are reluctant to trust our writing, though the skill should be easy to achieve. We have few problems with language when we speak with our friends, and often the letters we write present no difficulty at all. Yet when we are required to write a paper or report, especially in school and at work, the job of putting our thoughts down clearly may present grave problems. We put the task off until the last possible moment, and when we finally get down to it, few of us feel we have done our best. Are we afraid of making errors? Do we feel we have nothing to say? Are we embarrassed to commit our thoughts to paper, where others will read them?

But writing problems can be overcome. The suggestions and advice in this book are based on my work in helping many writers improve their ability to express themselves. I have taught for more than thirty years in colleges and universities; I have also edited the work of professional writers, scientists, engineers, and business people at Bell Labs, Du-Pont, American Telephone & Telegraph, United Technologies, and many other organizations. I have also written and edited many books of my own.

It is my hope that this book will help you improve your writing by showing you ways to organize your thoughts, and to overcome the almost universal problem of getting started on a piece of writing. It is also my hope that this book will provide answers to troublesome questions of grammar and usage.

Eugene Ehrlich
Department of English and
    Comparative Literature,
Columbia University

PART I

WRITING AS A SKILL

CHAPTER 1

Good Writing Is Good Thinking

ARRANGING YOUR THOUGHTS

Much of the writing done in schools and at work has the purpose of winning readers over to a point of view. Basic to a writer's effectiveness, then, are knowledge of the subject and a firmly expressed opinion. While it is generally quite easy to gather the necessary information, you may not always find it so simple to discover your own point of view, state it clearly, and stick with it throughout the argument in a convincing manner.

Few subjects worth writing about can be seen from a single perspective. Different opinions are persuasively and regularly expressed, for example, on such problems as inflation, energy, arms limitation, and national security. And national interest is only one of the many areas that engage the human mind. A technical report, for instance, may need to present, along with a recital of progress to date, good reasons for continuing or abandoning the particular project. A letter to the editor of the newspaper should convince readers, for example, to vote for or against a revision of the local charter.

You may believe that you know what you think when you sit down to write. But as you do your research and arrange your information, you will often find that you do not have sufficient understanding. Your work in collecting information will usually shape your attitude, and your final position on your subject may not emerge until you actually begin to write.

Writing is a way of expressing thinking. Writing sharpens stray thoughts; the full realization of where you stand on a question may become clear only *after* the first draft is completed. The job then becomes one of making certain that the second draft organizes the facts and supporting arguments in a way that will convince readers that your position is the correct one.

This process is most important for professional reports—arguing, for example, that the acquisition of five more computer terminals will improve office efficiency and increase business profits—and for political statements—arguing, for example, the desirability of a nuclear freeze. But a similar procedure applies to every kind of writing, even fiction. In describing a landscape, for example, the novelist must make certain that the types of trees said to surround a certain house really do grow in that part of the world; and that the way the description is worded conveys the sense of desolation or happiness or mystery that is an essential part of the story.

It is good to remember that the skills that make for effective writing differ only slightly for the various kinds of writing people do. The chapters that follow will deal with the most essential of the skills—organization, vocabulary, and grammar. But before any of the techniques can be usefully applied, before you pick up your pen or sit down at the typewriter, you have to prepare your most important tool: your mind. Logical thinking precedes effective writing and accompanies it down to the final revision.

COMMON ERRORS IN THINKING

Unsupported Opinion vs. Fact

One of the most common expressions we hear and read is *the fact that* . . . In truth what follows these three words is seldom a fact; what we usually get is the speaker's or writer's opinion.

When a writer states, *It is a fact that Victorians led highly moral private lives,* without giving any evidence in support, this claim does not convince an intelligent reader, who might suspect that Victorians were much like the people who preceded them and the people who followed them. In the absence of evidence to the contrary, then, the reader may believe that the entire statement is not true.

Unjustified Generalizing

Writers are free to make general statements, but they must present facts to support these claims. Unless a statement expresses common knowledge— Seattle has a great deal of rain, Japanese automobiles have found ready acceptance in the United States, ocean breezes are welcome on a hot day—it must be supported. Facts must be presented to support any claim that is not an obvious truth, and from these facts the writer must draw conclusions logically and convincingly in order to persuade the reader.

Contrary Evidence

When evidence exists that appears to contradict an argument you wish to make, you should never ignore such evidence. Rather, it must be presented and your case must be argued in the face of it, by presenting more convincing evidence to support your point. For example:

Although some baseball players undoubtedly are intelligent—Moe Berg was a linguist as well as a big-league catcher—some I have known and others I have read about have had difficulty even in signing their names on their multimillion-dollar contracts. Big-league baseball may not require a high degree of intelligence, but it is disturbing to many that baseball players receive handsome salaries while thousands of highly qualified scholars work for little—when they are fortunate enough to find work. It is this unfairness in the way our society distributes its rewards that makes one wonder whether we can expect to attract able people to careers in the arts, education, and government.

This brief paragraph strengthens the point it makes—everyone may suffer as a result of the wide differences in pay that society gives its working people—by immediately acknowledging that there are exceptions to the generalization presented: some baseball players are less intelligent than many people who are less amply rewarded. If the paragraph had started out with an unjustified generalization, *Baseball players are stupid*, the argument might have foundered right there.

Circular Reasoning

A writer may open a discussion with a statement intended to present a truth. Instead of supporting the statement with evidence, however, the writer may go on to restate the subject in a slightly different form and, at the end of the discussion, repeat the original statement as though it had been proved. This process is called *circular reasoning*.

We cannot solve our energy problems until we overcome our wasteful use of petroleum. Automobiles consume a great deal of fuel, as do home heating plants and private airplanes. When we begin to recognize the necessity of stopping our waste of petroleum, we will be able to solve the energy problem.

This paragraph has not supported its argument at all—indeed, nothing has been said about solving the energy problem. All the writer has done is list some examples of fuel use. The reader is none the wiser about energy problems and possible solutions after this example of circular reasoning.

After This, Therefore Because of This

Even when one event follows another, the first may not have caused the second.

I lost the race because I missed training for two days.

In truth, the loss may have been due to many other factors having nothing to do with missed training.

Appealing to Emotion Rather than to Reason

Emotional appeals have their place, but not in writing that calls for solid facts and sound logic. Erroneous appeals to emotion can appear in several guises.

Flattery   *Any intelligent person will agree with me when I say . . .*

Such words are designed to appeal to the reader's vanity. What is important is the claim that follows and how well it is supported. You gain nothing by starting a sentence this way.

Bandwagon   *Everybody in the college is now convinced that . . .*

Even if the claim were true—and it is highly unlikely that everyone in any college is convinced of anything—the statement that follows such words must stand on its own. The writer can convince readers only by presenting solid facts and by reasoning carefully from those facts. Trying to persuade readers to jump on a bandwagon—because everyone is doing something, you ought to do it too—is seldom effective when writing for intelligent readers.

The Golden Bandwagon   *The truly intelligent understand that . . .*

This cross between flattery and the bandwagon effect implies that the reader must be part of the group the writer claims as supporters. Again, the argument must be judged only on the facts presented and the logic of the reasoning that follows.

Name-calling   *The unscrupulous legislators who supported this bill will soon be turned out by the voters.*

Labeling legislators *unscrupulous* or anything else does not prove that they are wrong.

> *The dangerous notions of my fascist opponent would subvert good government.*

The words *dangerous*, *fascist*, and *subvert* are designed to appeal to the emotions. What support does the writer have for these words? The writer also speaks of *good government*. What proof has been presented that the writer's notion of government is worthy of being called good? What is needed instead is solid evidence that these emotionally charged words are justified by the facts.

THE WRITTEN ARGUMENT

Any paper, memorandum, proposal, or thesis—whether no more than a page long or hundreds of pages long—must be more tightly structured than a string of loose sentences, broken now and then into paragraphs. Each sentence you write must assist in the development of the paragraph of which it is a part. Each paragraph you write must deal with a single topic. Finally, the topic treated in each paragraph must relate directly to the subject of the entire work. When you have finished all your work—from your first vague thoughts on the subject through final rewriting, typing, and proofreading—you must have covered your subject to your own satisfaction and the satisfaction of your reader. What is necessary for a good paragraph will be discussed in Chapter 4, and sentence structure is dealt with in Chapter 5. But once again, before techniques can be effective, the thought processes underlying the paper's intention are of greatest importance.

You will satisfy your reader only if your entire paper shows the same sense of organization displayed in each well-organized paragraph and sentence. All your writing must be directed toward the theme discussed in the paper, and you must check your work after you complete your first draft to see that you have not strayed from that theme.

Just as you can most easily organize an individual paragraph by writing a topic sentence, you can best organize an entire paper by having your theme in mind before you begin to write. Knowing what you are trying to convey in the paper enables you to write confidently and easily. You may not know yet the precise conclusions your research will justify, but you ought to be clear in your mind, for example, whether your paper will deal with recent developments in electronics or with early discoveries leading to technological innovations or with both. If you do not have some concrete idea of what you want to say before you begin to write, you may make a number of false starts before you realize what you want to tell your reader.

Nevertheless, it is far better to begin to write without knowing where your thoughts will lead you than to sit and stare at a blank page while waiting for inspiration to strike or your thinking to sort itself out. If you begin by writing down anything that comes to mind, sooner or later a theme will emerge; this theme will organize your thinking and make it possible for you to write effectively. It is in the subsequent rewriting that you will sharpen your paper, making it unified and cohesive.

A well-organized piece of writing will fall roughly into three parts. These may be thought of as introduction, body, and conclusion.

An introduction tells the reader what the paper will discuss and stirs the reader's interest in the subject. The first purpose can be accomplished in several ways. You may state the theme of the entire paper; you may state the questions you are going to answer; or you may give the background of the questions or problems you are going to discuss. You may accomplish the second purpose—supplying the reader with good reasons to go on—by beginning with a striking quotation from a respected source you have been studying. You can dramatize your subject by citing a pertinent newspaper headline, a statement by a public official or expert in your subject, or facts that call attention to the importance of the subject. One of the best ways is to make the boldest claim you can. (But be sure to substantiate it later on.) By the time the reader has come to the end of the introduction—whether a single paragraph or several pages long—you will have made clear what the subject is and why the reader should continue reading.

The body of a paper develops and supports the theme established in the introduction, supplying the information that will convince the reader to accept the writer's point of view. Many types of paragraphs are appropriate to explain and expand and support the theme convincingly (see Chapter 4). To develop a particular point, you may relate facts or incidents chronologically, you may classify information, you may compare or contrast two ideas, and you may supply definitions. You may also divide large topics into their logical parts, and you may illustrate the truth of what you are saying by providing specific examples to support your points.

In a long paper a conclusion may be fairly detailed, summarizing for the reader every important point—but especially the overall theme. Without such a summing up the reader is left with the burden of putting together the full meaning of the paper. Instead of forcing readers to think back over everything they have read, any good writer supplies a summary of what has been discussed.

A short paper or report does not usually require a detailed conclusion. Because little information has been presented, the reader would be bored with repetitive details. Nevertheless, readers should not be abandoned abruptly once the body of the paper comes to an end. All that is necessary in a short piece is for the writer to state once again—in different words, of course—what the introduction raised as the subject of discussion. Having read this restatement of the theme, the reader will know that the writer did not quit suddenly before the end. The reader will also be aware that the paper has proved what it set out to prove.

When you plan and write your first draft, you risk setting yourself back unnecessarily by being too aware of the final structure of the paper. You may find it more useful to leave the final shaping for the rewriting stage, when you can play the role of reader rather than writer. As reader, you can take in what you have written and evaluate the way your paper is put together. You can easily make any structural changes that are needed. You can add words, phrases, sentences, and even whole paragraphs to complete your orderly presentation of ideas.

What usually begins as a shapeless topic, then, can be polished and repolished until you have a paper or report you are proud to submit. The necessary polishing takes time and care. It begins when you have completed your first draft and may continue even while you are doing the final typing.

The chief secret of a successful paper is simply this: think before you write, think while you write, think when you revise. And never fool yourself into believing that you can compose an effective piece of writing in one draft, no matter how carefully you have thought about the subject ahead of time. You will find that the act of writing will sharpen your thoughts and make it necessary for you to rethink, if not the entire topic, at least some of its subsidiary points. A second draft (and sometimes a third) is the way to transfer your best thinking to paper.

CHAPTER 2

The Act of Writing

All writers, students, and successful authors must begin at the same place: the first word. The page is always blank before you begin, and if the empty page frightens you, rest assured that many who make their living with the pen or typewriter or word processor find it just as threatening.

Inexperienced writers often are inhibited by the belief that they must know everything they are going to say before they begin to write. Professional writers do not make this mistake. While a succinct thesis statement and an outline can be useful, ideas and their organization can develop during the writing itself. Experienced writers know this.

The act of writing is a process of discovery. Good writing does not depend on thinking everything through in advance. As you write and rewrite, you will find out how much or how little you already know about your chosen subject. You will realize that some of the ideas you thought would be easy to explain and support are in fact not so clear. On the other hand, as you write, vague ideas may blossom into concrete and heartfelt convictions.

You may find that you have much more to say on a subject than you thought you would when you began. Jack London, for example, expected to complete *The Call of the Wild* as a 5000-word story. Within five weeks he had produced the 32,000-word novel we now consider a classic.

HOW TO BEGIN

Let us assume, for the moment, that a teacher has assigned a 500-word essay on one of the following topics:

1. a social problem of current interest;
2. a political event or controversy;
3. reform needed in school or college life;
4. a review of any book;
5. an incident that shaped your life;
6. choosing a career;
7. the value of education;
8. explanation of a difficult concept;
9. a comparison or contrast of any opposing points of view.

Do these subjects sound familiar? Have you met them before? Have you long since come to the conclusion that you do not have 500 words' worth on any of them? Your teacher sympathizes with you. In deference to your feelings, therefore, one more topic is added:

10. any subject of your own choosing.

To a student with nothing to say about nine suggested topics, a completely free choice may be the final blow. The only prospect worse than too few choices may be too many.

You have faced this dilemma before: not knowing what to write about. Yet you must find something to say, and when you have chosen a subject, you must make it specific enough to be manageable in the time and space available.

What can you do? The blank page that challenges you is the same white space that confronts any number of other writers—successful professionals, unknown amateurs, and unwilling students—before they get started.

You can make a statement about something in the world and then explore the reasons you feel the way you do about that particular condition or phenomenon. Or you can begin with a single word you like the sound of, check the dictionary to be certain of its meaning, and go on to build a sentence around it. The ideas in the sentence that emerges may be worth exploring further. If they are, you are on your way, even though in the end your paper may have no connection with the idea you started out with.

Above all, keep in mind that no word or series of words is final—except insofar as you must meet your deadline. In some cases writers may be pleased with what they find on the first try; but in most cases, as you well know, revision and rewriting are necessary. Some writers hate every word of their first drafts and start all over again; even when they like what they have written, they work to make it better. Regardless of how you prefer to work, even a poor first draft will be more productive than none.

Hate the assignment? There is an idea you can state with feeling: *I hate the assignment.* Why? Because it is forcing you to do something you don't like? Write that down too. Does it make you think about matters that otherwise would never have crossed your mind? Does it force you to examine your attitudes and search your memory for information? Is that what going to school is all about, or is it to train you for a place in the world? To be an engineer, a nurse, a lawyer, even a writer? You have returned to the sixth and seventh topics—

choosing a career and *the value of education. You have found something to say through the act of writing.*

BRAINSTORMING

The technique just discussed for finding a way to begin is a form of free association. Many organizations—particularly businesses—use a form of this process, called *brainstorming*, to find solutions for problems, choose new courses of action, and select goals. In such companies staff members meet in a conference room under the guidance of a group leader. They are encouraged to call out whatever ideas come to mind that may help solve the problem under study. Each idea is written on a blackboard as it is offered. No one criticizes; no one evaluates. The point of the exercise is to tap the imaginations of everyone present by encouraging the free flow of ideas instead of judging them. Only when the ideas stop flowing does the meeting turn to evaluation and discussion. Sessions like these produce many useful ideas.

Though you may not be part of an organization, you can brainstorm by yourself whenever you are searching for a topic or an idea—especially when you are seeking a theme for a paper.

Sit down with paper and pencil or typewriter. Jot down every idea that comes to mind; don't stop to consider whether the ideas are good. By not stopping to evaluate, you encourage the flow of ideas.

Say that you have been reading a novel about a marriage. Brainstorming about marriage may produce such topics as the following:

Marriage. Problems. Marrying too early. Bad communication between husband and wife. Children—planned and unplanned. Abolishing mar-

riage. Civil ceremonies. Church weddings. Bride wears white. Interracial marriage. Interfaith marriage. Role of husband. Working wife. Ideal marriage. Why I'll never marry. Why I will surely marry. Marriage between students. Living together. Parents' marriage. Marriage counseling. Divorce.

Stop for a moment. It took me just over two minutes to produce this list. The ideas began to come swiftly once the first one emerged. They slowed down about halfway through—a typical effect in brainstorming; once the first idea is written down, the rush of ideas is so great that we can hardly write fast enough to keep up. When the ideas slow down, we know that it is time to stop and look back at what we have.

Do any of the ideas appeal to you? I like a few, and I could probably write a short paper on any one of them. Since every one of these ideas offers the chance to take a side, try to figure out whether you know more about some of the topics than about the others. Explore one that may be pertinent to your present life. Jot down some notes. Again, use free association, as I will.

A topic I can handle easily is marriage between students. A high school sweetheart may seem like the only one, but that's probably not true. In my last year in high school, I thought I might be willing to take a chance. Charlie and I were going steady. Why did we decide against marrying? I guess I remember pretty well. We had a long talk about whether we should announce our engagement right away and marry after graduation in June. We talked about how surprised our friends would be and how there would be showers and parties. We also figured that our parents would object, and we talked about eloping. If we eloped and came back man and wife, our parents might feel resigned to giving us help while we were in college. Then there was the problem of getting into the same college, or at least two colleges in the same town, or one of us working while the other went to college. The problems began to look formidable. Then it was a question of what we really wanted to do with our lives. Charlie said he could live with the idea of working our way through, taking turns at chores, etc., but sooner or later he would want me to stay home and take care of the kids. I realized I didn't know him as well as I'd thought. High school romance offers a pretty narrow view of life. We agreed to put it off without breaking up. I meant it. I got a letter just a few weeks later. He was seeing someone else. So was I.

There you have the rough material that can be worked into an essay. Of course your own experience probably differs a great deal from that of the person who wrote these notes.

Try writing this paper now. You might title it "Marriage Between Students: Better Safe than Sorry."

You have your notes, you can make a rough outline:

1. The thing to do
2. Romance and rebellion
3. Struggling to make ends meet
4. Learning through experience

You can make a preliminary thesis statement:

High school sweethearts know so little of themselves and the world that any thoughts they have of early marriage will come to an end when they face reality.

If you want to work on this paper, begin writing it now. If, on the other hand, you have been developing a different theme, start to write while your thoughts are fresh. Do not let anything get away from you. It does not matter if your first draft strays far from the notes. It merely means that the act of writing has encouraged you to think further.

If your title, preliminary thesis statement, and outline turn out to bear no resemblance to the finished product, you shouldn't care; your thinking has led to something better. The main result is that you have what you wanted—a paper.

THE HABIT OF WRITING

When professional writers sit down to their day's work, they do not always have a good idea of what they are going to write. More often getting started is difficult and frustrating—ideas seem to disappear, words will not flow.

Some writers develop their own systems to get their work going. Ernest Hemingway used to stop work each day *just before he ran out of things to say*, so that when he resumed work the following morning at six, he wouldn't have to start cold. Once he had started by completing the previous day's work, he was ready for additional writing.

Other writers play out their string before they quit work on a given day. To get them started again the next morning, almost anything they put down on paper will serve. They may begin to write and find that what is appearing before them is a letter to a friend or a rebuttal to a newspaper editorial. They may merely blow off steam about the cruelty of life. No matter; writing anything leads to more writing and, finally, to the writing they must do.

Some colleges offer courses that encourage students to develop the habit of writing in just this fashion. These writing courses give credit for a certain number of words a day, every day, on any subject.

When you have no idea what to write about, try "free writing." Soon enough your mind will move you into productive work. The discipline that comes from writing regularly makes you a better writer, just as hours of practicing scales and easy pieces improve a pianist's work. Many important writers, Hemingway among them, started out as journalists. The pressure of deadlines and regular assignments on many subjects taught them to report concisely and clearly. Ben Hecht, a Chicago newspaperman who went to Hollywood, was able to write the movie *Underworld* in two weeks, even though it was the first screenplay he had ever tackled. His newspaper experience had made him a disciplined writer.

For each session of free writing, set a goal of a certain number of words, just as you would if you were taking a course or if your city editor told you to bring in one story a day every day. If possible, set aside the same time each day at the same desk. That time slot and that desk will help to establish your routine. As soon as you pick up your pen, begin to write. No planning, no thinking. Let the words flow. Dream. Complain. Write home. Review a book. Plan for the future. Rebuild society. Shape the world. Tell a story. Write anything. Write. Write a paper.

Don't look for polished writing. As you write each day, your writing will flow more smoothly. In time it will also be more persuasive, more gripping, more expressive of you.

AFTER THE FIRST DRAFT

Once you have a first draft and feel confident that what you have written is worth reading, your next job begins. You must read through your draft carefully to reorganize wherever necessary and make sure that you have written as well as you can. You want to check for clarity and for logical ordering of ideas. You want to make sure that your argument will convince your reader. You want to double-check all spellings and other essential details.

The checklist that follows spells out what to look for in reviewing a draft and preparing for the final draft. The material mentioned in the list is discussed in detail throughout this book. Use the index to locate the specific pages offering the information you need.

CHECKLIST FOR WRITERS

Information

1. Have I stated my thesis clearly?
2. Have I presented all my arguments convincingly and in logical order?
3. Have I omitted any important arguments that should be presented to convince the reader?
4. Have I kept to the point and been specific?
5. Have I answered opposing points of view, or have I merely attacked them?
6. Have I reasoned logically in every detail of the discussion?
7. Have I stated my conclusion clearly?

Style

1. Have I written as directly and clearly as I can, always speaking to the same reader and using language appropriate for that reader?
2. Have I written in the liveliest and most interesting style I can manage? Are my verbs as strong as possible? Do they convey the meaning I want? Are my adjectives and adverbs doing the job I want them to do?
3. Can I delete any words and thereby strengthen my paper?

Structure

1. Have I written an opening paragraph that makes clear what I am going to say and makes the reader want to go on?

2. Have I organized each paragraph logically and provided smooth transitions between paragraphs?
3. Have I closed my paper with a section or paragraph that ties my argument tightly together and leaves the reader convinced of the strength of my argument?
4. Have I deleted all sentences that add nothing to my meaning or to the strength of my argument?

THE FINAL DRAFT

When you are convinced that you have done everything as well as you can, you are ready for the final draft. Mark all the changes you want to make on your earlier version. Then copy carefully, taking as much time as is necessary to produce a clean page, legible and neat, with ample margins.

If you cannot use a typewriter, you may use pen and ink on ruled paper. (Instructors may specify how such handwritten papers are to look.) You should, however, learn to type as soon as possible in order not to penalize yourself as you advance through school or at your work.

For typewritten papers, use unruled white bond paper, $8\frac{1}{2} \times 11$ inches in size, unless you have been instructed to use another type or size of paper.

The following guidelines apply both to typewritten and handwritten papers:

1. Write on one side of the sheet only.
2. Provide margins of at least 1.5 inches at the left side of each page and at the top. Provide margins of 1 inch at the right side and at the bottom.
3. Double-space between lines except when writing footnotes or quotations of five lines or more. Footnotes are single-spaced. Lengthy quotations are single-spaced and indented an additional .5 inch on the left side.

4. Number all pages after the title page. Use Arabic numerals and place them in the upper right-hand corner.
5. Indent about an inch for paragraphs.
6. On the title page center the title, and provide all the other required information farther down on the page: class, instructor's name, date, your name.

The final job, proofreading, is not easy. After all, you are the parent of the words you have written, and parents tend to see their offspring as perfect. If you are going to catch all the errors you have made in the final typing, then it is best to leave as much time as you can between final typing and proofreading, so that the words will seem new to you.

While proofreading, proceed slowly and carefully. Read through everything at least twice. Read aloud if that practice helps to slow your reading. Find and correct every error: spelling, choice of words, grammar, and logic. Handwritten corrections in a typewritten paper are better than no corrections.

The last step is to check page numbers to make certain that the pages are in correct order. You have spent too much time on the text to let it be spoiled by foolish oversights.

CHAPTER 3

Building Your Writing Style

If only I could write with style. I think brilliant thoughts—at least I think they're brilliant—but when I put them down on paper, they just lie there and die. Good writing is more than using the appropriate words and structuring sentences properly. Good writers are concerned with how words relate to each other and whether they convey intended meanings. Good writers take special care to make sure that their sentences and paragraphs, long and short, flow into one another to give exactly the desired impression and exhibit enough variety to hold the reader's interest.

When you have completed your first draft, and are ready to rewrite, the time has come to think about your *style—your way of expressing yourself.*

You make stylistic choices even while writing your first draft. You are pursuing an idea, and you are addressing a specific audience. Your writing style cannot fail to be influenced by these considerations. Because you have developed an attitude about your subject and your audience, you unwittingly adopt a particular tone. You treat your subject fully, in a way that you think will make sense to your audience. The words you choose, the sentences you form, the paragraphs you structure, all reflect this attitude.

Now, in rewriting, you are ready to examine your *tone* and *diction*. You are ready to cut out any words and sentences, even paragraphs, that are not directly related to the topic, in order to make your work as *concise* as possible. In addition, you are ready to work toward a pleasing *variety of sentence structure*, and you want to make sure you have given your ideas appropriate *emphasis*. You also look out for the proper use of *figures of speech* to give your writing a vivid quality. These are the elements that make up style: tone, diction, conciseness, sentence variety, emphasis, and figurative language.

VOICE

As you work over your written material, you will realize that there are usually several choices you can make; there is not always one right word or one appropriate sentence length. The particular decision made in each case is often an expression of the writer's personality and outlook. In this sense, the clearer your thinking, the clearer your written paper or report. And the more you have thought through the ideas and suggestions you present, the more persuasive your writing will be. The final result will be an effective *voice*.

Tone

Tone can be defined as the characteristic of writing that reveals the writer's attitude toward the subject and the audience. Your tone is considered appropriate when you have addressed your subject with the degree of seriousness or humor it merits and treated your audience with the respect it deserves. When Art Buchwald, the satirist, takes aim at a target, his intent is to stick pins in human vanity and folly. When the President of the United States writes the annual State of the Union Message, his intent is to deal seriously with important matters that concern all citizens. Buchwald's material is meant to be chuckled over at the breakfast table; the President's, to be listened to carefully by all the leaders of government assembled on a solemn occasion while the rest of the nation looks on and listens. Obviously the tones adopted by these writers must be completely different.

Even when your intention remains the same, you will want to tailor your expression to the audience you have in mind. You may, for example, feel very strongly about the values of Little League baseball. The form in which you express your argument and present the advantages you see will be different depending on whether you are writing a letter to your ten-year-old nephew urging him to join a team or sending a proposal to your city council suggesting that the community establish a Little League team. In the former you will, of course, keep your vocabulary simple, your sentences fairly short, and your language vivid and figurative. In the latter you are more likely to use abstract nouns, structure your sentences to show connections and progressions, and employ language that is solid and weighty.

Communicating fairly with the reader

Writers who condescend to readers, endlessly repeating the obvious in words suitable for the nursery, may think that they are making themselves clear. Writers who talk over their readers' heads, using unnecessarily long words and peppering their messages with obscure references, may think that they are impressing their readers. In both cases the result is the same: the audience takes a walk, and the writer is left in an empty theater, reciting a monologue no one hears.

Treating the subject with the appropriate seriousness

When dealing with a matter of local interest, for example, you must treat it seriously, but you make a mistake if you write as though you were advising on national policy. Thus, an editorial for a student newspaper or an article for the newsletter of the PTA must not adopt a doomsday tone. If the problem you are discussing is student behavior in the cafeteria, you can deal with it in a sober manner (or with appropriate wit), but you should not make it sound more weighty than it is. On the other hand, you should not deal with matters of the highest importance, such as nuclear war, in terms that trivialize the weightiness of the topic.

Keeping the tone consistent throughout

As you read what you have written and begin to rewrite, you must remain aware of keeping your writing directed at the same audience—neither over the reader's head nor too simple—and maintaining the level of seriousness you started out with. When you are sure you have remained consistent, and when you are satisfied that your tone is appropriate to your subject and your audience, you have met the requirement of tone.

Objective Versus Subjective Tone

Objective tone is more appropriate when a balanced presentation of facts is more important than the author's feelings about those facts. Examples of objective tone are most often found in good technical writing, news reporting, and reports of research.

The writers of such material do not lack opinions, but they suspend them in the interest of supplying factual information. The following short paragraph, for example, remains objective throughout. The writer is introducing the subject of procedures that will ensure safe and efficient operation of a power plant.

> *There are four categories of plant procedures: operating, routine, administrative, and departmental. Because operating procedures and routine procedures affect safety, they must be approved by the governmental regulating authority as well as by the plant superintendent before they can be implemented. Since the other categories do not affect plant safety, approval by the plant superintendent alone is sufficient for implementation.*

This paragraph is objective in tone; it presents facts, not opinions. The writer's feelings do not appear.

    Subjective tone is appropriate when the writer's feelings about a subject are of great importance. The writer may make it clear that differing opinions exist, but these are shown to be less valid than the writer's opinion. Subjective tone is typically adopted by editorial writers, critics, satirists, and advocates of a particular point of view. The following paragraph, by a prominent social critic, treats the role of music in the second half of the twentieth century.

> *We have come a long way from the time when music was heard only on unique, formal occasions. When people heard music in concerts by live artists they expected the music itself to make the atmosphere. The event was the music. In a concert hall they listened to hear precisely what the composer or the performer had to offer at that particular moment. At home they listened while they themselves, a member of the family, or a friend sang or played an instrument. Nowadays, of course, we still have our occasional home concerts and special performances by particular artists in concert halls and auditoriums. Many of*

> *us play instruments. But this is no longer the
> commonest way music reaches us. Far commoner
> is the sound from the car radio as we drive
> along; or from the AM-FM radio while we cook a
> meal, wash the dishes, or work in our basement;
> or from the automatic-record-playing hi-fi as we
> play cards, read a book, or make conversation.
> A normal feature of upper-middle-class domes-
> tic architecture today is the hi-fi radio-phonograph
> system with a speaker in every room. We are
> music-soothed and music-encompassed as we go
> about our business. Now the appropriate music
> for any occasion is that which need not be fol-
> lowed but can simply be inhaled.*

In this paragraph from Daniel Boorstin's *The Image: Or What Happened to the American Dream*
(New York: Atheneum Publishers, 1962), the reader
is treated to a subjective tone. For example, listeners are described as *music-soothed*, *music-encom-
passed*, and the time's usual music is characterized
as *that which need not be followed but can simply be
inhaled*. The author was interested in putting forward his own thoughts about how music is treated
today. While he provides some factual evidence for
his point of view, he achieves his greatest effect by
adopting a subjective tone. This writing clearly contrasts with that of the engineer in objectively explaining power-plant procedures.

Avoiding Sex-specific Language

In recent years readers have become sensitive
not only to ethnic slurs and other offensive language
but also to a form of writing that implicitly excludes
women from the topic under discussion or segre-
gates and trivializes them in terms that have a
pejorative connotation. As women become more and
more visible in the marketplace, business writing
also needs to accommodate them in its statements.

Traditionally, the term *men* was used to refer
to all humanity—as in, *All men are created equal.*

While no one wants to rewrite the Declaration of Independence, writers now tend to avoid the term *men*. *Humankind* has a long history and can substitute for *mankind*. *People* and *everyone* can also serve in a number of instances. Sometimes the sentence can be rewritten to avoid the locution altogether.

Traditional	*Avarice is a trait found in all mankind.*
Traditional	*All men are avaricious.*
Sensitive	*All people are avaricious.*
Sensitive	*Avarice is a common trait all over the world.*

It has also been traditional to follow a singular indefinite noun with a form of the pronoun *he*.

| Traditional | *Each kindergarten pupil has his own box of crayons.* |

Such statements imply wrongly that only men and boys participate in the work of the world. Changing such statements to express gender results in various devices, some more awkward than others.

Awkward	*Each kindergarten pupil has his or her own box of crayons.*
Awkward	*Each kindergarten pupil has his/her own box of crayons.*
Smooth	*All kindergarten pupils have their own boxes of crayons.*
Smooth	*A box of crayons is given to each kindergarten pupil.*
Smooth	*Each kindergarten pupil has a box of crayons.*

In most instances turning the subject into a plural, turning the sentence around to make the original object the subject, or omitting the pronoun solves the problem adequately. When none of these is possible, it may be better to go with the awkward version than to overlook one sex.

Another device that works on a very few occasions is to arbitrarily alternate *he* and *she*. This device must be used with the utmost caution; it has a tendency to sound a little foolish. Consider the following example.

> *At the end of the schoolday, each student brings his story or her poem to the teacher's desk.*

There are, of course, occasions when *he* or *she*, *his* or *her* individually are correct.

> *Each Miss America contestant has her own chaperone.*
>
> *Each sophomore brought his father to the father-son banquet.*

The trivialization of women has taken a number of forms that modern writers are eager to correct. It goes without saying that women should never be referred to as *girls* or *gals*, let alone *broads* or worse. Nor should their occupations be given special forms. Traditionally, women poets have been referred to as *poetesses*, for example; *poet* is just fine for versifiers of either sex. Throughout society sex-specific occupational words have been changed as women (or men) have entered professions previously reserved for one sex or the other. Thus, *firemen* are now conventionally referred to as *firefighters*, *mailmen* as *postal carriers*, *stewardesses* as *flight attendants*.

Some publications still make another invidious distinction by referring to a man by his last name only while using an honorific title (*Mrs.* or *Miss*, usually; more rarely, *Ms.*) before a woman's name. A uniform practice for men and women should obtain throughout a piece of writing.

Diction

The basic unit of writing is the word. *Diction* is concerned with the words chosen and the way they are combined in phrases, clauses, and sentences.

Inexperienced writers who try hard to sound like eminent authorities may produce writing that is muddled and pretentious. Their mistake comes from attempting to use language beyond their control. Most of the writing we do in school and in business calls for everyday language, not the stiff wording we reserve for the most formal documents.

The following paragraph is by the economist Milton Friedman, from his book *Capitalism and Freedom* (Chicago: University of Chicago Press, 1981).

> *Government can never duplicate the variety and diversity of individual action. At any moment in time, by imposing uniform standards in housing, nutrition, or clothing, government could undoubtedly improve the level of living of many individuals; by imposing uniform standards in schooling, road construction, or sanitation, central government could undoubtedly improve the level of performance in many local areas and perhaps even on the average of all communities. But in the process, government would replace progress by stagnation, it would substitute uniform mediocrity for the variety essential for that experimentation which can bring tomorrow's laggards above today's mean.*

If you study this paragraph closely, you will discover that Professor Friedman is suggesting that the federal government stay out of important aspects of our lives that are under local control. The diction he employs makes the central idea a bit more difficult to understand than necessary. Friedman suggests that we would be most productive with the fewest government controls. Here is an attempt to rewrite the paragraph by changing the diction to make the central idea more accessible.

> *Government can never produce programs with the imagination and ingenuity shown by individuals working independently. By interfering with people's lives, government appears to make improvements in housing, nutrition, clothing, schooling, road construction, sanitation, and so forth. But we pay a high price for what we get. We end up with average living conditions, without any outstanding elements. Worse yet, people stop trying to do better. The result is that the majority of people will stop reaching for improvement in their own lives.*

The second version of this paragraph avoids the formality of Friedman's diction, which is surely appropriate for an audience of economists and social theorists. The diction now is closer to everyday speech and, therefore, more understandable—but without talking down to the reader. (See the *Dictionary of Usage* at the end of this book for specific entries that clear up questions about diction.) A few cautions are worthwhile here.

Avoiding Jargon

Jargon is specialized vocabulary useful or essential in particular trades or professions. Such words may not be understood outside their natural sphere. Since you want to write clearly for your audience, you must concentrate on using diction that expresses what you mean in a way that enables the reader to follow your discussion easily. If you are not writing for people in a particular trade or profession, you will improve diction by avoiding trade talk. To a general audience, for example, a *cat* is a furry domesticated feline, not a man or a musician. *Cash flow* has a clear and agreed-upon meaning in business, but when you want to explain your inability to pay your bills, you may say you have *no cash on hand*. The list of specialized terminology is long because modern civilization is highly diversified. But special terms become confusing jargon when they are used outside their normal field of application.

Avoiding Clichés

Clichés are words and phrases that have been used so often and have become so ingrained in daily speech that they have lost real meaning and do not express real thinking. Writers who employ clichés excessively face ridicule and rejection. (Those who find the *pen mightier than the sword* become *laughingstocks* and *suffer the slings and arrows of outrageous fortune* if they cannot *probe their unconscious minds* and strike *a mother lode* of words that are *as fresh as a daisy*.) Everyone will fall into an occasional cliché, but as with all other less-than-perfect practices, habitual use is far worse than an occasional indulgence. How do you know when you are in danger of writing a cliché? Ask of the suspected phrase: *Have I heard or read it a thousand times before?* If the answer is yes, look for a fresher way to express yourself. The trick at that point is not to consult a thesaurus, which may give you a word or phrase whose meaning is just a shade different from what you intend. Instead, try asking yourself what meaning you are trying to express. When you answer *I'm trying to say . . .* you are likely to express yourself clearly, in a fresh, interesting way.

Correct Meaning

Whenever you come upon a new word in conversation or reading and want to use it in your writing, you *must* consult your dictionary. Only if you find that the word means precisely what you want it to mean should you employ it in your writing.

Make sure also that the word has the appropriate

connotation as well as *denotation*. A pocket dictionary may give you all the information you need about the denotation of a word—its primary, or literal, meaning. But more than a pocket dictionary is needed to discover its connotation—the power of a word to produce an emotional response or association in the reader. Think, for example, of the different responses you will get from readers when you use any of the following pairs of words and phrases: *eat, dine; politician, statesman; assassin, freedom fighter; obscure the truth, tell a lie; controlled substance, drug; teacher, pedagogue.*

Avoiding Exotic Words

Your best words are the ones you encounter and use frequently. If you are a steady reader, your vocabulary will grow. If you listen carefully to people who express serious thoughts, ideas, and opinions about a variety of subjects, your vocabulary will grow. You will not find it necessary to dress up your writing with fine words and expressions from foreign languages, nor will you reach self-consciously for long words. Listen to a word before you write it. Does it sound like you? If so, it is probably a good word for a report or essay you are writing.

Conciseness

Whenever you write, you are striving for the reader's attention. Economical writing has a better chance of gaining and holding an audience than does long, rambling, overwritten prose. Training yourself to be concise has a further benefit: the sparer your writing, the clearer your thinking; the clearer your thinking, the greater your mastery of your subject.

In revising a first draft to make it concise, avoid the following.

Redundancy

Redundancy is the error of repeating an idea unnecessarily—a word, a phrase, even a sentence—in different words. *Several things have to be said if I am to be certain that I have covered everything I want to say. The key turning point . . . The one essential necessity . . .* Redundancy pretends to make a statement but in fact says nothing.

Fat Phrases

Perhaps trained by school assignments that call for a specific number of words, many writers tend to take the long way around. Thus, they *share in common;* they describe people who are *attractive and beautiful, wise and sagacious, witty and humorous;* they do things that are *useful and worthwhile.* They start every sentence with *it is* and *there is* (see entries for *it is, there is* in the *Dictionary of Usage*). They end up with longer and longer sentences and meanings that are less and less clear.

Vagueness

A sentence may puzzle the reader. Though the words may all have been chosen correctly, in combination they mean less than they should. Two examples will help demonstrate the subtle way in which vagueness works its undesirable magic.

From a school district report on language arts:

> *"Writing Through Literature" covers the total experience from the beginning thought process to the final writing of the complete composition.*

"Writing Through Literature" is the name of a course. Though the meanings of the individual words in the title are clear, taken together they mean nothing. Whose writing is to be covered—that of the students in the course or that of the great writers of literature? Perhaps writing will not be covered at all, but only something there is no other phrase for but *the total experience.* The fat phrase *beginning thought process* may mean *original idea.* The *final writing of the complete composition* is surely redundant, since it is scarcely possible to get to the final stage of anything without meaning to include completion.

From an Air Force publication:

> *Over a period of the last several years, the Air Force has experienced the development of an upward obesity trend.*

The statement leaves no doubt what its writer was trying to convey: Air Force men and women are fatter than they used to be. But one does wonder why the writer avoided saying so directly and concisely.

Toward the end of a long writing day, under the pressure of a deadline, or even without an excuse of any kind, a writer may fall into the traps of loose diction and excess verbiage. But once rewriting begins, good writers see immediately where they have fallen short. They eliminate whatever has crept into a first draft that must not be allowed to survive into the second.

Sentence Variety

Lively writing carries the reader along steadily, sustaining interest and attention. Lively writing, then, means sentences of varying lengths and constructions. While simple sentences have the virtue of clarity, a long series of simple sentences can be dull. Such a series, moreover, may fail to demonstrate to the reader the relationships between the elements of the ideas being discussed. The complexity of ideas that have been carefully thought through often demands sentences that also have a complex structure.

This does not mean that every sentence in a serious paper will be long and complex. As you write, your thoughts come in different forms: impressions, images, opinions, guesses, generalizations, facts, and so forth. A sentence that advances a belief or principle may vary in length from a few words to dozens of words. The complexity or simplicity of a thought will determine the length of a given sentence. Your job in rewriting is to make clear all the sentences you have written. The length of the sentences is one factor to consider.

As you read over your first draft, count the words in each of the first ten sentences. Next study the order of elements in your sentences. Are all the sentences of roughly the same length? Do all the sentences proceed routinely from subject to verb to object or complement? Perhaps you rely too much on simple sentences or on complex sentences that invariably begin with a dependent clause. Perhaps you have only one way of starting and finishing your sentences. Whatever the cause of the monotony, try to restructure your sentences to make them entirely clear and appropriately emphatic. You will then find that different constructions and different sentence lengths fit your purpose better—and you can revise your work accordingly.

By varying sentence structure, you can also indicate to the reader where it is best to read slowly, giving ideas time to sink in. Alternatively, you can convey to the reader some of your own excitement by a series of quick, snappy sentences. In any case, you will never put your reader to sleep if you shape each sentence and each paragraph to fit the meanings you wish to convey.

EMPHASIS

I went to the movies yesterday, and my sister won a lottery that will pay her $1,000 a week for life. What is wrong with this sentence? After all, the grammar, spelling, punctuation, and capitalization are all correct.

The sentence lacks emphasis. No distinction is made between the importance of going to the movies and winning a lifetime of financial security. The way the sentence presents these two thoughts in *coordinate* independent clauses implies that both are equally important. Whenever a sentence presents two or more ideas or information of unequal importance, the less important element should be made *subordinate* to the more important.

Coordinate: *of equal importance, rank, or degree*

Subordinate: *of secondary, or lesser, importance, rank, or degree*

Coordination

Coordinate constructions show that the ideas and information presented carry equal weight. These constructions may be coordinate clauses, coordinate phrases, or coordinate words.

> Use *coordinate constructions* for items worthy of equal emphasis.

Coordinate clauses.   *Once we were challenged by a world of unlimited resources available for the taking; now we face the greater challenge of a world with only a limited supply of life's necessities.* (Two equally important thoughts are presented in independent clauses.)

Coordinate phrases. *If our country is to survive, our democracy must provide for the family farmer as well as for the corporation executive, for the auto worker in Detroit as well as for the foundation executive in New York, for the municipal garbage collector in a small Southern town as well as for the college president in a sprawling California metropolis.* (Three equally important and contrasting pairs are presented in phrases repeating the same connecting words.)

Coordinate words. *We live in the age of special interests—religious, economic, political, social, sporting—all competing for as much as they can grab of available power and wealth.* (A series of equally important single-word modifiers is listed.)

Coordinate constructions can be more complex and utilize various forms of punctuation, as the following examples show.

Long or short, simple or complex, every scene in Ibsen's plays is significant. (Two pairs of equally important adjectives.)

Each day we spent together made us a little older, a little fonder, but no wiser. (Three equally important phrases, with reader interest reaching a climax in the last phrase.)

The company treated all its employees well, yet only a few of them gave the company a fair day's work. (Two independent clauses of equal importance joined by a coordinating conjunction.)

I consider myself a citizen of the world; you express nothing but narrow nationalistic feelings. (Two independent clauses of equal importance separated by a semicolon.)

A government must fall if it cannot provide work for the able-bodied, if it cannot assure housing for the poor, and if it cannot help its people live satisfying lives free from fear. (Three dependent clauses of equal importance supporting the main statement. The three dependent clauses are co-ordinate. All of them are subordinate to the main statement, *A government must fall.*)

Coordination assists the reader by directing equal attention to ideas and information of equal importance. In rewriting, the author can recast sentences to give equal emphasis to equally important ideas and information through coordination.

> Use *parallel structure* to express thoughts of similar importance.

Parallel structure is one of the principal ways of indicating coordination. It employs *grammatically parallel words, phrases,* or *clauses* for two or more *logically parallel thoughts.* Parallel structure can even be used to express logically parallel thoughts in two or more consecutive sentences.

The following examples illustrate some of the advantages of parallel structure.

While the rest of us sat *and* stared, *she* walked *slowly across the room,* lifted *her glass high, and* stared *straight ahead.* (A pair of parallel verbs followed by a series of three parallel verbs.)

There is no more eloquent tribute to the England of an earlier day than Shakespeare's in *Richard II*: *This royal throne of kings, this sceptred isle,/ This earth of majesty, this seat of Mars,/ This other Eden.* (Five parallel phrases, all beginning with *this.*)

Peasants in most parts of the world are apolitical: they do not vote, they never think about actions of their government, they care only about day-by-day survival. (Three parallel clauses, all beginning with *they.*)

That this nation, under God, shall have a new birth of freedom, and that the government of the people, by the people, for the people shall not perish from the earth. (Two parallel clauses with three parallel phrases in the second clause.)

Parallel structure gives emphasis by equally highlighting two or more ideas or thoughts that are logically parallel. The effect is particularly striking when key words are repeated within the parallel construction. In rewriting your own work, pay careful attention to opportunities for parallel construction for coordinate elements. But make certain that your constructions are grammatically parallel in every case.

Four Principles of Parallel Structure

- Use a series only for logically parallel items that can be expressed in grammatically parallel constructions.
- Repeat an article, preposition, or any other word when necessary to clarify a parallel construction.
- Use coordinating conjunctions to join parallel elements.
- Use parallel structure with pairs of conjunctions: *either . . . or, neither . . . nor.*

The reader is jarred by a grammatical flaw in what is intended as a series of parallel elements.

Confusing	*I regret that I looked on college only as four years of fun, a chance to meet people, and enjoying an all-expenses-paid vacation far from home.* (Two noun phrases in series with a gerund phrase.)
Clear	*I regret that I looked on college only as four years of fun, a chance to meet people, and an all-expenses-paid vacation far from home.*
Confusing	*Nursery school is the place for playing, learning to get along with others, and preparation for grammar school.* (Two gerund phrases in series with a noun phrase.)

Clear	*Nursery school is the place for playing, learning to get along with others, and preparing for grammar school.*
Confusing	*Most of today's company presidents are college graduates, hard workers, and they express themselves well.* (Two noun phrases in series with an independent clause.)
Clear	*Most of today's company presidents are college graduates, hard workers, and effective speakers and writers.*
Confusing	*We enjoy fishing, swimming, and to hunt.* (Two gerunds in series with an infinitive.)
Clear	*We enjoy fishing, swimming, and hunting.*

When you edit your work, be alert to faulty series. Remember that a series gives you the advantage of coordination only when you group logically parallel items in grammatically parallel constructions.

You will often find it useful to clarify a parallel construction by repeating an article, preposition, or other word. The repetition will also increase emphasis.

Confusing	*Vegetable plots are being cultivated widely now to help families fight the high cost of food and give pleasure to gardeners.* (The verbs *fight* and *give* appear to be linked, so that the sentence seems to say *vegetable plots help families give pleasure to gardeners.* This is not the writer's meaning.)
Clear	*Vegetable plots are being cultivated widely now to help families fight the high cost of food and to give pleasure to gardeners.* (Repetition of *to* clarifies the parallel verbs *help* and *give*. The reader sees the correct relation between the two verbs.)
Confusing	*All the old man wanted in his final days was a little peace and room to sleep in.* (This sentence implies that the man wanted room to sleep in.)

Clear   *All the old man wanted in his final days was a little peace and a room to sleep in.*

Another way of ensuring that parallel statements are clearly recognized by readers is to use *coordinating conjunctions* to join parallel items. The coordinating conjunctions are *and, but, for, nor, or*; sometimes *so* and *yet*. The items that are joined, must be grammatically parallel and must be seen by readers to be logically parallel.

Confusing   *Early man survived by hunting animals and ate them.* (The conjunction *and* appears to join *survived* and *ate*.)

Clear   *Early man survived by hunting animals and eating them.*

Confusing   *Many people used to avoid buying paperback books because of their cheap paper and they were bound badly.* (The conjunction appears to imply that *many people were bound badly*. A conjunction cannot be used to join a phrase and a clause that are not parallel.)

Clear   *Many people used to avoid buying paperback books because of their cheap paper and bad bindings.*

Clear   *Many people used to avoid paperback books because they were printed on cheap paper and were badly bound.*

Certain pairs of conjunctions, such as *either . . . or* and *neither . . . nor*, require parallel construction; the reader must find the same grammatical pattern after each of the conjunctions. If a verb follows the first, a verb must follow the second; if a phrase follows the first, then a phrase must follow the second, and so on.

Confusing   *I was impressed neither by his knowledge nor how he spoke.* (a phrase after *neither*, a clause after *nor*)

Clear	*I was impressed neither by his knowledge nor by his speech.* (phrase after *neither*, phrase after *nor*)
Clear	*I was impressed neither by what he knew nor by how he spoke.*
Confusing	*They liked neither bowling nor to fish.* (gerund after *neither*, infinitive after *nor*)
Clear	*They liked neither bowling nor fishing.*

Subordination

Subordination employs grammatically subordinate constructions for minor ideas and information. Subordination thus indicates to the reader that certain items are less important than others; at the same time, the construction lends desired emphasis to items of greater importance. The requirements of subordination are fulfilled through careful choice of grammatical constructions and careful placement of items within a sentence.

> Use *subordinate constructions* for items of lesser importance in order to give emphasis to items of greater importance.

One of the advantages of subordination is that it avoids monotonous strings of words, phrases, and clauses connected by *and*. Unskilled writers often string information together without regard for emphasis, giving the impression that they have not thought about what they have written. As soon as a new idea comes to mind, such writers merely add *and* and go full speed ahead. They seem never to look back while they are writing; in their rush to finish, they give equal value to everything.

Two Principles of Subordination

- Express main ideas in independent clauses.
- Express subordinate ideas in dependent clauses.

When you are rewriting, one of your biggest tasks is to make certain that your most important thoughts are not buried in phrases, dependent clauses, and other lesser constructions. Independent clauses must carry your principal ideas.

Confusing   *The drama group spent a good deal of money on lighting and scenery and they hired a professional director and still the production failed.*

The three independent clauses are strung together with *and*, mistakenly implying that all three statements are equally important. The three facts conveyed by the sentence are put in the order of when rather than how they happened. The reader should be guided by subordination to see that the message of the sentence is that the production failed despite efforts of the group. But the sentence merely recites the facts, leaving the reader to figure out the relation among them. The sentence lacks emphasis because it lacks subordination.

Clear   *Although the drama group hired a professional director and spent a good deal of money on lighting and scenery, the production failed.*

Now the relation is obvious. Coupling the first two statements of the original sentence in a single dependent clause links the two steps taken to prevent failure and subordinates them to the result, the main statement. The sentence now clarifies the writer's message: the production failed despite earnest efforts.

The example demonstrates how subordination can be used to emphasize ideas or information that merit emphasis by giving less prominence to ideas or information that do not merit emphasis.

> Arrange your major and minor
> sentence elements to express the
> exact meaning you intend.

You lose the advantages of subordination if the order in which ideas are presented within a sentence is faulty or ambiguous. The following sentences illustrate the way a shift of sentence elements can change the meaning.

Before the plant closes for vacation, complete your report on your present project, so you can get started on the new design.

Complete your report on the present project before the plant closes for vacation, so you can get started on the new design.

Complete your report on your present project, so you can get started on the new design before the plant closes for vacation.

Shifting a dependent clause changes the meaning of a sentence.

My son said he would go back to law school after a year's vacation.

After a year's vacation my son said he would go back to law school.

Moving the modifying phrase from the end of the sentence to the beginning changes the meaning completely.

Readers do not know what you have in mind when you write a sentence. All they know is what they read. The responsibility for what you write is yours. When you edit a draft of a paper or report, you must put yourself in the position of a reader coming upon your words for the first time. If you read carefully when you are rewriting, you will be able to tell whether you have written exactly what you intended to write.

> Place an emphatic statement either at the beginning or end of a sentence—do not bury your independent clause.

You have seen how rearrangement of sentence elements can affect the meaning of a sentence. Even when the same meaning emerges from two different arrangements, one may give greater emphasis to the more prominent idea. The opening and closing parts of a sentence attract the greatest attention.

Unemphatic   *When she was fired while on maternity leave, Lucy filed a suit in state court, not knowing that the federal courts offered a greater chance of relief.*

The opening clause of this sentence is properly a dependent clause, since *When she was fired while on maternity leave* is less important than what follows. Unfortunately this dependent clause occupies the opening part of the sentence, where it attracts more attention than the independent clause, *Lucy filed a suit in state court*. The thought that occupies the last part of the sentence merits the attention it gets by being in that position. The problem in this sentence lies in the burial of the independent clause in the middle—the least emphatic part—of the sentence.

Emphatic   *Lucy filed a suit in state court, not knowing that women fired while on maternity leave have a greater chance of relief in the federal courts.*

The original sentence related events in the sequence in which they happened instead of presenting them in the order that assigns the proper emphasis to the various parts of the thought. Now the most important part of the sentence appears at the beginning; the rest of the sentence acts as a long modifier of *Lucy*, the subject of the main clause.

The sentence may also be rearranged to give even greater emphasis to the idea that federal courts give greater chance for relief.

Emphatic   *Not knowing that the federal courts offer a greater chance of relief for women fired while on maternity leave, Lucy filed her suit in state court.*

> Emphasize important modifiers by placing them at the beginning of a sentence.

In some sentences a modifier deserves emphasis because it is of overriding importance. In a series of arguments to prove a point, for example, the elements of the argument can be ordered clearly for the reader as follows.

Emphatic   *First of all you must consider the conditions under which the children were reared.*

The independent clause *you must consider the conditions* and the dependent clause that follows contain the essential information provided by the sentence; but the sentence modifier *First of all* directs the reader's attention to the argument that follows. When the reader reaches the next point in development of the overall idea—which may be given in the next sentence or in a sentence further along in the paragraph—the writer will provide the proper signpost—*secondly, in addition,* or some other appropriate expression.

A sentence can also open with a modifier to signal a change of pace between what has gone before and what the writer is about to state.

Most people would rather work and live well than be idle and merely exist on whatever money the government is willing to provide. In fact, a recent survey of welfare recipients indicated that many of them try desperately to hide their condition from their neighbors.

The sentence modifier *In fact* attracts special attention because it opens the sentence. *In fact* points up the contrast between the previous thought and the one that follows—an excellent way to provide emphasis. There are many such modifiers that strengthen writing in the same way, especially when they open a sentence: *unfortunately, in view of these facts, in conclusion, as a result, thus, on the other hand,* and so forth. These modifiers are valuable tools for achieving emphasis.

FIGURATIVE LANGUAGE AND THE LANGUAGE OF COMPARISON

Figures of Speech

Writing clearly and forcefully does not mean abandoning all picturesqueness. The good writer keeps the reader's interest in a number of ways; one is through use of *figures of speech* to impart vividness to the ideas being expressed. While there are numerous such figures, the chief ones are *simile* and *metaphor*—two versions of comparison.

A simile introduces the comparison with *as* or *like.* Such clichés as *strong as an ox, silent as the tomb,* and *quiet as a mouse* are all similes. *A pretty girl is like a melody* is also a simile. A well-chosen, well-placed simile in a paper or report can concentrate the reader's attention either on the point you are about to introduce or one you have just finished making.

Simile   *Adding an X-ray machine to the equipment of the retirement home would be* like placing an elaborate computer in an infant nursery. *No one now on staff is trained to operate such a sophisticated diagnostic tool,*

> *nor does the overall health of the residents
> require its use more than once or twice a
> year.*

Simile
> *There seems to be a shared element in the
> natures of talented people that leads them
> to self-destruction more easily than ordi-
> nary folks. We need only think of Freddy
> Prinze, John Belushi, or Karen Carpenter
> to grasp the danger of sudden fame. In
> short, these brilliant performers seem as
> bent on self-destruction as lemmings dur-
> ing their annual rush to the sea.*

Metaphors make similar comparisons but in an
implicit way. In a metaphor the telltale *as* or *like*
disappears so that one thing becomes another rather
than being likened to another. *He was an ox of a
man* makes the same statement as *he was strong
as an ox* but without the explicit term of comparison. Many clichés in common use are, in fact,
metaphors—such as *rooted to the spot, he was putty
in her hands,* and *my new car is a lemon.* Metaphors give the reader an immediate entry to the
writer's thinking.

Metaphor
> *Only about five feet tall, Napoleon was a
> midget towering over the rest of Europe.*

Metaphor
> *The* United States Constitution *is the foun-
> dation on which the imposing structure of
> the state is built. Its architects could not
> know how high the edifice would rise. But
> they took care to make the masonry sub-
> structure solid enough to bear the weight of
> all the laws and regulations governing a
> unified society.*

You will probably find that appropriate figures
of speech do not occur to you when you write your
first draft. But as you revise your work, ask yourself whether a dull passage could not be made more
lively by some explicit or implicit comparison. If so,
how can you phrase your idea to produce an apt

comparison—one that can be readily understood, that fits the subject of your paper, and that is not so elaborate or striking as to detract from the thought you are expressing? Avoid the following.

Mixed metaphors

The rift between Burr and Hamilton grew more heated, until the duel was unavoidable. A rift (used metaphorically here for a difference of opinion), being a crack, can deepen or widen; an angry argument—or something that is already warm—can grow heated; but the two elements of this metaphor belong to different areas of reference in the natural world and cannot be used together. Check your metaphors to make certain that their separate parts are consistent.

Meaningless or inappropriate metaphors and similes

Working in a laboratory is like a kitchen—it may be true that a laboratory is like a kitchen, or that working in a laboratory is like cooking, but an activity cannot be compared with a place. Make certain that your similes compare comparable parts of speech. Make equally certain that the comparison is applicable to your meaning: *Sales this past quarter have risen sharply, like a Frisbee.* In fact, a Frisbee rises slowly and at a fairly slow speed. Above all, it does not attain any great height. The simile is therefore not appropriate.

Figures of speech that are too elaborate or extended

Sometimes a writer can get carried away by the simile and lose sight of the main thought that should be expressed. *Like Tarzan growing up in the jungle, learning the ways of the animals, confused when he first meets Jane but then adapting so well that by the time Boy comes along, his father can give him parental love, the three-year-old squatted down to observe the earthworm.* Here the writer is trying to convey to the reader the image of a child exploring nature; the extended simile about Tarzan introduces inappropriate comparisons and goes on so long that the important part of the sentence is completely lost.

Dead Metaphors

Some metaphors are so apt and so obvious that the temptation to use them is strong. But precisely for this reason they have been used so often before that they have become meaningless—in short, they are overused clichés, and are to be avoided. *Hair white as snow, skyrocketing prices, a burning passion*: such phrases no longer resonate for the reader and add nothing to your writing.

Terms of Comparison

Even without using figurative language, you will use comparison to describe and to explain the advantage of an idea or object. When handled correctly, comparison can be an effective technique. When handled loosely, comparison can obscure what you are trying to say or hold your writing up to ridicule.

In comparing one thing with another, your first concern is to make sure that the items can be compared. You must also make sure that the comparison is made in grammatically correct form. There are other requirements you must observe when you draw comparisons.

The Degrees of Comparison

Absolute   *She is a* good *driver.* (adjective) *She drives* well. (adverb)

Comparative	*She is a better driver than I am.* (adjective)
	She drives better than I do. (adverb)
Superlative	*She is the best driver in our family.* (adjective)
	She drives best at night. (adverb)

The absolute is the easiest form to use: *we run quickly; dogs make good pets.* Notice that *quickly* is an adverb, *good* an adjective. When you add a modifier to an absolute form, the modifier must be correctly selected. On pages 110–115 you will find the rules governing the use of adverbs to modify other adverbs and to modify adjectives: *we run very quickly; dogs make exceptionally good pets.* Once you have selected the proper modifier and placed it correctly—as close as possible to the word or words it modifies—you are correct. But there are problems to watch out for.

[Do not modify an absolute illogically.]

No sense	*Do you consider yourself more equal than someone else?*

Equal is equal. How can anything be more equal than anything else? George Orwell was being ironic in *Animal Farm* when he coined the slogan *Some pigs are more equal than others.*

Sensible	*Do you consider yourself better than me?*
Sensible	*Their pay finally became nearly equal to ours once several states ratified the Equal Rights Amendment.* (The absolute *equal* is correctly modified by *nearly.* The meaning is clear: *nearly equal* means a little less than equal.)

Many absolutes can give you trouble. Consider *complete, dead, fatal, impossible, infinite, perfect,* and *unique,* among others.

No sense	*The detective reported that the victim was very dead when she was brought to the hospital.* (How dead are the very dead?)
Sensible	*The detective reported that the victim was almost dead when she was brought to the hospital.*
Sensible	*The detective reported that the victim had been dead for half an hour when she was brought to the hospital.*
No sense	*Your work is more than perfect.* (Can anything be more than perfect?)
Sensible	*Your work is perfect.*
Sensible	*Your work is far from perfect.*
No sense	*I consider her painting very unique.* (Unique means *one of a kind.* Can anything be very one of a kind?)
Sensible	*Picasso was unique among twentieth-century artists in his consistent and prolific production of outstanding paintings over his entire career.*
Sensible	*Edward Weston was almost unique in his conception of photography; I can think of perhaps two or three others who were aware of the possibilities Weston found in the camera.*

Those who modify absolutes illogically show either the effects of slang—as in *very dead*—or an inclination to gush. Find the most appropriate absolute adjective or adverb, and in most cases you will not have to modify it.

> [Avoid the double comparative and double superlative.]

When we write that something is *stranger than . . .* , we have begun to draw a comparison. The *-er* ending of *stranger* gives the meaning of *more.* When we write that something is *the strang-*

est . . . , we have begun to present a superlative. Because the *-est* ending gives the meaning of *most*, *strangest* means *most strange*.

If we write that something is *more stranger than* . . . , we are guilty of a double comparative. If we write that something is *the most strangest* . . . , we are guilty of a double superlative. Modifiers ending in *-er* or *-est* are already comparative or superlative.

Double comparative	*Do you think your solution is more better than mine?*
Proper comparative	*Do you think your solution is better than mine?*
Double superlative	*I believe your suggestion is the most cleverest of all those I have heard.*
Proper superlative	*I believe your suggestion is the cleverest of all those I have heard.*

More and *most* are appropriately used with those adjectives and adverbs that cannot be given the endings *-er* and *-est*. As a general rule, one-syllable adjectives—such as *clean*, *swift*, and *great*—are modified by adding the *-er* and *-est* endings—*cleaner*, *swiftest*, *greatest*. Adjectives of more than one syllable, on the other hand, cannot be given these endings and must be modified by *more* and *most*—thus, *more fragile*, not *fragiler*; *most appreciative*, not *appreciativest*. But, like most grammar rules, this one has many exceptions—for example, *clever*, in the example used above, *can* be changed to *cleverest* (though some people find *cleverer* awkward). Let your ear be your guide, but never use both *-er* or *-est* with *more* or *most*.

[Avoid open-ended comparisons.]

Comparisons must involve at least two items: *Willows grow faster than oaks.* Careless writers, and advertising writers who may not always be dedicated to the truth, make comparative sentences with only one item. They tell us that one brand of beer is lighter, one cigarette milder. We must ask, lighter or milder than what? Lighter than ginger ale? Milder than a cheap cigar? Comparisons that do not identify the items being compared are said to be *open-ended,* and such comparisons are vague and possibly misleading.

Vague	*In my first day at work, I found that a supervisor can be more demanding.* (More demanding than what? Than whom?)
Specific	*In my first day at work, I found that a supervisor can be more demanding than a teacher or a father.*

Sometimes the basis for comparison is obvious.

Wait until you are older. (The meaning clearly is *older than you now are.*)

In some sentences the reader may have to keep in mind the content of previous sentences in order to complete a comparison. As long as the writer has made certain that the basis for comparison is apparent, such comparisons are acceptable. When you edit your work, make sure that your comparisons are clear. If you reword, make sure that you have not removed part of a comparison. Open-ended comparisons weaken anything else you write.

Open-ended	*Joe knew he could bat well enough to make the team. After losing ten pounds, however, he found he could run much faster.* (The first sentence does not mention Joe's running.)
Clear	*Joe knew he could bat well enough to make the team, but everyone said he ran too*

slowly. After losing ten pounds, however, he found that he could run as fast as anyone on the team.

[Avoid open-ended superlatives.]

The reader is entitled to know the basis for any statement containing a superlative. *She is the best* does not explain best at what. If you write, *She is the best surgeon on our staff*, the statement can be understood. If the superlative is true, it can be accepted. The reader has the proper frame of reference for judging the superlative *best*.

Open-ended   *They had the best won-lost record.*

Clear   *They had the best won-lost record in the American League.*

[Never compare two items that cannot be compared.]

It is clear that some things are unfit for comparison—for example, apples and oranges. But the writing problem is more subtle and centers on parts of speech.

Not comparable   *The children said that a trip to Vermont would be more fun than New Hampshire.* (A trip cannot be more fun than a state.)

Comparable   *The children said that a trip to Vermont would be more fun than a trip to New Hampshire.*

Comparable   *The children said that they would enjoy Vermont more than New Hampshire.*

Not comparable   *Most of the action in* Huckleberry Finn *is slower than* Tom Sawyer. (Action cannot be compared with a novel.)

Comparable   *Most of the action in* Huckleberry Finn *is slower than the action in* Tom Sawyer.

Writers often fall into the error of comparing things that cannot be compared; they know what they are trying to say as they write, but they forget the requirements of the reader. Care during rewriting will catch such errors.

> [Choose the correct words when drawing comparisons.]

Certain words of comparison are used often and misused almost as often. Refer to Appendix A, *Dictionary of Usage*, if you are uncertain of how to use such expressions as *like* and *as*, *compare to* and *compare with*, and *differ from* and *differ with*. The following sentences illustrate the correct uses of these and other expressions employed in drawing comparisons.

Usage: *Practices governing the manner in which a language is spoken or written.* (Use the appended *Dictionary of Usage* for guidance whenever you wonder how a word or phrase should be used.)

Like and *as*

Like   *Like his younger sister, Daniel always did his homework at school.*

As   *As close as pages in a book.*

Fewer and *less*

Fewer   *The end of summer means fewer games left to play, fewer campfires to enjoy, fewer country breakfasts to savor.*

Less   *The approach of spring means less snow to shovel, less wood to chop.*

Compare to, compare with, contrast with, contrast to, contrast between

Compare to

> The poet compared her life to the tropical seasons, in which long stretches of cruel heat were relieved only by uncontrolled storms.

Compare with

> You can no more compare football with baseball than a modern army with Robin Hood's merry men.

Contrast with

> The report contrasted the care taken in designing the forward fuselage with the carelessness shown in designing the landing gear.

Contrast to

> In contrast to your opinion, I would like to offer the correct solution.

Contrast between

> Have you noticed the contrast in style between Isobel's early sculpture and her latest work?

Differ from and differ with

Differ from
> She and her cousin differ from one another in fundamental ways.

Differ with
> They never differ with one another in front of strangers.

PART II

THE BUILDING BLOCKS OF WRITING

CHAPTER 4

Effective Paragraphs

The ideas and information contained in a letter, a paper, or a book need to be sorted out in some sensible way. And it is up to the author to arrange them for the reader in a way that makes the ideas and information understandable in their separateness and their connections. The first consideration in achieving clear arrangement is the paragraph.

FUNCTION OF THE PARAGRAPH

The simplest way to define a paragraph is to note that it expresses a distinct unit of thought or makes a complete point related to the topic of which it is a part. The most obvious way to recognize a paragraph is by its appearance. By employing special indentation before the paragraph begins, or by providing extra space between paragraphs, the writer indicates where a paragraph begins, and where it ends. The paragraph, then, is a way of showing the reader that a thought is complete or that a point has been made, and it is time to get ready for the next important unit of information.

When the information to be presented consists of a number of thoughts, it requires more than one paragraph; at such times transitions (see pages 73–75) are necessary to help the reader tie those thoughts, or paragraphs, together. Good paragraphing helps the reader think along with the writer, understand each part of the subject in the way intended, and perceive where the thoughts are going. Finally, paragraphing is a tool for making an understandable whole of the report, paper, or chapter you are writing.

The length of any paragraph should be determined by the nature of the information presented as well as by the reader's ability to understand what is presented. Just as there is no single best length for a sentence, there is no single best length for a paragraph. A paragraph is too short when the reader feels it to be incomplete; a paragraph is too long when the reader feels that it contains too much information. In the one case the reader has to connect thoughts the writer has left unrelated; in the other, the reader has to distinguish between thoughts the writer should have separated.

Your first goal in paragraphing, therefore, is to complete a single idea or topic within a single paragraph. When you come to the end of that idea or topic, you are at the end of a paragraph. You do not end a paragraph in the middle of a discussion, leaving important thoughts unwritten. You do not insert into the middle of a paragraph information unrelated to the rest of the paragraph. You stick to your point, dealing only with the main topic of the paragraph. When you have written everything you should write on that topic, or when you believe that your paragraph threatens to become uncomfortably long—and that the thought it contains probably consists of several distinct parts—start a new one.

Paragraphing is a device whose purpose is to

help the reader. It is easier for the eye to locate a particular sentence in a particular paragraph on a particular page than it is to search through line after line of unbroken text. Furthermore, bringing a paragraph to a comfortable close permits the reader to pause, think, and absorb.

In your writing, therefore, be kind to your reader. Place the greatest emphasis on expressing ideas and topics fully. Are you proud of a particular passage you have written? End the paragraph and let your reader stop to admire it. Have you written something that does not deserve to stand alone. Connect the thought with the one that follows. With care for your reader's needs, you will come up with good paragraphs.

Thus you will find yourself writing some long paragraphs and some short ones, and many of medium length. Extremely short paragraphs occasionally can be used to achieve a particular effect. A rule of thumb, however, says that even the shortest paragraph should consist of at least two sentences; only very accomplished writers (as Twain and Bellow, below) will be able to break the rule and get away with it.

Two selections are presented here to demonstrate how paragraphs of various lengths can be used to convey a writer's thoughts effectively. The first consists of the final two paragraphs of Mark Twain's essay "Fenimore Cooper's Literary Offences."*

The Cooper novel under discussion in this essay is *The Deerslayer*. Cooper wrote romantic stories of the French and Indian Wars. In the essay Twain attacks every aspect of the novel at great length, giving detailed examples of what he considered were Cooper's literary failings. The essay concludes with two paragraphs, one of medium length, the other extremely short.

---

*The modern spelling is *offenses*; Twain published his essay in 1895, at a time when the older spelling was still in common use.

A work of art? It has no invention; it has no order, system, sequence, result; it has no life-likeness, no thrill, no stir, no seeming of reality; its characters are confusedly drawn, and by their acts and words they prove they are not the sort of people the author claims they are; its humor is pathetic; its pathos is funny; its conversations are—oh! indescribable; its love-scenes odious; its English a crime against the language.

Counting these out, what is left is Art. I think we must all admit that.

The sarcasm of the final paragraph is crushing. In only fifteen words Twain climaxes the blood-letting of the previous paragraph and leaves *The Deerslayer* mortally wounded. Nothing can be removed from or added to either of these paragraphs without weakening the message. The contrast in length adds to their effectiveness.

The second selection is from "The Sealed Treasure," an article by the Nobel Prize novelist Saul Bellow, in which he evaluates the condition of Midwestern culture in the 1950s. The following four paragraphs open the article.

A few years ago I traveled through the state of Illinois to gather material for an article. It was brilliant fall weather, the corn was high and it was intersected by straight, flat roads over which it was impossible not to drive at top speed. I went from Chicago to Galena and then south through the center of the state to Cairo and Shawneetown. Here and there, in some of the mining counties and in the depopulated towns along the Mississippi there were signs of depression and poverty, but these had the flavor of the far away and long ago, for the rest of the state was dizzily affluent. "Pig Heaven," some people said to me. "Never nothing like it." The shops were filled with goods and buyers. In the fields were the newest harvesting machines; in the houses washers, dryers, freezers and refrigerators, air conditioners, vacuum cleaners, Mix-

*masters, Waring blenders, television and stereo-
phonic high-fi sets, electrical can openers, novels
condensed by the* Reader's Digest, *and slick magazines. In the yards, glossy cars in giddy colors,
like ships from outer space.*

*Down in Egypt, as the narrow southern end
of the state is called, a Negro woman, her head
wrapped in an old-fashioned bandanna, flashed
by in her blue Packard with a Boston bull terrier
affectionately seated on her shoulder. Here at
least was some instinct for the blending of old
and new. For the most part, everything was as
new as possible. Churches and supermarkets had
the same modern design. In the skies the rich
farmers piloted their own planes. The workers
bowled in alleys of choice hardwood where fouls
were scored and pins reset by electronic devices.
Fifty years ago the Illinois poet Vachel Lindsay
had visited these towns preaching the Gospel of
Beauty and calling on the people to build the
New Jerusalem.*

*Except for the main stem, the streets were
boringly empty, and at night even the main stem
was almost deserted. Restless adolescents gath-
ered in the ice-cream parlors or loitered before
the chain saws, vibrators, outboard motors and
garbage disposal units displayed in shop windows. These, like master spirits, ruled the night
in silence.*

*Some important ingredients of life were con-
spicuously absent.*

The first of these paragraphs is a hundred and
eighty words long, the second and third are shorter,
and the fourth consists of only eight words. The
reader drives along with Bellow as he tours the
state, through agricultural and mining areas, seeing
the objects that occupy people's lives and ambitions.
We move on to the southern end of the state, finding much the same focus of life. Finally we are in a
town at night, on an almost empty street. The description is complete. The brief final paragraph tells
what the journey has revealed.

Bellow has piled evidence upon evidence of what

life was like in Illinois in the 1950s. He has moved his readers from paragraph to paragraph as his automobile moved. By writing shorter and shorter paragraphs, he has prepared us for his final point. Bellow has taught us that paragraphs do not just happen: they are crafted.

UNITY AND COHERENCE

Like sentences and entire papers, paragraphs must have *unity* and *coherence*. The term *unity* demands that paragraphs deal with a single topic; the term *coherence*, that the relation between the parts of a paragraph must be clear to the reader. Coherence also applies to the relations between consecutive paragraphs.

As you put paragraph after paragraph down on paper, you will be expected to make each of them unified and coherent. When each paragraph is dedicated to a single topic, and every topic is related to the subject of the paper, a unified piece of writing results. When the reader can easily grasp the relation between all the paragraphs, and all sections of your paper, you have a coherent piece of writing.

This is not to say that in writing a first draft you must constantly consider whether the paragraphs are unified in themselves and coherent in relation to each other. (If you work from a careful outline, the job of achieving a unified and coherent paper is easier; see pp. 228–231.) It is in the second draft, when you examine every sentence and every paragraph you have written, that you find out whether you have stuck to the point (unity) and whether your ideas stick together (coherence). It is in the rewriting that you tighten up your writing and your thinking to make the greatest possible impact.

To promote unity and coherence in your writing, ask yourself the following questions as you read over your first draft.

- Will my readers easily follow the thought of this paragraph?
- Have I confused my reader by jumping back and forth among ideas?
- Have I wandered from the point I am trying to make?
- Will my readers easily see the relation between this sentence and the next? Between this paragraph and the next?

When readers can see that all the sentences in any paragraph deal with the same topic or topics and when all the paragraphs flow easily one into the next, the paper is unified and coherent.

The following paragraph by Waldemar Kaempffert, the late science editor of *The New York Times*, which appeared in *The New York Times Magazine* (April 2, 1950), is a good example of both unity and coherence.

> *Every hour the earth is deluged with as much energy as there is in twenty-one billion tons of coal. There is more energy in the small fraction of radiation that we receive from the spendthrift sun than there is in all the uranium in the world. According to Dr. Charles G. Abbot of the Smithsonian Institution, the state of New Mexico alone can supply from solar radiation over ten thousand horsepower-hours in a year—about thirty times the annual production of electrical energy in the United States. On a single day the land areas of the temperate and tropical zones are flooded with more energy from the sun than the human race has utilized in the form of fuel, falling water, and muscle since it came out of the trees a million years ago. The amount of coal, petroleum, and natural gas left in the earth is the energy-equivalent of only 100 days of sunshine.*

This paragraph deals from beginning to end with a single topic: the untapped potential of solar energy. In example after example, the writer indicates that such energy is abundant. The thought behind the paragraph can easily be followed. The writer has not jumped back and forth among ideas. The writer has not wandered from the point. The relation between each sentence and the next is clear.

In this same paragraph, the writer has used the word *energy* in every sentence. This repetition serves the purpose of linking every sentence in the reader's mind. Repetition of key words is a powerful tool for achieving coherence. But there are other ways of building coherence.

- *Varied conjunctions* Do not rely exclusively on *and*, *but*, and *or*. Find a conjunction that expresses exactly what you want to express. For example, *although*, *because*, *for*, and *unless* can be used to show that one thought is subordinate to another. They serve subtly to lead the reader along a line of logic, contrasts, analogies, or the like.
- *Varied sentences* Exclusive use of short sentences can rob a paragraph of coherence. Try linking two or more short sentences together in order to clarify the relation of the thoughts being expressed.
- *Making every sentence work* When a paragraph you have written consists of several sentences that work well together but also contains a sentence that is weak, eliminate that sentence. You judge weakness by whether a sentence adds to understanding or helps convince a reader.
- *Building bridges* When two sentences do not flow logically one from the other, add a sentence to make the necessary bridge for your reader.
- *Be elastic* Split a paragraph in two to help your reader see a difference between ideas; combine two paragraphs in one to show a close relation between ideas.
- *Repetition* Repeat key words to make things easier for your reader.

TRANSITION

Essential to coherence is effective use of *transition* from one paragraph to the next. A transitional element takes the reader comfortably from the topic of one paragraph to another—even when an entire series of paragraphs deals with the same general topic, as is so often the case.

Transitions between paragraphs have two functions. They show connection between paragraphs, and they relate the topic of a paragraph to the subject of the entire paper. You may find it easy to supply effective transitions between paragraphs, but it takes practice to learn to write transitions that also keep the reader aware of how each paragraph of a paper relates to the entire subject under discussion.

An excellent way to achieve effective transitions is to repeat the key term of a paragraph in the opening sentence of the next. In the two paragraphs by Mark Twain on page 68, the first begins with the query *"A work of art?"* It goes on to list all of Cooper's deficiencies in creating a work of art. Twain provides unity and coherence by repeating the words *it* and *its* regularly, so that the reader is aware that Twain is discussing a single topic, *The Deerslayer* as an example of Cooper's literary offenses. The second paragraph opens with *"Counting these* [the offenses] *out."* The pronoun *these* ties the two paragraphs together. With *"what is left is Art,"* Twain has repeated *art*, the key word of the first paragraph. Beyond creating a transition between paragraphs, Twain has connected these two paragraphs to the subject of the entire paper, "Fenimore Cooper's Literary Offences."

Besides key nouns and pronouns to provide transition between paragraphs, the entire range of *introductory phrases and clauses* is available. Bellow, in the excerpt from his work cited above, achieved transition by this device. The article, describing a trip through Illinois, moves the reader along in a unified description of what Bellow saw in the countryside and towns. The opening sentence of the first paragraph sets the stage for the description. The second and third paragraphs open with sentences that act as transitional elements, moving the reader first to Egypt and then to the main street of a town. Each of the opening sentences moves the reader's attention from one place to the next. Transition achieved in this way ensures the coherence of the writing.

Transition between paragraphs is best provided at the start of a paragraph, not at the end, as illustrated in the following material from James Baldwin's *Notes of a Native Son* (New York: Bantam Books, 1971). In this moving description of Baldwin's father and the relationship between father and son, the focus is primarily on the father. The description consists of seven paragraphs, and the opening sentence of each paragraph contains a reference to Baldwin's father:

> *I had not known my father very well.*
>
> *He had been born in New Orleans and been quite a young man there during the time that Louis Armstrong, a boy, was running errands for the dives and honky-tonks of what was always presented to me as one of the most wicked of cities—to this day, whenever I think of New Orleans, I also helplessly think of Sodom and Gomorrah.*
>
> *He was, I think, very handsome.*
>
> *When he died I had been away from home for a little over a year.*
>
> *He had been ill a long time—in the mind, as we now realized, reliving instances of his fantastic intransigence in the new light of his affliction and endeavoring to feel a sorrow for him which never, quite, came true.*
>
> *His illness was beyond all hope of healing before anyone realized he was ill.*
>
> *In my mind's eye I could see him, sitting at his window, locked up in his terrors; hating and*

*fearing every living soul including his children
who had betrayed him, too, by reaching towards
the world which had despised him.*

All the paragraphs are tied tightly together by the
repetitive use of *he*, *his*, and *him*; there can never
be a doubt that throughout Baldwin is speaking of
his father. The transitions tie the seven paragraphs
to the entire work as well as to each other.

Transition, then, strengthens your writing by
providing the reader with the logical associations
between paragraphs and by connecting every paragraph of a paper to the central subject of the paper.
As you review the first draft of any paper you
write, look for ways of making the necessary transitions:

- Repeat key terms.
- Repeat nouns and pronouns as appropriate.
- Employ introductory phrases or clauses that
  direct the reader's attention specifically to the
  topic and show its relation to what has gone
  before and to the overall theme.

THE TOPIC SENTENCE

Some paragraphs are strongest when their central thoughts are stated in topic sentences. The best
way to define a topic sentence is to say that it
expresses the essential idea of a paragraph or larger
unit of writing. A secondary definition states that it
announces the topic to be treated in a paragraph or
larger unit of writing. Such a sentence can open the
paragraph or it can be placed further on; it can even
recur. Not every paragraph, however, requires a
topic sentence.

The easiest way to build a paragraph is to state
its topic immediately and then go on to explain,
prove, expand, refute—in short, accomplish what-

ever you intend to accomplish with the particular topic. This method consists of *topic sentence* first, details later, as is done in the following paragraph.

> *The English have a highly developed sense of justice and of right. No phrase is more commonly used by the ordinary people than "it's right" or "it's not right," and that pretty much concludes the matter. They want to know where they stand, and they usually do. They believe in fair play, on the playing field and in the law courts and in business. They have little patience with subtlety or cleverness: they do not want rights that can be argued about. They hate all chicanery, all evasiveness and slipperiness. They are upright and downright, foursquare and simple and staunch. They carry their sense of justice over into the political realm—in large matters of national or international policy, in small matters which have their day as questions in the House [of Commons]. Their law is at once just and heartless, and in matters outside the law they are philanthropic but not charitable.*
> *Henry Steele Commager,*
> The Atlantic Monthly, *August 1948*

The topic sentence announces a characteristic of the English people. All subsequent information is given in support of that topic sentence, explaining what the author meant in the topic sentence. He conveys a picture of a population with standards, playing by the rules, shunning deviousness, and living by the same standards in its games as in its politics.

Commager's topic sentence is intended to meet the purpose of definition. (His supporting information tells us what he means by a sense of right and justice.) A number of other functions may be served by paragraphs, and the presence of a topic sentence can have a beneficial effect on paragraph coherence:

- Contrast: differences between ideas or information

- Classification: information grouped systematically
- Comparison: similarities between ideas or information
- Division: a large topic split into its logical parts
- Illustration: examples that clarify the topic under discussion

You will write all these types of paragraphs many times, and some of your paragraphs will have more than a single function. Comparison, for example, can often be made only when it is accompanied by contrast, since there are limits to the similarities between any two things. Without contrast, a comparison can mislead the reader.

In other cases, a definition may be followed by an illustration, since definitions tend to be abstract while illustrations are more vivid. Commager's paragraph about the English sense of what is right and just, for example, could be illustrated with another paragraph showing that sense in action among common people or at the highest level of government.

A topic sentence is a generalization, a summary, or a conclusion. It must always be supported by additional material to convince and inform the reader. The topic sentence *The English have a highly developed sense of justice and of right,* for example, might meet heavy argument without the author's supporting detail.

We have been dealing with topic sentences that open paragraphs. The logic of some paragraphs dictates other placement. The topic sentence may come at the end, as a conclusion based on evidence. It may come at the beginning and be restated at the end. Finally, a paragraph may have no topic sentence at all.

The following paragraph places its topic sentence at the end.

Those who have not grown up with computers generally find them more frightening than those who have. The legendary manic computer biller who will not take no—or even yes—for an answer, and who can be satisfied only by receiving a check for zero dollars and zero cents is not considered representative of the entire tribe; it is a feeble-minded computer to begin with, and its mistakes are those of the human programmers. The growing use in North America of integrated circuits and small computers for aircraft safety, teaching machines, cardiac pacemakers, electronic games, smoke-actuated fire alarms and automated factories, to name only a few uses, has helped greatly to reduce the sense of strangeness with which so novel an invention is usually invested. There are some 200,000 digital computers in the world today; in another decade, there are likely to be tens of millions. In another generation, I think that computers will be treated as a perfectly natural—or at least commonplace—aspect of our lives.

> Carl Sagan,
> The Dragons of Eden, *1977*

This paragraph builds up the necessary detail to show the ways in which computers have become a part of daily life, making it logical to close with the topic sentence. Note the repeated use of the word *computer*, which gives unity to the paragraph.

In the following paragraph the same topic sentence appears both at the beginning and the end, though not repeated word for word. In this method the second topic sentence generally appears as a restatement with amplification or with some difference in emphasis. After all, the remaining sentences of the paragraph have had their effect on the reader, making the reader ready for a modified thought.

The normal child, with some ability to reason, recognizes pressures. He rebels against them. He protests them. He runs away from them. He faces them. He fights them. But reason tells him

*that he must somehow manage to live with them.
The normal child's reason is, like the governor
on an engine, that balancing mechanism which
makes it possible for the child to live with pressures, almost all of which seem to be spiritual.
Other pressures, such as physical ones, are re-
lieved in sports and games. But the normal child
gives with pressures, takes pressure, as he par-
ticipates in a tug-o'-war that, in actual living, is
lifelong.*

> *Marion F. Smith with Arthur J. Burks,*
> Teaching the Slow Learning Child, *1954*

The second topic sentence amplifies the meaning of
the thought expressed in the first. By this means
the authors make certain that the reader grasps the
intended meaning and has read the thought twice.
This use of two topic sentences is reserved for
thoughts that may be difficult to express or that
merit repetition because of their importance. You
certainly would not want to repeat topic sentences
within most of your paragraphs.

BUILDING PARAGRAPHS WITHOUT
TOPIC SENTENCES

Many paragraphs in the work of our best writers contain no topic sentences at all. Nevertheless,
such paragraphs accomplish what their writers want
them to accomplish; readers have no trouble in following. Indeed, inserting a topic sentence in them
may do more harm than good.

When the idea conveyed by a paragraph is apparent without a topic sentence, the writer may
create a more striking effect by proceeding without
one. Consider the following paragraph, in which the
writer conveys an important message to the careful
reader.

*"You spend a billion here and a billion there,"
Everett Dirksen used to tell budget committees*

with mock solemnity, "and pretty soon you're talking real money!" It sounded pretty funny at the time but it's beginning to date. What's a billion any longer? Today, a single proposed aircraft carrier costs over two billion. We thought about that listening to President Carter discussing nuclear war at Annapolis last week. The latest example of a real war is Vietnam. George McGovern has an estimate for Vietnam, worked out for him by some government agency or other. The full bill isn't in yet, of course (the US paid pensions to veterans' widows for a century after the Civil War). Vietnam IOUs still pour in— medical costs, pensions and interest on the war debt. Total? Around $350 billion—the price tag for a small war. For comparison, the total federal budget receipts from all sources in fiscal year 1977 were $357 billion. Or, as an easy way to remember it, a third of a trillion. Trillion. We are moving into the vocabulary of astronomers.

TRB, The New Republic, *June 17, 1978*

Clearly the paragraph states that war has become so costly that it is rapidly exceeding the ability of nations to pay for it. The thoughtful reader gets the message.

Especially when you are writing of the feelings of people will you find that topic sentences are not needed—if you write expressively. In the work of Ralph Ellison we read this gripping paragraph, which needs no topic sentence.

I might well have waited until the end of the services, for I hadn't gone far when I heard the dim, bright notes of the orchestra striking up a march, followed by a burst of voices as the students filed out into the night. With a feeling of dread I headed for the administration building, and upon reaching it, stood in the darkened doorway. My mind fluttered like the moths that veiled the street lamp which cast shadows upon the bank of grass below me. I would now have my real interview with Dr. Bledsoe, and I recalled

Barbee's address with resentment. With such words fresh in his mind, I was sure Dr. Bledsoe would be far less sympathetic to my plea. I stood in the darkened doorway trying to probe my future if I were expelled. Where would I go, what would I do? How could I ever return home?

Ralph Ellison,
The Invisible Man, *1947*

Readers of narrative prose—writing that tells a story—do not want to be directed explicitly by the writer, do not want the writer to point out the significance of everything that happens. They want to find out for themselves, and they want to feel what the characters feel. A topic sentence in such paragraphs would get in the way.

The same is true for a paragraph of description, in which a topic sentence would appear artificial or stop the flow of the writing. The writer must direct the reader's eye to a scene the writer wishes to share. By building detail upon detail, the writer creates an image—and with it a feeling. There is no need for a topic sentence.

Whenever you describe a scene or a person, ask yourself what you want your readers to see. Then show it. Show it the same way your readers would see it in life. What would be seen first? What next? Or you may prefer some other order to build the effect you are after. Show the scene or person any way you wish that suits your purpose. But don't concern yourself with constructing topic sentences.

In the following paragraph from the first chapter of *The Great Gatsby* (New York: Scribner, 1981), F. Scott Fitzgerald masterfully guides the reader. The narrator of the novel has just entered the expensively furnished living room of the Buchanans on the north shore of Long Island.

The only completely stationary object in the room was an enormous couch on which two young women were buoyed up as though upon an anchored balloon. They were both in white, and their dresses were rippling and fluttering as if they had just been blown back in after a short flight around the house. I must have stood for a few moments listening to the whip and snap of the curtains and the groan of a picture on the wall. Then there was a boom as Tom Buchanan shut the rear windows and the caught wind died out about the room, and the curtains and the rugs and the two young women ballooned slowly to the floor.

The organization of the paragraph is primarily chronological. The opening sentence shows the couch the writer wants the reader to look at, because on it are perched two women important to the story. The second sentence describes the women briefly, and we listen to the wind until, in the third sentence, our sound-picture comes to an end and we begin to see again. The paragraph has no topic sentence and needs none. Nothing has happened. Four characters of the novel have been brought together in the rich, idle world of the novel. Two of them are young women suspended in time and space, and the author has made us ready for the scene about to unfold. There is no central idea that needs to be brought out in a topic sentence.

Novelists are not the only writers whose paragraphs often work best without a topic sentence. Anyone who narrates a story, whether based on fact or not, usually has no need for a topic sentence, as demonstrated in the following paragraph about modern German history.

On October 24, 1938, less than a month after Munich, Ribbentrop was host to Jozef Lipski, the Polish ambassador in Berlin, at a three-hour lunch at the Grand Hotel in Berchtesgaden. Poland, like Germany and indeed in connivance with her, had just seized a strip of Czech territory. The luncheon talk proceeded, as a German

Foreign Office memorandum stressed, "in a very friendly atmosphere."

> William L. Shirer,
> The Rise and Fall of
> the Third Reich,
> *1960*

This opening paragraph of Shirer's account of the fall of Poland does not require a topic sentence.

In your own writing, then, you must decide whether a paragraph can be strengthened by including a topic sentence. When a topic sentence can strengthen a paragraph, place that sentence at the beginning of the paragraph, at the end of the paragraph, at both the beginning and end of the paragraph—but never in the middle of the paragraph. Why force your reader to search for it amid all your other sentences? When a topic sentence is desirable, place it where it will do the most good.

CHAPTER 5

Sentences

As paragraphs are the building blocks of articles, reports, papers, and so on, sentences are the building blocks of the paragraph. Each sentence consists of a number of words arranged in a grammatical relationship that gives them meaning. At the least, a sentence consists of a *subject* and a *verb*. To these may be added a *direct object*, an *indirect object*, one or more *modifiers*, and one or more *complements*. The functions of the principal parts of speech will be covered in Chapters 6–8; for definitions, see the appended Appendix B, *Dictionary of Grammatical Terms*.

Subject	*performer of action indicated by an active verb:* The *boxer* fights. *receiver of action of a passive verb:* The *boxer* was beaten.
Verb	*word or words expressing action or state of being of the subject.* *(1) active verb:* The boxer *fights.* *(2) passive verb:* The boxer *was beaten.*
Direct[*] Object	*word or words that receive the action of a verb:* The boxer fought *the contender.*

Indirect Object	*word or words that receive the direct object of a verb:* The referee gave *them* a signal. (The subject is *referee.* The verb is *gave.* The direct object is *signal.* The indirect object *them* receives the direct object, *signal.*)
Modifier	*word or words that limit, describe, or make more precise the meaning of the word or words modified:* The boxer fought *hard.* He gave the contender a *knockout* blow.
Complement	*word or words that complete the meaning of a linking verb, a verb such as* be, feel, *or* seem: He is *a* fighter. He feels *strong. His opponent seemed* dazed.

All subjects and objects are nouns or substantives, words that function as nouns. Verbs fall into three categories. *Linking verbs* are verbs that take complements. Verbs that take direct objects are known as *transitive verbs.* Verbs that take neither direct objects nor complements are known as *intransitive verbs.* A few examples will help you identify the three types of verbs and learn the difference between direct objects and complements.

Transitive verbs

I hate hamburger. (The direct object of *hate* is *hamburger.*)

They see us every week. (The direct object of *see* is *us.*)

Intransitive verbs

The computer worked rapidly. (Because the verb *worked* has no direct object, it is intransitive. *Worked* is modified by the adverb *rapidly.*)

Sam eats all day long. (When the verb *eats* has no direct object, *eats* is intransitive. In this example, *eats* is modified by *all day long*. With a direct object, *eats* becomes transitive—*Sam eats hamburger all day long.*)

Linking verbs

Annette is an excellent teacher. (The verb *is* has the complement *teacher*. Do not confuse a complement with an object. One cannot *be* something in the same way that one can *hate* or *see* or *eat* something. A complement is needed to complete the thought expressed by a linking verb; the most common of such verbs is *be* in its many forms. The sentence *Annette is* means nothing—unless the preceding sentence has already supplied the complement: *Who is an excellent teacher? Annette is.*)

I feel ill today. (The verb *feel* has the complement *ill*. With the complement removed, the sentence means nothing.)

SENTENCE TYPES

Simple Sentences

All the sentences used as examples thus far are *simple sentences*—sentences that consist of a single clause.

Annette is an excellent teacher.

Sam eats hamburger all day long.

A clause is a group of words containing at least a subject and a verb. An *independent* clause is a clause that can stand as a sentence. A *dependent clause* cannot stand as a sentence. (See pp. 000–000.)

Additional elements can be contained in simple sentences.

Little Joan gladly gave Henry two books. (The adjective *Little* modifies the noun *Joan*, which is the subject of the verb *gave*. The adverb *gladly* modifies *gave*. *Henry* is the indirect object of *gave*. The indirect object receives the direct object, *books*. The adjective *two* modifies the noun *books*, which is the direct object of *gave*.)

Some supervisors rarely give their employees large raises. (The adjective *Some* modifies the noun *supervisors*, which is the subject of the verb *give*. The adverb *rarely* modifies *give*. The adjective *their* modifies the noun *employees*, which is the indirect object of *give*. The indirect object *employees* receives the direct object *raises*. The adjective *large* modifies the noun *raises*.)

England is an interesting country. (The noun *England* is the subject of the verb *is*. The article *an* and the adjective *interesting* modify the noun *country*, which is the complement of *is*.)

Compound Sentences

A *compound sentence* consists of two or more independent clauses. The clauses may be connected by coordinating conjunctions or by conjunctive adverbs. They may be separated by commas or by semicolons.

The most common *coordinating conjunctions* are *and, or, but, for, nor, so,* and *yet*. These conjunctions are generally preceded by a comma when they connect independent clauses of equal value.

We went to the movies, but our father and mother stayed home to watch television. (Because neither clause is given greater emphasis than the other, the clauses are taken to be of equal value. Notice the use of the comma before *but*.)

Charles spent the entire afternoon on the telephone, and I took the opportunity to complete my history paper.

Conjunctive adverbs are adverbs used as conjunctions. The most common ones are *consequently, furthermore, hence, however, moreover, nevertheless, therefore,* and *thus.* Conjunctive adverbs connect independent clauses that have a special relation. In the following example the relation is cause and effect.

> *The club treasury is in poor condition; consequently, we will not be able to sponsor our usual programs this fall.* (The meaning of the second clause results from the meaning of the first clause. Notice the use of a semicolon before *consequently* and a comma after it.)

In the following example the relation implies continuation of thought.

> *Many businesses are leaving the inner cities; furthermore, new residential building is declining.*

Because conjunctive adverbs require so much punctuation, they should be used sparingly. The two sentences would be improved if they were changed to include coordinating conjunctions: *The club treasury is in poor condition, so we will not be able to sponsor our usual programs this fall. Many businesses are leaving the inner cities, and new residential building is declining.*

When no conjunction is used between independent clauses, a semicolon is needed.

> *The two armies met in battle; the correspondents stayed with the heroic troops; the world waited for the outcome.*

The three independent clauses in the preceding compound sentence—and the independent clauses in all the other examples—can be written as simple sentences.

> *We went to the movies. Our father and mother stayed home to watch television.*

> *The club treasury is in poor condition. We will not be able to sponsor our usual programs this fall.*
>
> *Many businesses are leaving the inner cities. New residential building is declining.*
>
> *The two armies met in battle. The correspondents stayed with the heroic troops. The world waited for the outcome.*

However, the writers of the compound sentences elected to avoid simple sentences in these instances, because they wanted to show the relation between thoughts.

In analyzing a compound sentence, first identify the independent clauses. Then you can identify the principal elements within each clause, as was done in analyzing simple sentences.

Complex Sentence

A *complex sentence* consists of one independent clause and at least one dependent clause. A dependent clause cannot stand alone as a simple sentence.

> *A person who habitually misses work cannot expect to keep a job very long.* (The independent clause is *A person cannot expect to keep a job very long.* The dependent clause is *who habitually misses work*; as written, the latter cannot stand alone as a sentence.)
>
> *Snowfalls that come late in the season and term papers that require a great deal of research are equally unpleasant.* (The independent clause is *snowfalls and term papers are equally unpleasant.* The sentence has two dependent clauses: *that come late in the season* and *that require a great deal of research.*)

In analyzing a complex sentence, first identify the independent clause and the dependent clauses. Then you may identify the principal elements within the clauses.

Compound-Complex Sentence

A *compound-complex sentence* consists of two or more independent clauses plus one or more dependent clauses.

> *He rapidly stamped our passports while we waited nervously, and then his superior stepped forward toward us.* (The independent clauses are *He rapidly stamped our passports* and *then his superior stepped forward toward us*. The dependent clause is *while we waited nervously*.)

> *Many authors prefer to use a typewriter, even though most cannot type well, but poets are usually content to write with pen and ink.* (The independent clauses are *Many authors prefer to use a typewriter* and *poets are usually content to write with pen and ink*. The dependent clause is *even though most cannot type well*.)

Diagraming English Sentences

Diagraming is a time-honored technique for showing relationships among the parts of any sentence, and you may find the technique helpful in analyzing the sentences you write.

A simple two-word sentence will introduce you to diagraming.

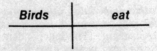

The subject *birds* and the verb *eat* are written above a horizontal line and are separated by a short vertical line. Notice that the vertical line goes through the horizontal line.

The addition of a direct object extends the horizontal line.

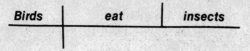

The direct object *insects* is placed above the horizontal line. Notice that the line separating *eat* (the verb) from *insects* (the direct object) does not go through the horizontal line.

Expanding the sentence to read *Wild birds usually eat many insects* results in the following diagram.

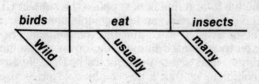

Because the subject *birds* is modified by *Wild*, the modifier *Wild* appears along a slanted line coming out of the horizontal line before *birds*. The modifiers *usually* and *many* also appear on slanted lines coming out of the horizontal line before the words they modify.

We have now shown how to treat subjects, verbs, direct objects, and modifiers. The next sentence element to be represented is the indirect object.

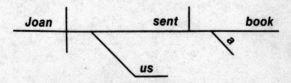

The indirect object *us* appears on a line below and parallel with the horizontal line on which appear the subject, verb, and direct object. Notice that its line is connected to the horizontal line by a slanted line. The fact that *us* is written on a horizontal line shows that it is an indirect object, not a modifier.

Notice also that the direct object *book* is modified by *a*, written on a slanted line.

The only remaining principal sentence element is the complement.

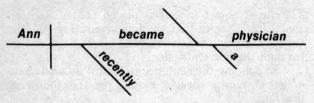

The horizontal line now supplies the subject (*Anne*), the verb (*became*), and the complement (*physician*). Notice that the verb and the complement are separated by a slanted line coming down to the horizontal line. This slanted line indicates that *physician* is a complement, not a direct object. Notice also that the verb and the complement are modified.

If you can diagram a simple sentence in this way, you can also diagram other sentence types. For example, the compound sentence *Jack spent his allowance, but I saved mine* may be diagramed as follows.

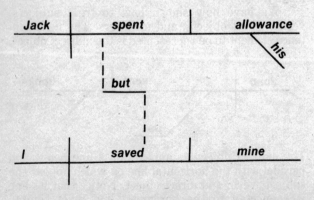

Notice that each independent clause has its own horizontal line and that the conjunction (*but*) sits between the two clauses connected by broken lines to each horizontal line.

In diagraming a compound, complex, or compound-complex sentence, each clause has its own horizontal line, and its modifiers and other sentence elements are treated in the same way they are treated in a simple sentence.

Let us now add prepositional phrases. (See Appendix B for definitions of *preposition* and *prepositional phrase*.) A representative sentence employing such elements is *The portrait in the museum was painted by her mother.*

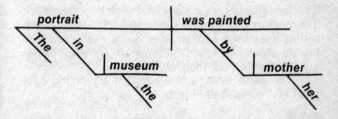

There are two prepositional phrases in this sentence: *in the museum* and *by her mother.* In each case the preposition (*in*, *by*) is written above a slanted line coming out of the horizontal line, showing it to be the first word in a modifier of a sentence element. The object of the preposition (*museum*, *mother*) appears above a horizontal line parallel with the main horizontal line. A vertical line precedes the object of the preposition. The modifiers of the objects of the prepositions (*the*, *her*) appear on slanted lines coming out of the horizontal lines beneath the objects of the prepositions.

When a sentence has more than one word serving as subject, verb, object, or complement, it is diagramed as follows.

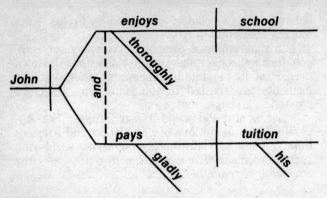

This sentence shows a compound verb (*enjoys*, *pays*). The conjunction *and* is connected to the two horizontal lines by a broken line. Since each verb also has an object, two vertical lines are shown separating the verbs from their objects.

The same system is used with compound subjects and compound objects.

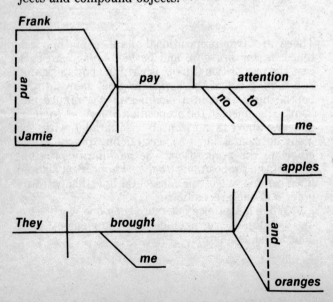

Until now diagrams of independent clauses have been shown. In conclusion, we will offer a few sentences containing dependent clauses.

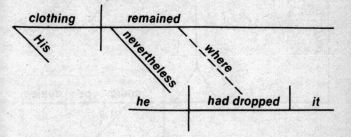

In the foregoing sentence, *where he had dropped it* is a dependent clause modifying the verb *remained* in the independent clause.

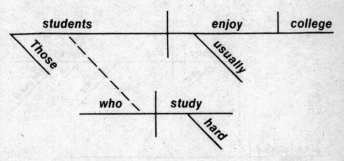

In the sentence above, *who study hard* is a dependent clause modifying the subject *students* in the independent clause.

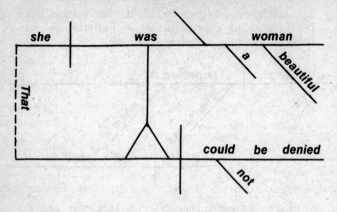

In the sentence above, the noun clause *That she was a beautiful woman* is the subject of the sentence: *That she was a beautiful woman could not be denied.*

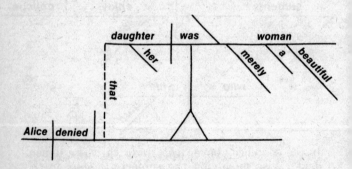

In the sentence above, the noun clause *that her daughter was merely a beautiful woman* is the direct object of *denied*.

CHAPTER 6

Verbs

The functions of verbs, whether transitive, intransitive, or linking, were discussed in the previous chapter. By definition, of course, any verb expresses an action, occurrence, or state of being. When a verb is used in a sentence, several considerations must be kept in mind: *tense*, *voice*, *mood*, and *person*.

TENSE

The first consideration is tense—the *time* of an action or state of being expressed by a verb. The following chart, listing the verb *choose* in all its tenses, gives the first-person singular form as a model for constructing verb forms. Note that *active voice* means that the subject performs the action, while *passive voice* means that the action is performed upon the subject. (For a full discussion of voice, see below.)

	Present (present action, habitual action, action true for all time)	Present Perfect (action begun in the past and continuing into the present)	Past (action completed in the past)
Active Voice	I choose	I have chosen	I chose
Passive Voice	I am chosen	I have been chosen	I was chosen
Progressive Active	I am choosing	I have been choosing	I was choosing
Progressive Passive (exists only in present and past)	I am being chosen		I was being chosen

	Future (simple future action)	Future Perfect (action completed before a future action)	Past Perfect (action completed before a previous past action)
Active Voice	I will choose	I will have chosen	I had chosen
Passive Voice	I will be chosen	I will have been chosen	I had been chosen
Progressive Active	I will be choosing	I will have been choosing	I had been choosing

[Use the correct sequence of tenses to express your thoughts exactly.]

The tenses of all verbs within a sentence must be in logical agreement. Such agreement is called *sequence of tenses*. When tenses are incorrectly combined, the result can be misleading or ridiculous. To ensure correct sequence of tenses, you must determine when the actions of the various verbs in a sentence occurred or will occur. Ask yourself what happened first? What happened next? What is happening now? What will happen then? What will happen after that? The following sentences illustrate the logic of proper sequence of tenses by showing the *perfect tenses* in combination with other tenses.

Present perfect

I have now chosen my candidate and am not changing my mind. (Present perfect active with present progressive active.)

I have chosen my courses for next year and will not change my schedule. (Present perfect active with future active.)

I have been considering all possible choices for three days and will announce my decision tomorrow. (Present perfect progressive active with future active.)

Past perfect

She had completed her application and was waiting to hear from the employment office. (Past perfect active with past progressive active.)

Jill had wanted to delay her decision until her summer vacation ended. (Past perfect active with past active.)

Future perfect

You will not have completed your work by the time the editor arrives. (Future perfect active with present active. Notice that in this sentence *arrives* indicates future action.)

[Use logical and consistent tenses.]

Anne's interest in medicine grew steadily as time went by. (Two past actions, two verbs in the past tense.)

The schedule says that the planes leave every hour on the hour. (Two actions true for all time, two verbs in the present tense.)

Hope for her recovery diminishes with each day that passes. (Two present actions, two verbs in the present tense.)

Two of my sons will settle in England, but my third son will remain with us in California. (Two future actions, two verbs in the future tense.)

VOICE

Voice is the name given to the characteristic of verbs that indicates whether the subject is acting (*active voice*) or being acted on (*passive voice*). Writers may select either the active voice or the passive voice when they are using transitive verbs. Active verbs make strong sentences; passive verbs make remote, formal, often abstract sentences.

Active   *The* Bill of Rights *guarantees free speech in the United States.*

Passive   *Freedom of speech is guaranteed in the United States.* (By whom? By what? The sentence does not tell us.)

Passive   *Freedom of speech is guaranteed in the United States by the* Bill of Rights. (Now we know the source of the guarantee, but it appears in a prepositional phrase.)

Active   *Monthly statements tell bank customers the state of their accounts.*

Passive   *Bank customers are informed monthly of the state of their accounts.*

While these examples may begin to show the advantage of active verbs, it is a mistake to think that passive verbs are never justified. In certain circumstances, in fact, they are preferable.

Active   *The waves pounded the rocky shore.*

Passive   *The rocky shore was pounded by the waves.*

Passive   *The rocky shore was pounded.*

Notice that since passive verbs always require some form of the verb *be* as an *auxiliary verb*, passive verb forms are longer than their active counterparts. But consider the difference in effect on the reader of the active and passive sentences. The first sentence makes us see the waves pounding. The active verb *pounded* focuses our attention on the subject, *waves*, and on the action. The second sentence, using the passive verb *was pounded*, focuses our attention on the shore being pounded. We feel that we are reading an account of an earlier incident rather than participating in an incident while it is going on. We no longer see the action; the waves are given secondary attention. In the third sentence, we do not see the waves at all. Many passive sentences omit the performer of the action of the verb entirely. Perhaps that is why corporations and other institutions prefer the passive voice in their correspondence. The reader does not know *who* or *what* has done what has been done, *whom* or *what* to question when something has gone wrong.

Active verbs mean active subjects—someone or something is doing something. *Passive verbs mean passive subjects.* The active voice and the passive voice both have places in your writing.

> Use *active* verbs to emphasize the *performer* of an action, *passive* verbs to emphasize the *receiver* of an action.

Active   *The committee passed the bill just before the legislature recessed.* (The emphasis is on *committee* and secondarily on *legislature*.)

Passive   *The bill was passed by the committee just before the legislature recessed.* (The emphasis is on *bill*.)

In writing of the event described in the above sentences, you would choose the active voice if your focus should be on the actions of the committee. If you were focusing on the progress of the bill, you would choose the passive. Even so, you can express most thoughts without passive verbs if you are willing to try. The same thought, for example, can be expressed with the use of *passed* as an intransitive verb while still emphasizing the bill.

Active   *The bill passed the committee just before the legislature recessed.*

Most newspaper writers prefer the active voice in their writing, and the above example was taken from a newspaper column.

[Use active verbs when describing]
[action.]

The following paragraph seems to come to life before the reader's eyes. (All active verbs have been flagged to call attention to them.)

> *The waves* pounded *the rocky shore all day as the angry lake* did *its best* to drive *us from our cabin. We* watched *the water* rise *steadily until it* took *away our shed. It* was *getting dark. How much more* could *the cabin* take? *We* made *our decision. We* would pack *everything and* move it to higher ground. But the same storm that whipped *the lake* poured *heavy rain on us as we* carried *each pathetic load up the slope. We* lost *our footing again and again, and soon mud* covered *us from head to foot, so thick even the rain* did *not* wash *it off. It* was *no use. We* abandoned *the rest of what we* owned *and* wrapped *ourselves in canvas to sit before the little cave that* held *the few things we* had saved. *Just as we* settled *down, the lake* had *its way. The water* swallowed *our cabin.*

The paragraph contains no passive verbs. All are active transitive verbs, linking verbs, or intransitive verbs. Even one infinitive, *to drive*, is in the active voice.

When the same paragraph is changed by converting the active verbs to passive wherever possible, it fails in its intention to describe action. (In this case all passive verbs have been flagged.)

> *The rocky shore* was pounded *all day by the angry lake, doing its best to drive us from our cabin. The steadily rising water* was watched *until our shed* was taken *away. It* was getting *dark. How much more punishment* could be taken *by the cabin? Our decision* was made. *Everything* would be packed *and* moved *to higher ground. But we* were whipped *by the same storm by which the lake* was being whipped *as each pathetic load* was carried *up the slope. Our footing* was lost *again and again, and soon we* were covered *by mud from head to foot, so thick it* could *not* be washed *off by the rain. It was no use. The rest of what* was owned *by us* was abandoned, *and our bodies* were wrapped *in canvas so we could sit before the little cave in which* were held *the few things that* had been saved. *Just as we settled down, the will of the lake* was satisfied. *Our cabin* was swallowed *by the water.*

The second paragraph does not seem as interesting as the first paragraph. Instead of presenting the actions of endangered people watching their dreams vanish, it reads more like a dispassionate report of storm damage filed by an insurance-claims adjuster. Active verbs bring action to life; passive verbs deaden action.

> Use the passive voice in business and technical reports, which often emphasize information rather than the people who developed the information.

In most business and technical writing, you will be required to emphasize *what* is being reported rather than *who* is reporting it. Technical reports usually announce that a new method has been established, a new procedure found promising, a problem solved. The people responsible for the work are of no interest. This traditional attitude of science and technology may account for some of the dullness of technical writing.

Passive   *After the acceptance tests were completed, full-scale deliveries were made.* (The reader is presumed to have no interest in who conducted the tests or who made the deliveries.)

Passive   *The total area of the site under construction was surveyed and found incapable of supporting a plant of the size now being designed.*

Both the above sentences can be written in the active voice without loss of clarity and with some benefit.

Active   *After we completed the acceptance tests, the production department made full-scale deliveries.*

Active   *The site-selection committee surveyed the site that management is now considering and found it incapable of supporting a plant of the size the construction department is now designing.*

By putting people into these two sentences and using active verbs, we have breathed life into the sentences. In most engineering companies the choice of active voice over passive voice depends on the taste of the chief engineer. Be aware, however, that a preference for the passive is not entirely without merit.

> Don't switch needlessly between active voice and passive voice.

    From sentence to sentence, the active voice and the passive voice should be used as they are appropriate to the purposes. There is no need to sustain one voice consistently through a paragraph unless the paragraph has a single, unchanging purpose. Within individual sentences, however, you will do better to adopt either the active or passive voice and stay with it. Otherwise you may find yourself burdened with awkward sentences.

Awkward *Once she located the faulty transistor, re-soldering of the circuit board was begun.* (The first subject is *she*, and its verb— *located*—is active; the second subject is *resoldering*, and its verb—*was begun*—is passive.)

Consistent *Once the faulty transistor was located, re-soldering of the circuit board was begun.* (Two passive verbs identify neither performer of the actions.)

Strong *Once she located the faulty transistor, her assistant began to resolder the circuit board.* (Two active verbs have people as subjects.)

MOOD

Beyond tense and voice, verbs also present problems of mood. One sure way to confuse and annoy readers is to shift unnecessarily and too frequently from verbs of a particular mood to verbs of another mood. Make certain when you use a mood shift that it is essential and effective.

Mood: *characteristic of a verb that shows the manner in which a statement is thought of by the writer. The three moods are* indicative, imperative, *and* subjunctive.

The *indicative* mood states a fact, a condition, or a question.

Lynn runs the mile in just over four minutes.
If I go home early, I will rest.
Have you eaten lunch yet?

The *imperative* mood states a command, makes a request, gives directions, or advises.

Attack at dawn.

Give me the book, please.

Follow the main road.

Speak lovingly.

The *subjunctive* mood expresses a wish, a condition contrary to fact, or a speculation.

We wish she were not staying.

If I were directing this project, I would budget more carefully.

[Avoid needless shifts of mood.]

When the intention shifts within the same sentence, it is logical to shift the moods of the verbs.

Logical   *Find another profession when your work begins to bore you.* (Imperative mood to indicate advice, followed by indicative mood to indicate a factual condition.)

Logical   *I would find another profession if I were sure that this work is wrong for me.* (Indicative *would find*, to indicate condition, followed by subjunctive *were sure*, to indicate speculation, followed by the indicative *is*, to indicate the fact underlying the speculation.)

But needless shifts of mood disturb the logic of the sentence in which they appear and therefore confuse the reader.

Confusing   *First make certain that all tools for the job are at hand and then you will decide on the order in which to do the work.* (The verb *make* is in the imperative: the writer is giving directions. The second verb, *are*, is indicative: the writer is stating a fact to be determined. The third verb, *will decide*, is in the indicative. It should be in the imperative, the same mood as the first, since it, too, is giving directions.)

Logical　　*First make certain that all the tools for the job are at hand and then decide on the order in which to do the work.* (Both verbs giving directions are now in the imperative.)

Logical　　*First you make certain that all the tools for the job are at hand and then you decide on the order in which to do the work.* (All the verbs are in the indicative.)

Confusing　　*They consider it essential that each employee buy savings bonds and names a family member as beneficiary.* (The first verb in the dependent clause, *buy*, is in the subjunctive and the second, *names*, is in the indicative, even though both have *employee* as subject and express parallel thoughts.)

Logical　　*They consider it essential that each employee buy savings bonds and name a family member as beneficiary.* (Both verbs are in the subjunctive, to indicate parallel wishes.)

PERSON

Verbs must reflect the person or persons about whom they make statements.

Person:　　*characteristic of verbs (and pronouns) that indicates the person speaking, spoken to, or spoken about. There are three persons singular: (first person—I; second person—you; third person—he, she, it); and three persons plural: (first person—we; second person—you; third person—they).*

[Avoid needless shifts of person.]

Many sentences require a shift of person in order to convey the correct meaning. Consider the sentence *I know that you are telling the truth even though most members of the club are not.* It contains all three persons: first (*I know*), second (*you are telling*), and third (*most are*). But other sentences shift person inappropriately.

Inappropriate	*Scientists are guilty of serious error if you ignore evidence opposed to your hypotheses.* (The subject of the first clause, *scientists*, is logically the subject of the second clause as well. Thus, *you ignore* should be *they ignore*, and the pronoun *your* should be *their*.)
Appropriate	*Scientists are guilty of serious error if they ignore evidence opposed to their hypotheses.* (Third person consistently.)
Appropriate	*As a scientist you are guilty of serious error if you ignore evidence opposed to your hypotheses.* (Second person consistently.)
Inappropriate	*A writer finds a quiet place in which to work and they go there every day.* (Third person singular, third person plural.)
Appropriate	*A writer finds a quiet place in which to work and goes there every day.* (Third person singular.)
Appropriate	*Writers find a quiet place in which to work and go there every day.* (Third person plural.)

The correct use of verbs is not difficult, but requires careful attention to tense, voice, mood, and person.

CHAPTER 7

Modifiers

Modifiers are essential sentence elements. When writers use them skillfully, readers understand readily the precise intention of what is on the page. But when modifiers are carelessly used, readers may be confused.

Modifiers are words and groups of words that describe or limit elements of a sentence. The most familiar modifiers are single-word adjectives and adverbs, but phrases and clauses also may act as modifiers.

Modifiers

Adjectives: *words that modify nouns, pronouns, and noun phrases (beautiful* clouds, *those* ones, *sleepy* Little Boy Blue*).*

Adverbs: *words that modify all other parts of speech (almost* complete confusion, moved *quickly).*

Adjective
phrases: *phrases that modify nouns and pronouns* (the boy *with blue eyes,* the one *on the left).*

Adverb phrases:	*phrases that modify all other parts of speech* (They arrived *in the evening*, the contract was awarded *after the first competition*.)
Adjective clauses:	*clauses that modify nouns and pronouns* (all *who attend*, the time *we spend together*).
Adverb clauses:	*clauses that modify all other parts of speech* (*After they arrived*, they sat and waited. John hesitated *because he was torn between the two job offers*.)

You will have little trouble placing adjectives correctly within a sentence if you place them as close as possible to the elements they modify. But while you are editing your work, make certain that adjectives—whether *single words*, *phrases*, or *clauses*—clearly modify the elements they are intended to modify.

ADVERBIAL MODIFIERS

Adverbs are a different matter. Unless they are placed properly—and placement is sometimes difficult—your writing will be awkward or your meaning obscure. To illustrate the pitfalls of placement, examine the following two sentences.

They frequently ate late at night.

They ate frequently late at night.

Consider first the adverb phrase *late at night*. It occurs at the end of each of the sentences, because such phrases are usually placed after the verb. This is a question of idiom; any native speaker of English would place this phrase where it has been placed.

Idiom: *a characteristic way of expressing a thought
in a language—whether grammatically cor-
rect or incorrect.*

The adverb *frequently* in the two sentences poses
a different problem. Both sentences are correct and
both are idiomatic. But moving the adverb *frequently*
from before the verb *ate* to after the verb *ate* changes
the meaning of the sentence. The first sentence
describes night owls; the second describes gluttons:
why else would they eat frequently? Thus, where an
adverb is placed can be critical.

> Place most adverbs *before* or *after* the
> *verbs* they modify *or* at the *end* of
> a *clause or sentence.* Be sure that
> your sentences convey the exact
> meaning you intend.

As long as the meaning is clear, the placement
is correct. All four of the following sentences are
clear.

He immediately went to the hospital. (The adverb is placed before the verb.)

He went immediately to the hospital. (The adverb is placed after the verb.)

*He went to the hospital immediately, but we
waited at home for his mother's arrival.* (The
adverb is placed at the end of the clause.)

He went to the hospital immediately. (The adverb is placed at the end of the sentence.)

Take care when placing an adverb at the end of a
clause or a sentence: the result may be ridiculous.

*She went to the cemetery to see the boy buried in
a taxi.*

The writer of this sentence did not mean to modify *buried* with the adverb phrase *in a taxi*. The intended meaning is clear in the following sentence.

> *She took a taxi to the cemetery to see the boy buried.*

> [Think twice before placing an adverb
> between a verb and the direct ob-
> ject of the verb.]

Many sentences will appear unidiomatic when an adverb falls between a verb and its direct object, although some sentences can have this construction without risking awkwardness. *They answered slowly the reporter's questions* may be technically clear, but it sounds wrong, perhaps because the adverb appears between the verb *answered* and its direct object, *questions*. But there is no problem when the sentence reads, *They slowly answered the reporter's questions*, or *Slowly they answered the reporter's questions*, or *They answered the reporter's questions slowly*.

The only way to know when an expression is or is not idiomatic is by living and reading and listening. In the following sentences the adverb falls in various positions.

Idiomatic   *Helen sensed quickly that her opponent's backhand was weak.*

Idiomatic   *Helen quickly sensed that her opponent's backhand was weak.*

Misleading   *Helen sensed that her opponent's backhand was weak quickly.*

In the sample sentence the adverb cannot be placed at the end and still make the intended sense. Adverbs can be a nuisance.

> When a verb has both a *direct* object
> and an *indirect* object, think twice
> about where to place an adverb.

The usual position of the adverb is immediately before the verb.

My employer never gives hourly workers a bonus.

The direct object is *bonus*. The indirect object is *workers*. The adverb *never* has no place in this sentence except immediately before the verb.

In many other sentences you may place the modifier elsewhere, especially when you are editing a short sentence.

Idiomatic   *The old couple frequently mail packages to their sons.*

Idiomatic   *The old couple mail packages frequently to their sons.*

Now add a few words to this sentence and see what happens to the position of the adverb.

Awkward   *The old couple mail packages of home-cooked food frequently to their sons.*

Reading the last sentence, the reader sensitive to idiom feels uneasy. What is *frequently* supposed to modify now? The sentence can be rewritten in still other ways.

Idiomatic   *The old couple frequently mail packages of home-cooked food to their sons.*

No one is likely to write, *The old couple mail frequently to their sons packages of home-cooked food.* It simply sounds wrong—unidiomatic.

Your first impulse, therefore, should be to place adverbs directly before the verbs they modify—especially when you are dealing with verbs that have both direct and indirect objects. Most of all, ask yourself whether a construction sounds right. In time you will become increasingly sensitive to the demands of English idiom.

Split
infinitive: *an infinitive in which one or more words occur between* to *and the verb form; for example,* to love *(regular infinitive) and* to always love *(split infinitive).*

Split infinitives no longer are considered mortal sins, yet few sentences are improved by their use. When a modifier of an infinitive falls easily between the two parts of the infinitive, there is no need to move the modifier simply to satisfy an old-fashioned rule against split infinitives. But when such placement results in an awkward expression, the modifier should be moved. As a guideline, remember that when infinitives are split by more than a single word, the expression is probably awkward. As you become experienced in good writing, your eye and ear will tell you when you must not split.

> [Split an infinitive only to improve a sentence.]

Awkward *Once I mastered the art of making my customers feel at ease, I was able to, without violating any laws, sell them almost anything I wanted to sell.*

In the sentence above, readers are left hanging so long between the first *to* and *sell* that they may forget what the sentence is about.

Smooth *Once I mastered the art of making my customers feel at ease, I was able to sell them almost anything I wanted to sell without violating fair trade laws.*

Even when only one word splits an infinitive, the resulting construction may be awkward. In such a case, do not split the infinitive. The following two examples show acceptable split infinitives.

I hope you will find a way to quickly balance *all our financial accounts before the annual audit.*

The efforts of many of our politicians are not intended to really help people *in the inner cities.*

When moving a modifier out of an infinitive would not markedly improve the sentence, the split infinitive may stand.

PROBLEM CONSTRUCTIONS

Verb
phrase: *a verb plus its auxiliary verbs. (They have adopted our customs.) The most common auxiliary verbs are be, do, and have. Other common auxiliary verbs are can, may, might, must, ought, shall, should, will, and would.*

Split verb phrases may be as awkward as split infinitives. Your job as editor of your own writing is to identify all the parts of a verb phrase and then decide whether separating the phrase by a modifier improves a sentence or makes it awkward. *Verb phrases split by more than a single word are usually awkward.*

> Split a verb phrase only to improve a sentence.

Awkward *Many companies are, by requiring employees to take their vacations within a single two-week period, finding that they can install heavy equipment on assembly lines without disrupting normal work flow.* (The parts of the verb phrase *are finding* are too far apart.)

Logical   *Many companies, by requiring employees to take their vacations within a single two-week period, are finding that they can install heavy equipment on assembly lines without disrupting normal work flow.* (The verb phrase is now intact, but the subject, *companies*, and the verb, *are finding*, are too far apart.)

Smooth   *By requiring employees to take their vacations within a single two-week period, many companies are finding that they can install heavy equipment on assembly lines without disrupting normal work flow.*

Awkward   *John and Janet are, now that they have saved enough money, buying the new television set they want.*

Logical   *John and Janet, now that they have saved enough, are buying the new television set they want.* (The subject and verb are too far apart.)

Smooth   *Now that John and Janet have saved enough money, they are buying the new television set they want.*

A single-word modifier often finds a welcome home within a verb phrase.

They have quickly become accustomed *to life in a retirement community.*

As my father grows older, he finds that he is easily moved *to tears.*

Any tenants slow in paying rent will rapidly regret *their dilatory ways.*

If you try moving any of the adverbs in these three examples, you will find that no other arrangement is as clear. When a modifier fits naturally within a verb phrase, let it stay there.

As was said earlier, adverbs modify everything but nouns, pronouns, and noun phrases. This means that they modify adjectives and adverbs as well as verbs and entire clauses and sentences. The requirement to keep adverbs close to the elements they modify is strongest when adverbs modify adjectives and adverbs. Failure to do so will almost always result in unclear and misleading sentences.

> [Keep adverbs close to the adjectives]
> [and adverbs they modify.]

The following are examples of sentences that keep the adverbs close to the words they modify.

> *She played tennis so well that we thought she was a professional.* (The adverb *so* modifies the adverb *well*. Both are well placed. They cannot be moved anywhere else in the sentence.)

> *Your actions in support of our cause were quite welcome.* (The adjective *welcome* complements the verb *were*. The adverb *quite* modifies *welcome* and is best placed before it.)

> *You ought to get rid of that thoroughly disreputable hat before going out on job interviews.* (The adjective *disreputable* modifies *hat*. The adverb *thoroughly* modifies *disreputable* and cannot idiomatically be placed elsewhere.)

Moving any of these adverbs about would create confusion.

Another pitfall in the correct placement of modifiers is offered by the *modifier that looks both ways*, a difficulty sometimes referred to as the *squinting modifier*.

> *I wanted immediately to notify him.*

In the sentence above, what does *immediately* modify? It is looking both at *wanted* and at *to notify*. Moving *immediately* before *wanted* results in one meaning; putting it at the end of the sentence produces another. As a writer, you must decide which meaning you intend. You then will know where to place *immediately*.

> [Beware of modifiers that look both ways.]

Ambiguous — *The book he was reading quickly bored him.* (This sentence can be understood perfectly by anyone *listening* to it, because the speaker will pause either before or after *quickly*. In print, however, the sentence gives no clue as to which of two possible meanings is intended.)

Clear — *The book he was reading bored him* quickly.

Clear — *He was bored by the book he was reading* quickly.

Murphy's First Law of Writing

> [Anything that can be misunderstood will be misunderstood.]

Ambiguous — *Many neighbors I know would have reacted the same way.* (Does *I know* modify *neighbors* or the entire sentence?)

Clear — *I know many neighbors would have reacted the same way.*

Clear — *Many neighbors would have reacted the same way, I know.*

Clear — *Many neighbors, I know, would have reacted the same way.* (This last sentence has the same word order as the original awkward sentence, but the pair of commas enables *I know* to function as a sentence interrupter, or parenthetical expression.)

Ambiguous	*She said when the play ended she would change her clothes and go to the party.* (Does the clause *when the play ended* modify *said, would change, go,* or *would change and go?*)
Clear	*When the play ended, she said she would change her clothes and go to the party.*
Clear	*She said she would change her clothes when the play ended and go to the party.*
Clear	*She said she would change her clothes and go to the party when the play ended.*
Dangling modifier:	*a word or group of words that appears to modify an element it cannot modify.*

Dangling modifiers can make for unintentionally ridiculous writing even though readers usually understand exactly what is meant. Dangling modifiers can be *gerunds, participles,* or *infinitives* used alone or as parts of phrases or clauses. They can also be *prepositional phrases* or *dependent clauses.* Modifiers are said to dangle when they are badly placed—most often at the beginning of a sentence. You can cure a dangling modifier by straightening out the grammatical relation in the offending sentence. This job often requires changing the dangling modifier to a complete clause or supplying the noun or pronoun the modifier logically describes.

Dangling	*After working so hard in the garden, the vegetables rewarded us with a delicious meal.* (Vegetables do not work in gardens, yet the dangling gerund, *working,* implies that they do.)
Logical	*After working so hard in the garden, we were rewarded with a delicious meal of fresh vegetables.* (The pronoun *we* gives the gerund phrase something to modify.)
Dangling	*To be accepted by most graduate schools, a recent photograph is required.* (The infinitive *To be accepted* here refers to *photo-*

graph. But photographs do not usually apply to graduate schools.)

Logical — *To be accepted by most graduate schools, applicants must supply a recent photograph.* (Now the noun *applicants* is modified by the infinitive phrase.)

Dangling — *At age seven, my sister married her childhood sweetheart.* (Surely the sister did not marry that young, as implied by the phrase *At age seven.*)

Logical — *When I was seven, my sister married her childhood sweetheart.* (The phrase has been changed to a clause that makes the real meaning clear.)

Absolute phrase: *a phrase closely related in meaning to the rest of a sentence but grammatically independent of it.*

Do not confuse *absolute phrases* with *dangling modifiers.* A verb form in an absolute phrase is complete within the phrase—*the table set, all the guests gone, the dishes done.* Because the verb forms are complete, absolute phrases such as the following can stand independently.

All things considered, the evening was a great success.

The concert ended, the musicians packed their instruments and waited to be paid.

The absolute phrases shown above do not dangle. They tell the reader what was *considered* and what *ended.*

CHAPTER 8

Pronouns

Pronouns are essential elements of well-crafted sentences. Note the number of pronouns in the following sentence.

> *The hardships you mention in your letter are mere abstractions for those of us who have never experienced them.*

Of the nineteen words in the sentence, six are pronouns—*you, your, those, us, who,* and *them.* Strict grammarians use the term *pronominal adjective* for words such as *your;* but in the discussion that follows, pronominal adjectives will usually be referred to as pronouns, since they come from pronouns and resemble them so closely.

Pronominal
adjective: *an adjective formed from a personal pronoun and appearing only in the possessive:* my, your, his, her, its, one's, our, your, their. *Pronominal adjectives modify nouns or noun substitutes.*

Pronouns are not difficult to manage once you learn the rules that govern them. These rules concern *agreement, case,* and *reference,* covering such matters as when to use a plural pronoun; when to use first person, second person, or third person; and when to use the subjective, possessive, and objective cases.

AGREEMENT

> Make sure that every pronoun agrees with its antecedent in number, person, and gender.

Number: *singular or plural*

Person: *identifies the performer of the action of a verb, or the subject of the condition described by a verb:*
      first person: *I am, we are*
      second person: *you are*
      third person: *he is, she is, it is, they are*

Gender: *masculine, feminine, neuter*

In the following sentences there is full agreement in number, person, and gender.

John left his telephone number with his mother. (The antecedent, *John,* is third person singular, so the sentence uses the third person singular masculine pronoun *his.*)

John thanked his mother for her generosity in paying his debts. (The pronouns clearly related to *John* are the masculine *his; her* clearly relates to the feminine *mother.*)

Michael wrote to Eileen and Anne, asking that they check the completeness of their study before submitting their request for funding. (The third person plural feminine antecedent *Eileen and Anne* takes the third person plural pronouns *they* and *their.* Plural pronouns do not show gender.)

It is not difficult to choose the correct pronouns in simple sentences. As sentences grow in complexity, problems may arise.

Collective Nouns

[Use a *singular pronoun* to refer to a]
[*singular collective noun*.]

A *collective noun* designates an aggregate of people or things—*police*, *flock*, and *army* are good examples. Collective nouns are treated as singular when they are thought of as representing a singular meaning. In the sentence *The company is firing all employees with less than three years' service*, the collective noun *company* is thought of as a single unit and is therefore followed by a singular verb. But in *The company had arrived early and were going home at last*, the collective noun *company* is thought of as many people counted individually and therefore takes a plural verb.

Awkward *The engineering design group, at the request of the subcommittee chairman, has decided to defer their final recommendation until wind-tunnel tests are complete.* (The antecedent of *their* is *engineering design group*, a collective noun. It should be treated as singular in this sentence, because the group is acting as a single body making a recommendation. Notice the singular verb *has decided*.)

Logical *The engineering design group, at the request of the subcommittee chairman, has decided to defer its final recommendation until wind-tunnel tests are complete.*

[Use a *plural pronoun* to refer to a]
[*plural collective noun*.]

Logical *When the theater manager announced the bomb threat, the audience left their seats and walked quickly to the street.* (*Audience*, a collective noun, is here thought of as consisting of many individuals, each with a seat and each walking.)

When you must decide whether to use a singular or a plural pronoun to refer to a collective noun, consider whether you intend the collective as a singular or as a plural. When you edit your work, pay careful attention to this question and make sure that you treat each collective noun consistently.

Indefinite Pronouns

[Use a *singular pronoun* to refer to a
  singular indefinite pronoun.]

Indefinite
pronoun: a pronoun that does not specify the identity
             of its antecedent—*all, both, few, several,
             some, somebody*—and the like

English has a great many indefinite pronouns. Some are singular, others are plural, and a small number may serve in either capacity. The singular indefinite pronouns include:

another	either	much	oneself
any	everybody	neither	other
anybody	everyone	nobody	somebody
anyone	everything	no one	someone
anything	little	nothing	something
each			

Five indefinite pronouns are always plural:

both	many	several
few	others	

Five other indefinite pronouns may be used either as singulars or plurals:

all	none	such
more	some	

Your concern as a writer is to make certain that you treat singular indefinite pronouns as singular, and plural indefinite pronouns as plural. This requirement affects the *verbs* you use with indefinite pronouns as well as the *pronouns* you use to refer to indefinite pronouns. The following sentences illustrate how agreement is required in pronouns that refer to indefinite pronouns.

Mixed
: *Each of the five courses I registered for in my first year in college made their demands on my future.* (The antecedent of the plural *their* is the singular indefinite pronoun *Each.* The plural noun *courses* between *each* and *their* misled the writer.)

Consistent
: *Each of the five courses I registered for in my first year in college made its demands on my future.*

Mixed
: *We welcomed anybody who came to the stag party and gave them plenty to eat and drink.* (The antecedent of the plural *them* is *anybody*, a singular.)

Consistent
: *We welcomed anybody who came to the stag party and gave him plenty to eat and drink.*

Consistent
: *More was given than we expected, but it was still too little.* (The indefinite pronoun *More* is singular here, referring to an amount rather than to a number. Therefore, the verb following is *was given*, and the pronoun is *it*.)

[Use a *plural pronoun* to refer to a *plural indefinite pronoun*.]

The plural indefinite pronouns *both, few, many, others*, and *several* count things and people. All the following sentences consistently use plural pronouns.

Once the work had officially ended, all agreed that their project had been ruined by company indecisiveness and inadequate funding. (The antecedent of *their* is the plural *all*—here standing for all the people involved in the work.)

More of the marketing personnel being hired this year will find their field experience helpful if our training staff is able to do everything it plans. (*More* is plural in this sentence because it refers to *marketing personnel*, people who can be counted.)

Several are taking their CPA examinations next spring.

Many will be assigned to the project even though they have explicitly requested other assignments.

Compound Nouns

Compound
subjects
and objects: *two or more nouns or pronouns joined by* and *and serving as subject or object of the same verb or verbs.*

Expressions joined by *and* usually refer to more than one subject and are therefore plural. Sentences built on such compounds use plural verbs because their subjects are plural. Any pronoun referring to these subjects must therefore also be plural.

[Use a plural pronoun to refer to a compound joined by *and*.]

Unemployment and inflation added their special miseries to lives already damaged by food shortages, pollution, and political crises. (The antecedent of *their*, a plural, is the plural compound subject *Unemployment and inflation*.)

A dictionary and thesaurus find their way onto almost every writer's desk.

Frank and Anne are completing the mural they started last year.

Fear and crime go together; the one causes the other, and both take their toll.

Exception. Some compounds, though joined by *and*, are considered singulars—*eggs and bacon; the red, white, and blue;* and so on—because they stand for a singular concept, such as a dish of food or a flag.

Fish and chips sinks to new depths as a sustainer of life when you order it in a fast-food outlet. (The antecedent of *it*, a singular, is the singular compound subject *Fish and chips*.)

> Use a singular pronoun to refer to a compound antecedent consisting of *singulars* joined by *or* or *nor*.

When *or* or *nor* separates the parts of a compound subject, the meaning implies that, in effect, only one of the subjects will operate in the sentence. Agreement is served by having a singular verb and singular pronouns.

The federal government or the state government will have to pay its share of the cost of the new highway before work can begin. (The antecedent of *its* is either part of the compound antecedent— *federal government* or *state government*. Both are singular, connected by *or*.)

Neither the engineering department nor the marketing department has the substantial personnel reserve needed for its work in the coming year.

> Use a plural pronoun to refer to a compound antecedent consisting of *plurals* joined by *or* or *nor*.

When the individual parts of the compound noun are already in the plural, agreement demands plural verbs and pronouns.

> *The company officers or the directors will have to make their opinions known in this matter.* (The antecedent of *their* is either part of the compound antecedent *company officers or the directors.* Both parts are plural.)

> *Neither the boys nor the girls can expect to get precisely what they want when their disagreement is resolved.* (The antecedent of *they* and *their* is either part of *the boys nor the girls.*)

> *Either the separatists or the nationalists are going to have to give ground if they are to find a peaceful resolution for the problem Canada faces.*

> *Potatoes or green vegetables have been served with every meal since we arrived, and I must warn all careful diners to avoid them.*

> When a compound antecedent joined by *or* or *nor* consists of a singular and a plural, use a pronoun that agrees in number with the part of the compound closest to the pronoun.

A choice has to made about agreement when a singular and a plural noun are linked by *or* or *nor*. The verb and pronoun are then controlled by the second, or last, noun in the compound. This rule is not as difficult as it seems. A *magazine or books* is a compound antecedent consisting of a singular noun and a plural noun joined by *or*. In a sentence in which this compound serves as the antecedent of a pronoun, the pronoun should be plural, because the plural *books* follows the singular *magazine*. In practice the plural part of a compound joined by *or* or *nor* is almost always made the last element in the compound. Otherwise, the sentence would sound awkward.

In the sentence that follows, the awkwardness

resulting from failure to follow this practice will become obvious.

Awkward	*Either the instructors or the department head chooses the committee members she wants.*
Smooth	*Either the department head or the instructors choose the committee members they want.*
Smooth	*Commercial fishermen report that neither a single shrimp nor more than ten soft-shell crabs are found in their customary beds.*
Smooth	*We will not be able to handle all the anticipated work if the design award or the prototype contract or the three production contracts we expect are announced before we complete staffing for them.*

CASE

Pronoun
case:
the form of a pronoun that shows its relation to other parts of a sentence:
subjective: *I, you, he, she, it, one; we, you, they*
possessive: *mine, yours, his, hers, its; ours, yours, theirs*
objective: *me, you, him, her, it, one; us, you, them.*

The case of a pronoun is determined by its function in a sentence. When the pronoun is the *subject*, the subjective case is used. When the pronoun expresses *ownership*, the possessive case is called for. And when the pronoun is the person or thing *to whom the action is done*, the objective case is appropriate. In most sentences selecting pronouns of the correct case is easy, but there are many constructions that trouble all but the most experienced writers. The rules that will be presented for pronoun case deal with these problem constructions.

If you can identify the parts of a clause and know the function of each part, you will be able to select all pronoun cases correctly in all sentences. Two simple examples of sentences employing pronouns will illustrate their proper use.

> *I hear they will soon be joining the group.* (The subject of the verb *hear* is *I*; the subject of the verb *will be joining* is *they*.)

> *Tell the librarian we are leaving soon.* (Since the subject of *are leaving* is *we*, it is in the subjective case.)

Exception. A sentence such as *It is me* does not follow the rules that will be presented in the following pages. It would seem that the complement of a linking verb should be subjective: *It is I*—meaning *It is I who stand here* (or some other full response to the question *Who is there?*). *It is me* is therefore illogical. But in such an instance grammar has lost out to idiom. Most people say, *It is me* or *It's me*, but some careful writers use *It is I* in formal usage.

> Use the *subjective* case for a pronoun acting as subject of a verb or complement of a linking verb.

Illogical   *You and me cannot agree on anything.* (*You* and *me* are subjects of the verb *cannot agree*. Since *you* has the same form in the subjective and objective, it is correct; but the objective *me* is incorrect for a subject.)

Logical   *You and I cannot agree on anything.*

Illogical   *I thought the winners of the contest would be Janet and me.* (The personal pronouns are complements of the linking verb *would be* and must be subjective.)

Logical   *I thought the winners of the contest would be Janet and I.*

Illogical	*The only person who will not attend is her.* (The pronoun *her* is the complement of the linking verb *is* and must be subjective.)
Logical	*The only person who will not attend is she.*

> [Use the *objective* case for a pronoun]
> acting as object of a verb or object
> [of a preposition.]

Illogical	*The manager told Jim and I to work late last night.* (The verb *told* has two objects— *Jim* and *I*. The noun *Jim* is correct, since nouns do not have different forms for subjective and objective. The mistake is in *I*, which should be in the objective case—*me*.)
Logical	*The manager told Jim and me to work late last night.*
Illogical	*I suppose they will choose Al and she as district leaders.* (The pronoun *she* is an object of the verb *choose*.)
Logical	*I suppose they will choose Al and her as district leaders.*

It is easy to determine the case of a pronoun when it is the *single object* of a preposition.

One of them will have to make the choice.

Two of us will be rooming together.

But many writers run into trouble when a preposition has more than one object. The way to test for the case of pronouns after a preposition is to treat each pronoun individually, as the following examples illustrate.

Illogical	*The community school board will have to find jobs for we and they.* (The pronouns are both objects of the preposition *for*.)
Logical	*The community school board will have to find jobs for them and us.* (By custom, the first person pronoun is placed last.)

Illogical	*Ellen was seated between he and I.* (The pronouns are both objects of the preposition *between*.)
Logical	*Ellen was seated between him and me.*
Illogical	*Do you think Bob wants to go to the party with his sisters instead of with you and I?* (Would anyone write *with I*?)
Logical	*Do you think Bob wants to go to the party with his sisters instead of with you and me?*
Illogical	*Many of we students are interested in organizing a protest meeting.* (The pronoun is the object of the preposition *of*. The noun *students* is in *apposition* with the pronoun. When a noun is in apposition with a pronoun, the grammatical relation does not change. The pronoun is still the object of a preposition and must be in the objective case.)
Logical	*Many of us students are interested in organizing a protest meeting.*

No matter the position of the pronoun in the sentence, and no matter how the pronouns are compounded, prepositions always determine that pronouns are in the objective case.

> Use the *possessive* case for pronouns appearing before a *gerund*. Use the *objective* case for pronouns appearing before a *participle*.

Gerunds and Participles

The *-ing* verbals—gerunds and participles—are look-alikes that function differently. They also have different requirements for pronouns that appear before them.

Gerund: *a verbal ending in -ing that functions as a noun.*

Participle: *a verbal ending in* -ing *that functions as an adjective.*

Pronouns appearing with gerunds take the *possessive case*, whether the gerund functions as a subject, object, or complement, as the following examples show.

> *Her diving impresses me.* (The subject of the verb *impresses* is the gerund *diving*.)

> *We question his acting in this manner.* (The gerund *acting* is the object of the verb *question*.)

> *I was affected by her crying.* (The gerund *crying* is the object of the preposition *by*.)

> *My principal objection was their lying under oath.* (The gerund *lying* is the complement of the linking verb *was*.)

Pronouns used with participles take the *objective case*, as the following examples show.

> *I saw him running from the fire.* (The participle *running* is part of a phrase modifying *him*. The pronoun *him* is objective because it is the object of the verb *saw*.)

> *I found them diving off the highest rocks.* (The participle *diving* is part of a phrase modifying *them*. The pronoun *them* is objective because it is the object of the verb *found*.)

> *We saw a few of them waiting for autographs outside the star's dressing room.* (The pronoun *them* is the object of the preposition *of*. The participle *waiting* is part of a modifying phrase.)

To determine whether a pronoun before an *-ing* verbal should be possessive or objective, the function of the verbal must be clear. If the verbal functions as a noun, the possessive case applies to the pronoun before it. If the verbal functions as a modifier, the objective case fits the pronoun before it.

When a noun occurs before a gerund or participle, the noun must also be in the correct case. *Nouns have distinctive forms for the possessive* (though their forms are identical in the subjective and objective).

> *The boy* (subject) *walked to the blackboard.*
>
> *The boy's* (possessive) *mistakes were overlooked by his teacher.*
>
> *I saw the boy* (object) *in the classroom.*

The rules for noun case before gerunds and participles are the same as for pronoun case.

> *Clara's diving impresses me.* (possessive before a gerund)
>
> *I saw Willy running from the fire.* (objective before a participle)

Exception. In a few constructions, *a noun is objective before a gerund.* The objective case may precede the gerund when a noun is plural, when the noun is inanimate or abstract, and when a phrase appears between the noun and the gerund.

Appositives

Appositive: *a noun or noun substitute placed next to another noun or noun substitute to explain or identify it—also known as a noun repeater.*

Pronouns as well as nouns may function as *appositives.* Because the case of a pronoun appositive depends on the case of the word or words with which it is in apposition, the relation between the appositive and its referent is important. They must be identical.

> Use the same case for an appositive—
> pronoun or noun—that you use for the
> word it relates to.

Illogical   *I must remind you that the jury found both of us—Hilda and I—innocent of the crime.* (The pronoun *us*, the object of the preposition *of*, is in the objective case. The appositives of *us* must therefore also be objective.)

Logical   *I must remind you that the jury found both of us—Hilda and me—innocent of the crime.*

Illogical   *All three partners—Jane, Ken, and her— must work as a team or the business will fail.* (The noun *partners* is the subject of the verb *must work*. The appositive must therefore also be subjective.)

Logical   *All three partners—Jane, Ken, and she— must work as a team or the business will fail.*

Illogical   *Your grandmother intended to give the present to the couple—Johnny and she—not to Johnny alone.* (The noun *couple* is the object of the preposition *to*. The appositives must therefore also be objective.)

Logical   *Your grandmother intended to give the present to the couple—Johnny and her—not to Johnny alone.*

Logical   *The fault was the principal's, hers alone.* (The noun *principal's* is possessive, and its appositive *hers* is also possessive.)

Incomplete Clauses

> Use the same case after *than* or *as*
> in an incomplete clause that you
> would use if the clause were complete.

Rather than repeat words unnecessarily in certain sentences, we write what are called *incomplete*, or *elliptical, clauses.* Such clauses are usually introduced by *than* or *as*. For example, we may write, *Fred gives you more trouble than I do*. We may express the same thought but leave the final clause incomplete—*Fred gives you more trouble than I*. In both these sentences, *than* is a conjunction joining the two clauses. *I* is subjective in both sentences because it serves as the subject of the verb *do*, even when *do* is understood rather than stated.

Incomplete clauses may omit various parts of speech. In the following sentence, both the verb and subject are missing from the incomplete clause: *Fred gives you more trouble than me*. This sentence expresses the thought *Fred gives you more trouble than he gives me*. The pronoun *me* is objective in both sentences because it is the indirect object of *gives*, whether *he gives* is stated or unstated.

Illogical	*We found you as worthy of praise as she.* (The final pronoun should be objective, because it is the object of the verb *found*, unstated.)
Logical	*We found you as worthy of praise as her.*
Illogical	*We found you were as worthy of praise as her.* (The omitted part of the incomplete clause is *was*. The subjective case is needed.)
Logical	*We found you were as worthy of praise as she.*
Logical	*I am older than he.*
Logical	*I am older than he is.*
Logical	*I hope you will never be as poor as we are.*
Logical	*I hope you will never be poorer than we are.*

REFERENCE

Pronoun
reference: *relation of a pronoun to its antecedent*

Simply put, pronouns must refer clearly and correctly to their antecedents. But mistakes in pronoun reference occur more often than you might suspect, and such mistakes are not always easy to see. Be alert to the function of every pronoun you use and make certain that it expresses your intention.

> [When clarity is at issue, rewrite to avoid pronouns.]

When pronoun reference becomes complex, the use of nouns is preferable. In a technical or legal document, for example, a vague pronoun can have far-reaching effects. Do not hesitate to remove a vague pronoun and repeat the noun that is its antecedent. Repetition is far better than risking misunderstanding. If you do not like the resulting construction, rewrite the sentence.

Vague   *Mary and Alice decided to work together on her project.* (The antecedent of *her* can be either *Mary* or *Alice*.)

Clear   *Mary and Alice decided to work together on Mary's project.*

Clear   *Mary and Alice decided to work together on Alice's project.*

Vague   *Dr. Atkins wrote to the director of the environmental laboratory to report that the program schedule did not permit his participation in the project.* (The antecedent of *his* can be taken to be either the *director* or *Dr. Atkins*.)

Clear   *In a letter to the director of the environmental laboratory, Dr. Atkins wrote, "The*

> *program schedule does not permit my participation in the project."*

Clear | *In a letter to the director of the environmental laboratory, Dr. Atkins wrote, "The program schedule does not permit your participation in the project."*

Clear | *Dr. Atkins wrote to the director of the environmental laboratory to report that the program schedule did not permit the director's participation in the project.*

Vague | *Some travel guides offer little information on such things as local customs, wines, foods, and history. The traveler is left to his own resources, wondering whether they are worth considering. (They might refer to resources, travel guides, customs,* and so on.)

Clear | [first sentence unchanged] *The traveler is left to his own resources, wondering whether the travel guides are worth considering.*

Clear | [first sentence unchanged] *The traveler is left without information on these matters.*

Because many of the problems posed by pronoun reference occur when *relative pronouns* are used, it is worthwhile to review relative pronouns here.

Cases of relative pronouns

subjective	possessive	objective
who	whose	whom
that	of that	that
which	of which, whose	which, whom

Who refers to people.
That refers to objects or people.
Which refers to animals, situations, objects, or collective nouns.

[Use the appropriate relative pronoun
in the appropriate case.]

The following sentences illustrate the appropriate use of relative pronouns.

> *A member of Congress who wishes to get along in politics is well advised to go along with the leaders.* (*Who* is the subject of *wishes.*)

> *The table that you bought will not take much rough use.* (*That* is the object of *bought.*)

> *I will not buy a dog whose tail has been docked.* (*Whose* is the possessive form of *which*, referring to *dog.*)

> *The audience before whom (or before which) you performed is unlike audiences you will meet in most concert halls.* (The relative pronoun *whom* is the object of *before.*)

Typical problems of reference of relative pronouns are worth reviewing here.

> When a verb has a relative pronoun as subject, make sure that the verb agrees in number with the *antecedent* of the relative pronoun.

A relative pronoun often serves as subject of a verb in a dependent clause. In the sentence *I like a waiter who enjoys his work*, the relative pronoun *who* is the subject of *enjoys.* The writer must decide whether the verb *enjoys* in this sentence should be singular or plural. If the antecedent of *who* is singular—and it is: *waiter* is singular—then *who* is considered to be singular, and its verb is correctly singular. If the antecedent of a relative pronoun is plural, then the relative pronoun is plural and any verb depending on that pronoun will also be plural. In the sentence *I like waiters who enjoy their work*, the verb *enjoy* agrees in number with its subject, *who*, whose antecedent, *waiters*, is plural. In writing, take special care with verbs whose subjects are relative pronouns.

In the following sentences, note especially the antecedents of the pronouns.

Confused   *Sally is the only one of our executives who have advanced degrees.* (The antecedent of *who* is *one*, so *who* must be singular.)

Clear   *Sally is the only one of our executives who has advanced degrees.*

Smoother   *Sally is our only executive with advanced degrees.*

Confused   *Sally is the only one of our executives who has advanced degrees who was not promoted last year.* (The antecedent of the first *who* is *executives*, not the pronoun *one*, so the first *who* is plural.)

Clear   *Sally is the only one of our executives who have advanced degrees who was not promoted last year.*

Smoother   *Sally is the only one of our executives with advanced degrees who was not promoted last year.*

Confused   *She was one of the actresses who was considered for that role.*

Clear   *She was one of the actresses who were considered for that role.*

Confused   *She is one instructor who are interested in her students.* (This mistake is easy to spot: the antecedent of *who* is *instructor*.)

Clear   *She is one instructor who is interested in her students.*

Clear   *The club owner wants to hire a pitcher and two outfielders who play aggressive baseball.*

Clear   *The executive vice president asked to speak with one of the members of the operating committee who are going to staff the new program.*

Be especially careful when dealing with *one of* and the relative pronoun that is almost sure to follow. In all instances, a good way to check is to turn the sentence around in your mind. For example, *Of the few instructors, she* is *one* . . . Careful analysis will see you through.

> [Use *who* and *whoever* as subjects,]
> [*whom* and *whomever* as objects.]

In everyday speech *who* is winning out over *whom* in all instances except as the object after a preposition. The same holds true for *whoever* and *whomever*. No one is likely to say *To who did you give the message?* Many people will also avoid the grammatically correct form *To whom did you give the message?* The most common conversational version now is *Who did you give the message to?* As long as the preposition—in this example, it is *to*—does not appear immediately before the pronoun, most people are content with *who*.

But speech is not writing. In writing, the distinction between *who* and *whom* and between *whoever* and *whomever* is still observed. Luckily, the pronouns *who* and *whom* can often be omitted from sentences in which the traditional form is awkward. The rules are not so difficult that you are forced to rely only on replacing these useful pronouns. All of the following are acceptable.

> *The young woman who is waiting outside does not have an appointment.* (The subject of *is waiting* is *who*.)

> *The young woman waiting outside does not have an appointment.*

> *Many critics whom you admire will be at the performance.* (The object of *admire* is *whom*.)

> *Many critics you admire will be at the performance.*

> *The engineers whom you sent for will be here promptly.* (The object of the preposition *for* is *whom*.)

The engineers you sent for will be here promptly.

They will admit whoever appears at the gate before the game begins. (The pronoun *whoever* is the subject of *appears*. It is not the object of *admit*. The entire dependent clause, *whoever appears at the gate*, is the object of *admit*.)

They will appoint whomever you nominate. (The pronoun *whomever* is the object of *nominate*. The entire clause *whomever you nominate* is the object of *appoint*.)

Do not be misled by sentences that include such parenthetical expressions as *I believe, I insist, you might say,* and the rest.

Parenthetical
expression: *an expression inserted in a sentence but having no grammatical relation to it—also known as an* interrupter.

Parenthetical expressions do not affect the case of *who, whom, whoever,* or *whomever*. If an expression such as *I think* or *we believe* can be removed from a sentence without damaging the sentence, the expression is parenthetical. It is good practice to determine the case of the pronoun correctly without the parenthetical expression, and then put the parenthetical expression back in. Note the following examples.

Confused   *The assistant vice president of the bank is the person whom I think can answer that question best.* (The expression *I think* is parenthetical—it can be removed without damaging the sentence—and has no object. The relative pronoun *whom* is the subject of *can answer* and should therefore be in the subjective case.)

Clear   *The assistant vice president of the bank is the person who I think can answer that question best.*

Confused *Sally is a woman whom we believe is trust-worthy.* (The expression *we believe* is parenthetical. The pronoun is therefore the subject of *is* and should be in the subjective case.)

Clear *Sally is a woman who we believe is trust-worthy.* (Notice that both preceding examples can be written without the pronoun *who*.)

> Use the pronouns *this, that, it,* and *which* to refer to an entire clause or sentence only when the reference is clear.

In speech you will often hear such constructions as: *The manager asked me to work through the weekend, even though she knew my wife and I were planning a trip to celebrate our first anniversary. This I refused to do.* We cannot argue that anyone hearing this statement does not understand precisely what the speaker has in mind. The terse *This I refused to do* is emphatic.

In writing, however, it is preferable to avoid placing so great a burden on the pronoun *this* or on its cousins *that, it,* and *which.* Otherwise the pronoun reference may be obscured. In the example given in the previous paragraph, the reader would have to locate the infinitive phrase *to work through the weekend* to identify the antecedent of *this.*

Clear *I refused when the manager asked me to work overtime. She knew my wife and I were planning a trip to celebrate our first anniversary.*

The requirements of the written language are more stringent than those of spoken English. *This, that, it,* and *which* may, of course, be used to refer to whole clauses and sentences, but the reference must be clear.

Obscure
A few of our competitors, eager to win new contracts, are even willing to pay bribes to foreign officials. This is the difference between our company and our competitors. (*This* can be taken to refer either to *eager to win new contracts* or to *willing to pay bribes.* The reader cannot be certain.)

Clear
We are as eager as our competitors to win new contracts but, unlike them, we are unwilling to bribe foreign officials.

Obscure
The discussion ended with a statement that further price increases were inevitable, which infuriated all of us. (What was it that *infuriated all of us,* the fact that the *discussion ended with the statement* or that *further price increases were inevitable*? The antecedent of *which* is not clear.)

Clear
The discussion ended with the statement that further price increases were inevitable, and the thought that prices would go up made all of us furious.

Clear
The discussion ended with the statement that further price increases were inevitable, and we all became infuriated when no chance was given for further argument.

Obscure
The seed catalogue contained a beautiful color photograph of the new hybrid rose, so Tom decided to buy it.

Clear
The seed catalogue contained a beautiful color photograph of the new hybrid rose, so Tom decided to buy the rose (or the catalogue or the photograph).

[Be sure that every pronoun you use]
[has a clear antecedent.

It may seem elementary to state that a clear antecedent is needed for every pronoun, but many writers neglect this requirement. The following sentences show how easily a writer can make the mistake of writing a sentence in which a pronoun has no antecedent.

Missing
antecedent
Allan's therapist told him that he was anxious because of the demands of his job and that she thought it would disappear only when he found an easier job. (The pronoun *it* has no antecedent. The writer may have had the word *anxiety* in mind.)

Vague
antecedent
Allan's therapist told him that his anxiety was caused by his job and that she thought it would disappear only when he found an easier job. (Now there is an antecedent for *it*, but the reader may be misled into thinking that the antecedent is *job* rather than *anxiety*.)

Clear
antecedent
Allan's therapist told him he was anxious because of his job and only an easier job would eliminate his anxiety.

Vague
Dr. Mazzilli told his department head that he had made a terrible mistake in refusing to review the experimental data. (It is not clear what the antecedent of *he* is.)

Clear
Dr. Mazzilli told his department head, "I have made a terrible mistake in refusing to review the experimental data."

Clear
Dr. Mazzilli told his department head, "You hace made a terrible mistake in refusing to review the experimental data."

Vague
The President informed his foreign policy advisers that he would oppose giving aid to foreign governments as long as they persisted in their opposition to disarmament. (It is not clear whether *they* refers to *advisers* or to *foreign governments*.)

Clear   *The President informed his foreign policy advisers that he would oppose giving aid to foreign governments as long as those countries (or as long as his advisers) persisted in their opposition to disarmament.*

CHAPTER 9

Punctuation

Good punctuation plays a vital role in helping readers understand the writer's thoughts. It groups closely related words and thoughts, separates words and thoughts less closely related, and helps in giving the intended emphasis. You will find that following certain conventions of punctuation will enable you to write more clearly.

PRINCIPAL USES OF PUNCTUATION

Sentence Marks

. *Period* closes a sentence; indicates abbreviations.
? *Question Mark* closes a question.
! *Exclamation Point* closes an exclamation or heavily stressed sentence.

Internal Marks

, *Comma* indicates a separation between words, phrases, and clauses; indicates separation between parts of a series; has many other conventional uses.

; *Semicolon* indicates a separation greater than that of the comma and less than that of the period; occurs chiefly between independent clauses.

: *Colon* indicates that something follows—an explanation, a formal quotation, or a series of some importance; also has other routine uses: after the salutation of a business letter, within bibliographic entries, and others.

() *Parentheses* enclose an explanation, clarification, or illustration inserted within a sentence and not related grammatically to the sentence.

[] *Brackets* enclose a writer's comments on quoted material.

Other Marks

" " *Quotation Marks* enclose directly quoted material, words that need to be set off within the sentence for irony or some other purpose.

— *Dash* shows a degree of separation stronger than achieved by the comma, breaking into the construction of a sentence to make a point with some emphasis; dashes may surround words or phrases or clauses in apposition.

... *Ellipsis* shows omission of word or words within a quotation.

- *Hyphen* connects parts of a compound.

' *Apostrophe* shows omission of letters within a word, possession, and plurals. (Not considered a mark of punctuation by some authorities.)

PERIOD

Statements

A period is used after sentences expressing statements and ordinary commands. (For emphatic commands, an exclamation point is used.)

Statement	*Many college students have great difficulty during final examinations.*
Statement	*The letter asked us why we had not contributed to her political campaign.*
Command	*Empty the ashtrays.*
Command	*Leave the room.*

Abbreviations

A period is used after abbreviations.

Mr. Ms. Sgt. A.D. J.D. Ph.D. A.A. i.e. e.g.

Only one period follows a sentence that ends in an abbreviation.

Some universities now offer a five-year program leading to the B.A. and M.A.

When a sentence is followed by a question mark or exclamation point, these marks are placed after a period used for an abbreviation.

Where will Susan take her LL.B.?

How I wish I had my R.N.!

Exceptions.   No period follows certain current abbreviations.

AFL-CIO USAF CIA LSAT NBC

Periods are not used for technical abbreviations unless the abbreviations form a word.

AMP cm hp

in. (inch) *tan.* (tangent)

Dictionaries list abbreviations, either in a special section at the back or in the general vocabulary, and show standard practice for the use of periods in a particular abbreviation.

QUESTION MARK

A question mark is used after a direct question.

Where has the boy gone?

He has gone to the movies again? (Though phrased as a statement, the sentence is intended as a direct question.)

No question mark is used in an indirect question.

Misleading *He asked me where we went last night?*

Clear *He asked me where we went last night.*

A question mark in parentheses indicates information that is open to doubt.

Chaucer, 1340(?)–1400, is best known for writing The Canterbury Tales. (Chaucer's birth date has not been established with certainty.)

The word "caucus," from Algonquian(?), means a private meeting of leaders of a political party. (The derivation of *caucus* is in doubt.)

Notice that no space is left between the information open to doubt and the question mark enclosed in parentheses. If the information open to doubt is itself enclosed in parentheses, no additional parentheses are necessary.

> *Chaucer (1340?–1400) is best known for writing*
> The Canterbury Tales.

> *The word "caucus" (Algonquian?) means a private meeting of leaders of a political party.*

No space is left between the information open to doubt and the question mark.

It is best to avoid the question mark as a means of indicating irony or humor.

Awkward	*I read her poems (?) last night.*
Effective	*I read her so-called poems last night.*
Awkward	*His funny (?) stories brought no laughter.*
Effective	*The audience found nothing to laugh at in his stories.*

EXCLAMATION POINT

The exclamation point is used after an emphatic interjection.

> *No! Ouch!*

You must decide whether an interjection is worthy of the emphasis given by an exclamation point. If it is not, a period will do—*No. Ouch.* After an unemphatic interjection within a sentence, use a comma.

> *No, I will not do what you ask.*

An exclamation point is used after exclamatory phrases and sentences.

> *Not again!*
> *What a mess!*

How I hated them!

What a courageous woman Sarah is!

An exclamation point is used after a sentence expressing a strong command. We distinguish between ordinary commands and strong commands by the amount of stress that would be used if we were speaking the command.

Empty the ashtrays.

Leave the room.

Don't ever speak to me that way again!

Run for your life!

Only the writer can decide whether an exclamation point or a period is appropriate after a written command. What matters is the spirit in which the command is given. In the examples above, one command is made in an angry voice: *Don't ever speak to me that way again!* In another, an emergency is clearly apparent: *Run for your life!*

If you save your exclamation points for situations that demand them, you will not fritter away the emphasis they supply. If you use them carelessly, the effect of those that are properly placed will be lost.

COMMA

The many uses of the comma are difficult to memorize. The comma is used principally to separate coordinate words, phrases, and clauses and to set off subordinate words, phrases, and clauses. It has a large number of other uses that may appear to be nothing more than empty conventions, but in fact a valid reason exists for each. The comma, above all, prevents misreading.

Items in Series

Commas are used to separate items in a series.

Words	*English majors read Hawthorne, James, and Melville in a single semester.*
Phrases	*A good supply of sun-tan oil, dark glasses, and a good book made the beach a perfect place to spend a summer day.*
Clauses	*All afternoon the cat played with a ball of yarn, the dog slept near the radiator, and the children watched television.*

Some writers omit the comma before the final *and* in a series. Specifically, newspaper and magazine style usually requires that the comma be left out. In books, on the other hand, the so-called serial comma is generally used.

If you choose to omit commas in series, be certain the omission does not confuse the reader.

Unclear	*We packed a good supply of food: three kinds of cereal, plenty of powdered milk and pork and beans.*
Clear	*We packed a good supply of food: three kinds of cereal, plenty of powdered milk, and pork and beans.*

Little is ever gained by omitting the comma before *and* in a series. Using the comma every time will help your reader.

A final comma is always used when *and* is omitted before the final item in a series.

Empty suitcases, paper cartons, dirty dishes, old newspapers littered the apartment.

A comma is used before *all* when that word precedes the verb.

Hairpins, combs, brushes, all are part of her makeup kit.

Independent Clauses

A comma is used to separate independent clauses connected by a coordinating conjunction.

Juanita tried again to surpass her old record, but the winds and tide were against her.

We wanted to buy a four-wheel-drive truck for the Service Department, so our supervisor asked us to get bids from at least three suppliers.

When there is no chance of confusing the reader, the comma may be omitted between short independent clauses connected by a coordinating conjunction.

Sales are declining and profits have almost disappeared.

Introductory Elements

Clauses

A comma is used after any introductory clause—that is, an introductory statement that includes a verb.

After Congress adjourned, the committee meeting was delayed for several weeks.

A comma is used after introductory verbal phrases—phrases that include a participle, gerund, or infinitive.

Participle   *Moving as quickly as he dared, the scout soon found the trail through the dark forest.*

Gerund   *On arriving at the concert, we found that the promoters had sold twice as many tickets as there were seats.*

Infinitive   *To demonstrate his courage, the boy jumped
              from one roof to the next.*

Phrases

It is not necessary to use a comma after a short
introductory phrase.

This morning I skipped school.

*To all intents and purposes I was now president
of my class.*

When an introductory phrase is long and complex, however, or when the omission of a comma
might make the meaning of the sentence unclear, a
comma should be used.

*For the sake of our long and intense friendship,
I decided against moving away from Milwaukee.*

*From childhood on, my sister showed a stubborn
streak.*

Adjectives

Commas are used to separate adjectives that
independently modify the same noun. Such adjectives are called *coordinate adjectives*. To test a pair
of adjectives, try placing the word *and* between
them. If the phrase still makes sense, the adjectives
are coordinate. Otherwise, the adjectives are not
coordinate.

Coordinate   *After the calm, clear statement he made,
              we were all surprised by his strange actions.*
              (The adjectives *calm* and *clear* independently
              modify the noun *statement.*)

Not
coordinate   *They spent most of their time tutoring three
              young children.* (The word *and* cannot be

> inserted between *three* and *young* in this
> sentence; the adjective *three* modifies the
> noun phrase *young children*, and *young* mod-
> ifies *children*.)

Another way to determine whether adjectives
are coordinate is to reverse their order. If the phrase
still makes sense, the adjectives are coordinate; otherwise, the adjectives are not coordinate.

Note. Commas are never used between a final adjective and the noun it modifies.

Erroneous
comma   *We admire an assured, skillful, player.*

Clear   *We admire an assured, skillful player.*

Nonrestrictive Modifiers

Phrases and clauses

Commas are used to set off nonessential modifying phrases and clauses. Some modifiers are needed
to identify the sentence elements they modify—"*my
present job*," "*the house* I live in," "*a sight* you will
never forget." Without these modifiers the reader
would not know which job, house, or sight was
being discussed. These so-called *restrictive modifiers*
restrict the sentence element modified to a particular member of a class of persons, places, or things.

Other modifiers, called *nonrestrictive modifiers*,
do not identify the sentence elements they modify;
the information they present is in addition to an
already identified element.

> *Ronald Reagan, who was elected by a large mar-
> gin, attempted to make sweeping changes in the
> operation of the United States government.* (The
> modifier *who was elected by a large margin* is

not needed to identify *Ronald Reagan*, the sentence element the clause modifies.)

Nonrestrictive modifiers can be left out of the sentence without damaging its meaning.

> *Ronald Reagan attempted to make changes in the operation of the United States government.*

Nonessential (nonrestrictive) modifiers are set off by commas, while essential (restrictive) modifiers are not set off. In some sentences the use of commas is the only guide to meaning. Without commas the modifiers are taken as essential to meaning. If the writer uses commas, the modifiers are taken as unessential to meaning.

Nonessential
> *Social workers, who consider the needs of the children they place for adoption, perform a valuable service.* (In this sentence, the reader is given to believe that all social workers perform a valuable service. The modifier *who consider the needs of the children they place for adoption* is seen as nonessential to meaning.)

Essential
> *Social workers who consider the needs of the children they place for adoption perform a valuable social service.* (This sentence leads the reader to understand that only those social workers who consider the needs of the children they place for adoption perform a valuable service. The punctuation is the key to meaning.)

If a nonessential modifier consists of a number of words, the meaning may be made even clearer by setting it off between dashes. See pages 179–180.

Noun repeaters

Commas are used to set off unessential noun repeaters. Noun repeaters, also known as *appositives*, appear often—*John the Baptist, the novel* The Godfather, *my eldest son* Henry. Noun repeaters may be essential to meaning or unessential to meaning. When they are essential, they are not set off by commas. When they are unessential, they are set off by commas.

Unessential	*Her first poem, "Summer at the Beach," showed a child's pleasure in simple joys.* (Because *Her first* identifies the poem sufficiently, *"Summer at the Beach"* is an unessential noun repeater and is therefore set off by commas.)
Essential	*The poem "Summer at the Beach" showed a child's pleasure in simple joys.* (The poem is not identified sufficiently by *The*. The title is therefore an essential noun repeater and should not be set off by commas. Without the title we would not know which poem was being discussed.)

Sentence interrupters

Commas are used to set off sentence interrupters. Interrupters function as modifiers of an entire sentence or of one of its elements. They break into the expected movement of a sentence.

She is, I believe, most likely to be appointed to the position.

Hitchcock's early films, according to some critics, are far superior to his later work.

They found, to their surprise, that they were welcomed heartily.

I do agree, however, that you have been treated unfairly.

When interrupters are set off by commas, the reader is helped to understand the relationships between the elements of a sentence. Expressions used as introductory modifiers are followed by a comma.

According to most critics, Hitchcock's early films are far superior to his later work.

To their surprise, they found they were welcomed heartily.

However, I do agree that you have been treated unfairly.

Absolute phrases

A comma is used to set off a phrase consisting of a noun and a participle. Such a phrase is known as an *absolute phrase*. This type of phrase, which modifies an entire sentence, usually appears at the beginning or end of a sentence.

Our work accomplished, we sat down to a hearty dinner.

We finally were able to relax, all danger having passed.

Sometimes the participle does not appear in the phrase, but it is understood.

All their possessions (moved) out of the apartment, the young couple waited unhappily for the van.

Place Names, Addresses, and Dates

Place names

In punctuating place names, the larger geographic unit is considered a nonrestrictive modifier of the smaller geographic unit and is set off by commas.

> *Wilmington, Ohio, is the home of Wilmington College.*
>
> *Our new factory will be located in Austin, Texas.*
>
> *Brighton, England, is a pretty coastal town.*
>
> *She did graduate work in Munich, Germany.*

Addresses

In writing out addresses, the various items are set off by commas. House numbers are considered part of street addresses.

> *He lived all his life at 409 Elm Street, Elmira, New York.*
>
> *They moved to an apartment in "The Gables," 18 Fifth Street, Tampa, Florida.*
>
> *He can be reached at his place of work, the International Biographical Centre, Cambridge, England.*

Exception. ZIP codes follow the name of the city without being set off by a comma. Similarly, the foreign equivalents of ZIP codes, which either precede or follow the name of the city, are not separated from the city name by any punctuation. (In some foreign addresses, house numbers follow the street name.)

*Her friend moved to Bahnhofstrasse 25, Zurich 2,
Switzerland.*

*The private detective gave her all the informa-
tion she needed: John Williams could be found
at 409 Third Avenue, New York, New York 10017.*

Dates

In written dates, commas surround the year.

December 30, 1976, is Karen's birth date.

Exception. So-called military style reverses the
order of day and month and omits the comma.

*Williams was inducted into the United States
Army 30 July 1977.*

When the date consists only of month and year,
a comma may be used or may be omitted. You are
free to follow your preference, but you should use
the same style consistently throughout any one piece
of writing.

He will retire in May 1980.

*His replacement will come to work in April,
1980.*

When a day of the week precedes the precise
date, a comma is used to separate them.

*The apartment will be ours on Saturday, June
2.*

*Saturday, July 11, is the date for the Feigert
family reunion.*

No commas are used when the date modifies
another expression of time.

Alice was hired during the 1977 summer session.

She was appointed for fiscal year 1977–1978.

Note. For certain phrasings it is preferable to insert another word rather than use the comma.

Awkward *We first met in summer, 1982.*

Smooth *We first met in the summer of 1982.*

Other Uses

Titles

Commas are used to set off titles that follow an individual's name.

Ernest Smith, president and chief executive officer of the corporation, will preside at the stockholders' meeting.

Commas do not set off titles that precede an individual's name.

Treasurer Janice McCord has been reappointed for another year.

Many Democratic candidates sought to run against President Reagan in 1984.

Msgr. Dougherty will sing the Mass.

Commas are used to set off degrees that follow an individual's name.

Jonathan Muddlesdorf, Ph.D., is our new chairman.

Benjamin Spock, M.D., wrote a highly successful book on child care.

Interjections

Commas are used to set off unemphatic interjections within a sentence.

Yes, you will be welcome.

Quotations

Commas are used to set off expressions that introduce a quotation. There are many such phrases: *he said, she wrote, he repeated,* and so on. The introductory expression may come before, after, or within the quotation.

Before	*The team captain insisted, "We will win tonight's game."*
After	*"The General Assembly will complete its work in a week or less,"* CBS reported.
Within	*"I plan to attend a school of dental technology,"* David said, *"because I like mechanical work and I can always be sure of a job."* (Notice that this quotation is a single sentence requiring a comma after *technology* and a comma after *said.* Notice also the placement of the commas, period, and quotation marks.)
Within	*"All the places have been filled by now,"* the director of admissions wrote. *"You may be sure we will reconsider your application if any students withdraw."* (Notice that this quotation consists of two sentences. Notice the placement of the commas and periods.)

See page 168 for the use of colons to introduce long or formal quotations.

Letters

A comma is used after the salutation and closing in personal letters.

Salutation   *Dear Bill, Dear Mother,*

Closing   *Very truly yours, Sincerely yours, Sincerely,*

Exception.   In formal business letters a colon follows the salutation.

Omission

A comma is used to show omission of a word or words from a sentence.

> *Joan is planning to attend Southern Connecticut State College; her sister, Fairfield Community College.* (The comma after *sister* indicates omission of the words *is planning to attend*.)

> *Showing impatience with a bridge partner is discourteous; communicating with a partner during bidding, unforgivable.* (The comma after *bidding* indicates the omission of *is*.)

See pages 000–000 for a discussion of ellipsis, the mark used to show omission of words from a quoted sentence.

SEMICOLON

More emphatic than a comma, less final than a period, the semicolon, with only four uses, is not often needed. Used correctly, the semicolon separates sentence elements in order to clarify meaning.

Independent Clauses

A semicolon is used between independent clauses not connected by a conjunction.

Mobile homes have the advantage of costing less than any other type of private housing; they also have disadvantages that may make them questionable investments.

Such independent clauses can, of course, be written as two separate sentences. The advantage of the semicolon is that it indicates a connection between the two expressed ideas that would not otherwise be clear. But the construction should be used sparingly. If a page is peppered with semicolons, the punctuation mark loses its effectiveness.

A semicolon is also used between independent clauses connected by *therefore*, *thus*, or any other conjunctive adverbs.

Incorrect *Many labor unions have worked hard to secure worthwhile pensions for their members, moreover, they have established health-care facilities that have improved the lives of their members and members' families.*

Correct *Many labor unions have worked hard to secure worthwhile pensions for their members; moreover, they have established health-care facilities that have improved the lives of their members and members' families.*

Notice that the conjunctive adverb is followed by a comma.

A semicolon is used between independent clauses connected by a conjunction when the first independent clause contains commas. A comma is ordinarily used between independent clauses connected by a conjunction. But when the first of two such clauses already contains commas, a semicolon is necessary in place of the comma between clauses to emphasize the change in subject.

Instead of dealing primarily with our common problems, the meeting was a series of confrontations over such minor matters as where to hold the next meeting, how to conduct meetings, and how to establish agendas; yet everyone participated freely and sensed the bond of community essential for continuing development.

Items in Series

A semicolon is used to separate parts of a series when the parts themselves contain commas. Parts of a series are separated usually by commas, but when the parts themselves are complex enough to require commas, semicolons must be used to separate the parts.

The largest cities of the world are Tokyo, Japan; New York, United States of America; London, England; and Shanghai, People's Republic of China.

Note. The semicolon is used just before *and*, not only between the previous items in the series. Even if only one item in the series contains a comma, all are separated by semicolons.

Polls indicate that the candidate is leading in Pennsylvania; Washington, D.C.; Rhode Island; and Georgia.

COLON

The colon alerts readers to pay attention to what they will read next. (This function is never performed by the semicolon.)

Principal Uses

Lists

A colon is used before a list or enumeration.

To provide maximum protection in the diet, nonmeat proteins must be eaten in combination: milk products with grains, grains with legumes, legumes with seeds.

By the end of the meeting, our objectives were clear: (1) extension of the profit-sharing plan to all employees, (2) reduction of the work week to 35 hours, and (3) abolition of mandatory retirement at age 65.

Exceptions. The colon is not generally used to introduce a list or enumeration when a preposition appears before the list or enumeration.

Uncommon	*We offer to assist you in:* • *curriculum planning,* • *course design, and* • *instructor training.*
Customary	*We offer to assist you:* • *in planning* • *in course design* • *in training*
Customary	*We offer to assist you in* • *curriculum planning,* • *course design, and* • *instructor training.*

The colon is not used to introduce a list or enumeration when a verb appears before the list or enumeration.

Incorrect	*They bought: chairs, tables, and kitchen appliances.*
Correct	*They bought chairs, tables, and kitchen appliances.*

Formal constructions

The colon is used to introduce formal statements, questions, and quotations. A colon implies greater formality than does a comma, which can also be used before quotations (see page 163).

He announced his candidacy with a simple, direct sentence: "My name is Jimmy Carter, and I'm running for President of the United States."

Only one doubt remains: Will we have the courage to stick by the decision we have made here tonight? (The word *will* can also be written without a capital letter, but customary usage suggests that the capital be used for a full sentence and a lower-case letter for a phrase or sentence fragment.)

Thomas Wolfe's opening sentence in Look Homeward, Angel *sets the tone for the rest of that brilliant first novel:*

A destiny that leads the English to the Dutch is strange enough, but one that leads from Epsom into Pennsylvania, and thence into the hills that shut in Altamont over the proud coral cry of the cock, and the soft stone smile of an angel, is touched by that dark miracle of chance which makes new magic in a dusty world.

Independent clauses

A colon is used between independent clauses not connected by a conjunction when the second clause explains, amplifies, or illustrates the first. The colon is used instead of a semicolon between such clauses to announce that the second clause stands in a special relation to the first clause. Although the two clauses are grammatically independent, the colon serves to indicate the logical relationship.

He had no desire to remain with the company for the rest of his working life: Management's lack of a definite plan for expansion and its refusal to grant executives earned recognition forced him to look elsewhere.

Manhattan is Treasure Island for anyone interested in the arts: On any single day it offers more plays, more museum exhibitions, more concerts of every kind, more old and new films of quality than can be found in an entire month anywhere else in the world.

Minor Uses

A colon is used between hours and minutes.

12:30 P.M. the 6:30 news.

A colon is often used after the speaker's name in a play.

HAMLET: *Do you think I mean country matters?*
OPHELIA: *I think nothing, my lord.*

A colon is used after the salutation in a formal letter.

Dear Mr. Walton:

A colon is often used between city and publisher in a bibliographic entry.

Leary, William G. Shakespeare Plain. *New York: McGraw-Hill, 1977.*

PARENTHESES

Parentheses are sometimes used by writers to set apart from the rest of a sentence material that, though not related to the sentence grammatically, clarifies or illustrates some part of the sentence. Parentheses may also be used to set apart entire sentences from the paragraphs in which they appear, or entire paragraphs from the body of a report or other paper. (See also pages 171 and 180 for similar uses of brackets and dashes.)

Parentheses are used to enclose information worth including in a sentence but not essential to it.

> *His first novel* (Liza of Lambeth, *1897*) *was not considered a success, but Maugham came into his own with* Of Human Bondage *(1915).*

> *Their third production (the first two were failures) established them as the leading producers of musical comedy.*

> *We first met George in his laboratory, where he was completely at ease working in the middle of what looked like a jungle of complex apparatus. (He never seemed comfortable outside his laboratory, at least during the many days we spent with him.) George was working then on his most promising research in plasma physics.*

Parentheses are also used to enclose numbers or letters in an enumeration.

> *We can easily list all the things you will need for such a trip: (1) two complete sets of clothing for street wear, (2) at least one bathing suit, (3) a light coat, (4) two pairs of good walking shoes and one pair of beach sandals, and (5) a wallet filled with money.*

BRACKETS

Brackets are used to indicate additions or changes in a quotation. Such additions and changes are often necessary to explain, clarify, or correct a quotation used in writing.

Brackets are used to enclose any material added to a quotation.

According to Caruso, "A contract [for a full sea-son with La Scala] was withheld until I had established myself as an outstanding box office attraction." (The writer quoting this sentence has supplied information judged necessary for full understanding of the quotation.)

Brackets are used to enclose any corrections added to a quotation.

In his memoirs Preston wrote, "Early in April of that year [actually in May 1975], the troops were up to full strength again." (The writer quot-ing the sentence has corrected the writer of the sentence.)

Note that brackets for explanations and correc-tions are used only in connection with words written by someone else and quoted directly.

Brackets are used to enclose *sic* after an error in quoted material to indicate that the error occurs in the original. Because the word *sic* is Latin for *"thus," sic* must be italicized or underscored. *Sic* is enclosed in brackets because it is a writer's com-ment on material being quoted.

Her letter concluded with these words: "Under no condishuns [sic] will I send you the money."

Brackets are used to enclose parenthetic mate-rial that occurs within parenthetic material. You will need brackets occasionally, especially when writ-ing footnotes and bibliographies, to indicate a pa-renthesis within a parenthesis; the practice should be avoided in text narrative.

³See Chapter 3 (Elizabeth Jenkins, Elizabeth the Great *[New York, 1959]) for a full description of Elizabeth's first public appearance during Mary's reign.* (In one common bibliographic style, the place of publication and the date of publication of a book are normally enclosed in parentheses. Since in the example the reference to the entire book is already within parentheses, brackets enclose the city and date.)

QUOTATION MARKS

Principal Uses

Quotation

Quotation marks are used to enclose directly quoted speech and writing. (See below for placement of other punctuation marks in conjunction with quotation marks.)

> *My brother angrily told me, "I will not go along with you on this or any other deal."*

> *One of Ben Franklin's maxims in* Poor Richard's Almanack *reveals an interesting side of his character: "Remember that time is money."*

Titles

Quotation marks are generally used to set off titles of short literary works that are published within books or magazines, titles of songs and similar short musical compositions, and titles of individual television programs. The titles of longer works in all these categories are usually printed in distinctive type and should be underlined when typewritten. Names of paintings and of ships also are usually treated this way.

Book chapters

> *Berton Roueché writes narrative accounts of medical detective work that are unsurpassed: "The Fog," in his collection entitled* Eleven Blue Men, *recounts the infamous Donora, Pennsylvania, pollution episode.*

Magazine articles

"To Heaven by Subway" appeared in Fortune *in August 1938.*

Short poems

Who does not know Poe's "Annabelle Lee"?

Song titles

Have you heard John McCormick's recording of "I'll Take You Home Again, Kathleen"?

Talks

The title of the commencement address was "A Time for Rejoicing," but we thought it should have been something like "A Time for Snoozing."

Full-length work published within a collection

Nine Plays by Eugene O'Neill *(New York: Random House) includes "Desire Under the Elms" and "Strange Interlude."*

Television

"Morning Comes to Minneapolis" is my favorite episode of The Mary Tyler Moore Show.

Words

Quotation marks are used to set off words intended to be understood as words rather than as their meanings. Though printers generally use italics for words intended to be understood as words, quotation marks are more common for this use in typewritten or handwritten papers.

He argues that "ain't" should be accepted by all of us as a useful word that only snobs avoid.

The word "run" has more than one thousand meanings.

They use "and" too often in their writing.

Do you know how many c's and m's there are in "accommodate"?

Quotation marks are sometimes used for nicknames or stage names.

Nat "King" Cole was very popular in the 1950s.

Andrew Jackson—"Old Hickory"—was the seventh president of the United States.

With Other Punctuation

Some procedures have been established for punctuation used with final quotation marks.

Periods and commas

Periods and commas are always placed inside final quotation marks.

She said, "The committee will meet tomorrow."

"Let the group decide," he said.

"I will go along with your wishes," she said, "if you agree that from now on I will have a voice in the decisions."

Colons and semicolons

Colons and semicolons are always placed outside final quotation marks.

Dictionaries give two meanings for "fresco": the art of painting by pressing colors dissolved in

*water into fresh plaster, and a painting made on
fresh plaster.*

*The rule states: "Nobody may use the pool with-
out permission"; however, I do not believe members are required to ask permission every time
they want to swim.*

Question marks and exclamation points

The placement of question marks and exclamation points depends on meaning. They are placed
inside final quotation marks when a quotation is a
direct question or exclamation.

*Rousseau asked, "What wisdom can you find
that is greater than kindness?"*

Job says, "How forcible are right words!"

They are placed outside final quotation marks
when a quotation is part of a sentence that is a
question or exclamation.

Did he really say, "I know nothing of this affair"?

*What greater mistake can one make than to say,
"I never make mistakes"!*

When a quotation requires a final question mark
or exclamation point and the sentence it is in requires the same mark, the punctuation is placed
inside the final quote.

*Have you ever heard anyone ask, "Are there any
honest people left in the world?"*

*What a foolish mistake he made when he wrote,
"How guilty I am!"*

When Quotation Marks Should Not Be Used

There are a number of instances when the use of quotation marks is not appropriate, though writers are sometimes tempted to use them.

Indirect quotation and paraphrase

Quotation marks are never appropriate for setting off an indirect quotation or a paraphrase.

Inappropriate	*My brother angrily told me "he would not go along with me on this or any other deal."* (The words in quotation marks could not have been the speaker's exact words.)
Appropriate	*My brother angrily told me he would not go along with me "on this or any other deal."*
Appropriate	*Concerning the deal I had proposed, my brother wrote me he would not go along with it—nor with any other I might suggest.*

Other quotations

Quotation marks are not customarily used to signal lengthy prose quotations. Long citations (one rule of thumb puts the dividing line at five lines; another specifies a hundred words; still another, more than two sentences) are better set off as so-called extracts—typed as separate paragraphs and with a left margin wider than normal. Extracts may be typed single-space, though if your material will go through any kind of editorial process (for printing in the company magazine, for example), double-spacing of extracts is preferable.

Her letter contained so many questions you must answer promptly that I have decided to give you her exact words:

It will be helpful if you explain just how many projects will take me out into the field during the first year. I also want to know whether I will have sole responsibility for field projects; whether I will be able to return home from time to time during the year and, if so, for how long and at whose expense; whether my field expenses will be paid in advance or whether I will have to pay these expenses from my own funds and eventually be reimbursed; and whether I will be eligible for pay increases during my year in the field.

Do not use quotation marks when quoting poetry of three lines or more. When the quoted material is extracted poetry, no quotation marks are used.

To see the world in a grain of sand,
And heaven in a wild flower:
Hold infinity in the palm of your hand,
And eternity in an hour.

You would, of course, use quotation marks if the poetry were not extracted.

It was Alexander Pope who wrote, "One similie that solitary shines / In the dry desert of a thousand lines."

Quotations within quotations are marked with single quotation marks.

On page 230 of The Coming of the New Deal, *we get further insight into the relationship between the President and the Secretary of State: "There was, perhaps, another victor. 'Before you sail,' Roosevelt cabled to Cordell Hull, 'I want you to know once more of my affectionate regard for and confidence in you.'"*

For words and phrases that can stand alone

Writers sometimes hope that quotation marks will add a special quality to their words, such as humor or emphasis. On other occasions they expect quotation marks to protect them against accusations of using slang or vulgar language. In fact, quotation marks do not absolve the writer from working on the words themselves to achieve special qualities and appropriate vocabulary. Vulgarity and ethnic slurs are never appropriate; slang, when it fits the subject and tone, can legitimately be used in all but the most formal writing.

Unnecessary marking of slang	*After my friend moved to California, he seemed to specialize in being "laid-back" and "mellow."*
Proper use of slang	*After my friend moved to California, he seemed to specialize in being laid-back and mellow.*
False apology for insult	*The 1980s saw politicians wooing the "Spic" vote.*
Proper wording	*The 1980s saw politicians going after the Hispanic vote.*
Meaningless emphasis	*They consider themselves "insiders."*
Proper indication of emphasis	*They insisted that they were insiders—that is, their special status gave them access to all company secrets.*

Quotation marks are superfluous after the use of such introductory remarks as *so-called* and *self-styled*.

> *Hank Aaron and Roger Maris broke home-run records set by Babe Ruth, the so-called Sultan of Swat.*

DASH

A dash shows a degree of separation greater than that indicated by a comma. A typewritten dash is made of two consecutive hyphens, with no spacing before or after the dash. A handwritten dash is twice as long as a handwritten hyphen, with no spacing before or after the dash. Dashes are used to set off material that interrupts the logical development or grammatical structure of a sentence. If material enclosed in dashes were removed, the sentence would still retain its primary sense.

Dashes are used to set off abrupt breaks in thought.

> *Life was proceeding as well as we could hope—we are surprised if our New England winters do not give us at least one solid month of freezing temperatures—until the last day of February, when our water line cracked and our pickup truck died.*

A single dash is used to set off an abrupt break in thought that ends a sentence.

> *The chairman went on for more than an hour, drearily telling us facts we already knew about the economy, the fuel shortage, inflation—you know his boring manner.*

Dashes are used to set off nonessential noun repeaters that include commas. Nonessential noun repeaters, also known as *nonrestrictive appositives*, are not sufficiently set off by commas if the repeaters already contain commas.

> *The Watergate Committee—that group of senators seeking the whole truth, some of the truth, and, in at least one case, anything but the truth—held the fate of the nation in its hands for months.*

Dashes are used to gain special emphasis for any nonessential noun repeater. This function of dashes carries with it the risk of overuse. Choose your spots carefully. It is better not to use dashes when commas will do.

> *The most urgent needs of our society—adequate energy resources and employment for all who seek work—were attacked boldly by the new administration.*

A dash is used to set off a summary that follows a series.

> *Goldfinches, evening grosbeaks, cardinals—these are the most colorful birds you will find at your feeder.*
>
> *Oil, gas, coal, and nuclear fuel—all conventional sources of energy have their drawbacks and all will probably be used for years to come.*

A dash is used to indicate an interrupted sentence.

> *We worked as hard as we could on the project and then—but why go on? You know nothing came of it.*
>
> *"My mother told me"—he paused for effect—"that I'm adopted."*

ELLIPSIS

Ellipsis is used to indicate the omission of words, clauses, or sentences, usually from a quotation. The basic mark of ellipsis is three spaced periods (. . .).

In quoting part of a paragraph or part of a sentence, missing words are indicated by ellipsis. The following sentence from the beginning of Nathaniel Hawthorne's *The Scarlet Letter* will serve as an example. It is first given in full.

> *A throng of bearded men, in sad-colored garments and gray, steeple-crowned hats, intermixed with women, some wearing hoods, and others bare-headed, was assembled in front of a wooden edifice, the door of which was heavily timbered with oak, and studded with iron spikes.*

The following quotation omits portions of the sentence.

> *We come first upon "bearded men . . . assembled in front of a wooden edifice . . . ."*

The first omission is the beginning of the quoted sentence—*A throng of*. Ellipsis is not used when a quotation begins within the sentence being quoted. The second omission is shown by three spaced periods, which represent many missing words, beginning with *in* and ending with *was*. The last omission is shown by four spaced periods, because the missing words include the last word in the sentence, which is followed by a period in the original.

Depending on the writer's intention, it is not always necessary to use ellipsis at the end of an unfinished sentence in quotation.

> *Hawthorne's "bearded men . . . assembled in front of a wooden edifice" set the mood for what is to come.*

If an ellipsis occurs at the end of a sentence
punctuated by an exclamation point or question mark,
three spaced periods and the exclamation point or
question mark are used.

Here is another sentence from *The Scarlet Letter*.

> *"Come along, Madam Hester, and show your
> scarlet letter in the marketplace!"*

If the last three words are omitted, the punctuation
becomes:

> *"Come along, Madam Hester, and show your
> scarlet letter . . . !"*

A full line of spaced periods is used to show the
omission of a line or more of poetry.

In quoting the first two and last two lines of
Shakespeare's Sonnet Number 55, omission of lines
3–12 would be shown as follows.

> *Not marble, nor the gilded monuments*
> *Of princes, shall outlive this powerful rhyme;*
>
> . . . .
>
> *So, till the judgement that yourself arise,*
> *You live in this, and dwell in lovers' eyes.*

Similarly, a line of spaced periods is used to
show omission of a paragraph or more in prose
extracts. Teachers and editors seldom agree on this
final use of ellipsis.

HYPHEN

General guidelines exist for most uses of the
hyphen, but few strict rules can be laid down. For
example, compounds of recent coinage (*super-duper*)
and nonce usages (*post-orthodoxy*) tend to be hyphenated. As these compounds come into wide use,

they are usually treated as unhyphenated single words. *Co-operate* is now *cooperate, re-elect* is now *reelect, pre-eminent* is now *preeminent,* and *pre-existing* is now *preexisting.* Yet the hyphen is always retained if closing up the word would put two *i*'s together (*anti-intellectual, semi-illuminated*). When the question of whether or not a word should be hyphenated must be settled, there is no substitute for a good dictionary. Which dictionary to use is a matter of choice. It is important, however, that the dictionary show American usage of recent years. A dictionary published in Great Britain or one published more than twenty years ago will not reflect current American usage.

Compound numbers for twenty-one to ninety-nine are always hyphenated.

> *twenty-six*
> *one hundred forty-seven*
> *two hundred forty*
> *three hundred twelve*

Compound adjectives before a noun are always hyphenated.

> *Our school produced well-trained accountants.*
>
> *They chased the all-important dollar.*
>
> *Jonathan had jet-black hair.*
>
> *Well-read students enjoy their university studies.*

Compound adjectives are not hyphenated after a noun unless the dictionary uses the hyphen.

> *Our accounting graduates are well trained.*
>
> *They thought that money was all-important.*
>
> *Jonathan's hair was jet black.*
>
> *Everyone agrees that Joan is well-read.*

Notice that the compound adjective *well-read* retains the hyphen even when it does not precede a noun. This expression does not convey the same meaning without the hyphen. Compare *Everyone agrees that Joan is well-read* with *Everyone agrees the passage was well read.* For similar reasons, dictionary usage requires the hyphen in *all-important* in all circumstances. Consult a dictionary when you are in doubt about hyphenating a compound adjective that does not precede a noun.

The dictionary decides whether a prefix is followed by a hyphen. Some prefixes are followed by hyphens to avoid confusion with another word or to avoid awkward combinations of letters. Examples of such prefixes are *ex-* and *self-*.

> *Ex-presidents of major companies enjoy handsome pensions.*
>
> *I particularly disliked his self-serving statements.*

A hyphen is always used between a prefix and a proper *(capitalized)* noun.

> *Her primary interest is the culture of pre-Christian societies.*
>
> *Opposition to the Concorde was mistakenly attributed to anti-British and anti-French attitudes.*

A hyphen is used to prevent confusion with a different word.

> *The divers managed to recover the bodies.*
>
> *Are you going to re-cover your couch?*
>
> *I cannot recollect the conversation.*
>
> *Our town decided to re-collect the garbage next week.*

Follow established practice in hyphenating at the ends of lines. Most writers avoid hyphenating

words at the end of a line. Rather than concern
themselves with the question of where to break a
word, they end their lines with complete words.
This is not a bad practice, even though right-hand
margins may look ragged. For the ambitious writer,
four rules cover the hyphenation of words at the end
of a line:

> Divide between syllables. (It is not
> possible to divide one-syllable words.)
>
> Divide after prefixes and before
> suffixes.
>
> Divide at the hyphen if a word
> already has a hyphen.
>
> Never hyphenate in such a way that
> a single letter stands alone at the
> end of or the beginning of a line.

Continuous dates and page numbers are always
hyphenated.

*The period 1968–1974 will be remembered for a
long time as The Nixon Era.*

We will hold the fair June 13–15.

*Refer to pages 212–217 for a complete discussion
of this question.*

*The treatment of slaves (pages 93–97) is particu-
larly interesting and illuminating.*

Certain compound nouns are always hyphenated. Others are not. Once again, the dictionary is
the final arbiter.

Have you met my father-in-law?

We have painted our kitchen-dinette.

They always eat in the dining room.

Queen Victoria had many ladies-in-waiting.

She was clearly a lady of the evening.

Love-in-a-mist is a kind of buttercup.

Horse manure has become a rare fertilizer.

APOSTROPHE

The apostrophe has three uses: It is part of the possessive form of certain nouns and pronouns, it indicates missing letters in contractions, and it is part of the plural form of letters as well as optional in plurals of numerals and abbreviations.

Possession

The apostrophe is used variously to show possession. The controlling factor is the final consonant sound.

Add apostrophe plus *s* to nouns that do not end in *s*.

a boy's life	*Mary's husband*
a man's career	*men's careers*
a woman's career	*women's careers*

For singular nouns ending in *s*, add apostrophe plus *s* if the additional *s* is pronounced as a syllable.

Yeats's poetry	*a seamstress's work*
Arthur Burns's policies	*Mrs. Jones's husband*

Add apostrophe alone to plural nouns ending in *s*.

girls' hobbies

the Smiths' residence

libraries' endowments

Add apostrophe alone if the extra syllable becomes awkward to pronounce.

Euripides' dramas

Cesar Chavez' leadership

Dickens' novels

Note. There is some disagreement over which sounds are awkward. Some writers prefer *Yeats' poetry, Chavez's leadership,* and *Dickens's novels.* You can make your own decision, but be consistent throughout the work.

Add apostrophe plus *s* to indefinite pronouns that do not end in *s.*

one's interests   *another's choice*

Add apostrophe alone to indefinite pronouns ending in *s.*

others' choices

An apostrophe is never used to show possession with pronouns.

his   hers   its   ours   yours   theirs

Note. *Its* is the proper spelling of the possessive form of *it.* (*It's* is the proper contraction of *it is.*)

President Lyndon Johnson was criticized for picking up his beagle by its ears.

An apostrophe (plus *s* when appropriate) is used only with the last noun when showing joint possession by two or more nouns.

Procter and Gamble's logo had to be changed.

Paul and Daniel's room is not large enough for two boys.

An apostrophe (plus *s* when appropriate) is used with each noun when showing individual possession by two or more nouns.

Carlos' and Luis's rooms will always be ready for them whenever they decide to return home.

Mrs. Gardner's and Mr. Brokaw's classes go to the zoo once each term, but Ms. Dalley's class goes at least twice.

An apostrophe (plus *s* when appropriate) is used with only the last word of a compound to show possession.

Your sister-in-law's investments will probably be sufficient to support her when she retires.

By mistake he put his gym suit in somebody else's locker.

Contractions

An apostrophe is used to show omission of one or more letters or numbers in a contraction.

We haven't (have not) *been able to complete the project.*

She's (she is) *a friend of mine.*

Are you a member of the class of '81 (1981)?

Be sure to be there by seven o'clock (of the clock).

It's (It is) *not my fault.*

Letters, Numbers, and Words

An apostrophe plus *s* may be used to form the plural of letters and numerals.

Remember to dot your i's and cross your t's.

The department will hire only people who have their Ph.D.'s.

Many economists forecast a shortage of E.E.'s and Ch.E.'s during the next decade.

The 1960's were devastating years for young Americans.

Europeans cross their 7's.

In military, business, and technical writing, however, the apostrophe is usually omitted. Some writers in less specialized fields also prefer to omit the apostrophe.

He came of age in the 1960s.

Several RFPs have been neglected in the past month.

We sent three TWXs before we received an answer.

The U.S. Army bought thousands of HU-1s.

They fly only 747s.

Some MIAs are still unaccounted for, but almost all the POWs have returned.

An apostrophe plus *s* is used to form the plurals of words used as words.

Do you realize how many the's *you use in a typical paragraph?*

I soon tired of his sorry's *and* soon's *and looked elsewhere for the help I needed so desperately.*

GOOD STRATEGY FOR WRITERS

When you have finished revising the first draft of your paper, you may find it useful to read it through one last time to check all your punctuation. Sensible punctuation helps readers understand exactly what the writer is expressing.

PUNCTUATION REVIEW CHECKLIST

1. *Consistency.* Have you used the same mark of punctuation for the same purpose throughout your paper?
2. *Amount of Punctuation.* Do you appear to require much punctuation in every sentence you have written? A little restructuring may eliminate excessive reliance on punctuation to clarify meaning. Have you fallen into the bad habit of inserting punctuation wherever you might pause in reading your paper aloud?

   Do your sentences seem to require hardly any punctuation? Perhaps you are too free in forgiving yourself.

   Read the paper carefully from beginning to end, pretending that you are reading it for the first time. That is how your readers will read.
3. *Applying Experience.* Look back at your earlier papers. What criticism of punctuation have you had? Do not repeat the same mistakes.
4. *Applying the Rules.* Even though punctuation rules are not applied uniformly, read the appropriate rules again whenever you are unsure.

CHAPTER 10

Word Conventions

SPELLING

Of the thousands of words used in writing, a few hundred present spelling problems. We seem forever to be going back to the dictionary to check once again the spelling of words we have looked up many times before. Even though spelling rules do not work all the time, they are worth learning because they give some guidance. The following pages may help you save time.

Suffixes

Doubling a final consonant before adding a suffix

Before adding a suffix to a base word ending in a single consonant—*hit (hitting), treat (treatment)*—the final consonant is doubled under certain circumstances.

The final consonant is *never* doubled when the added suffix begins with a consonant.

abandon + ment =   harm + ful =
   abandonment   harmful
meaning + less =   tender + ness =
   meaningless   tenderness

The rest of this section deals with base words to which *suffixes beginning with a vowel* are added.

In words of one syllable, the final consonant of a word ending in a single consonant preceded by a single vowel is always doubled before a suffix beginning with a vowel.

spot + ed = spotted   stop + able = stoppable
beg + ar = beggar   god + ess = goddess
big + er = bigger   sit + ing = sitting

The final consonant of a word ending in a single consonant preceded by two vowels is never doubled before a suffix beginning with a vowel.

beat + er = beater   seat + ing = seating
goad + ing = goading   wood + en = wooden

In words of two or more syllables, the final consonant of a word ending in a single consonant is doubled when (1) the final syllable of the base word is accented and (2) the accent does not shift after the suffix is added.

This rule can be illustrated by the example of the word *prefer* and some of the words formed from it. *Prefer* has two syllables and ends in a single consonant. The final syllable is accented: preFER. When we add *-ed*, the accent does not shift: PreFERRED and the *r* doubles. When *-ing* is added, we get preFERring. All conditions of the rule have been met once more; the *r* doubles.

Let us leave *prefer* for a moment to ask why the final consonants are not doubled before suffixes in the following words.

broaden + ing =   fester + ing =
   broadening   festering
deepen + ed =   lengthen + ed =
   deepened   lengthened

The answer is clear. In each of the base words the accent is not on the final syllable.

Let us return to the word *prefer*. When -*ence* is added, the accent shifts: PREference. When -*ential* is added to *prefer*, the accent shifts: preferENtial. In both instances the *r* does not double. The rule remains valid that the final consonant doubles only when the accent does not shift from the final syllable of the base word.

Dropping the final silent *e* before adding a suffix

When adding a suffix to words ending in silent *e*—such as *arrange* and *service*—the *e* is kept in some cases and dropped in others. There are no firm rules in this matter, so the exceptions will be presented along with the generalizations. One key to this spelling problem is found in the first letter of the suffix and the last consonant of the base word.

Before suffixes that begin with a vowel, the silent *e* is dropped in most words.

arrange + ing = arranging	live + able = livable
change + ing = changing	live + ing = living
insure + ing = insuring	notice + ing = noticing
hinge + ing = hinging	replace + ing = replacing
home + ing = homing	service + ing = servicing

Exceptions. When a suffix begins with *a* or *o*, the silent *e* is often retained when it follows *c* or *g*. (The *e* keeps the *c* or *g* soft; the *c* in *nice* and the *g* in *gesture* are soft, while the *c* in *count* and the *g* in *golf* are hard.)

change + able = changeable	outrage + ous = outrageous

courage + ous =   replace + able =
    courageous   replaceable
notice + able =   service + able =
    noticeable   serviceable

Notice how the absence of a silent *e* affects pronunciation:

practice + al = practical (hard *c*)
practice + able = practicable (hard *c*)

In some cases the silent *e* is kept to prevent confusion with other words. The *e* in *singeing* prevents confusion with *singing*. The *e* in *dyeing* prevents confusion with *dying*. The *e* in *hoeing* helps in pronunciation. (Try pronouncing *hoing*.) The silent *e* is retained in most words before suffixes that begin with a consonant.

amaze + ment =   hope + less =
    amazement   hopeless
arrange + ment =   lone + ly =
    arrangement   lonely
live + ly =   naive + ly =
    lively   naively
argue + ment =   nine + th =
    argument   ninth
awe + ful =   true + ly =
    awful   truly
due + ly =   true + th =
    duly   truth
judge + ment =   whole + ly =
    judgment   wholly

Plurals

The plurals of most nouns are formed by simply adding -*s*.

appetite + s =   typewriter + s =
    appetites   typewriters

Nouns ending in *y* preceded by a consonant change the *y* to *i* and add *-es*.

pantry + es =   sentry + es =
  pantries   sentries

Nouns ending with the sound of *ch*, *s*, *sh*, or *x* add *-es* to form the plural.

porch + es = porches
mass + es = masses
brush + es = brushes
mix + es = mixes

Nouns ending in *z* double the final *z* and add *-es* to form the plural.

fez + es = fezzes   quiz + es = quizzes

Some nouns ending in *o* after a consonant form the plural by adding *-s*. Others add *-es*. And still others allow the option of either. This is surely an instance of where the dictionary will help.

    Add *-s* only:
      alto: altos
      piano: pianos
    Add *-es*:
      echo: echoes
      potato: potatoes
    Optional ending:
      buffalo: buffaloes, buffalos
      cargo: cargoes, cargos
      banjo: banjos, banjoes

Words ending in *y*

When words ending in *y* are followed by plural endings, verb tense endings, or other suffixes, certain rules (which have few exceptions) decide whether the spelling of the base word remains unchanged or whether the *y* changes to *i*.

Spelling of base word unchanged in plurals of proper names ending in *y*.

Goodbody + s =   Jay + s =
  Goodbodys   Jays

in plurals of nouns in which the final *y* follows a vowel:

boy + s = boys   valley + s = valleys
way + s = ways   guy + s = guys

in the third-person singular form of regular verbs when the final *y* follows a vowel:

annoy + s = annoys   obey + s = obeys
say + s = says   buy + s = buys

in the past tense of regular verbs when the final *y* follows a vowel; the past tense is formed by adding -*ed*:

annoy + ed =   obey + ed =
  annoyed   obeyed

in the comparative and superlative of adjectives when the final *y* follows a vowel:

coy + er = coyer   gay + est = gayest

when adding any other suffix to words ending in *y* when the *y* follows a vowel:

joy + ful = joyful   gray + ness = grayness

The final *y* in the base word changes to *i* in plurals of nouns when the final *y* follows a consonant; the plural is formed by adding -*es*:

actuary + es =   history + es =
  actuaries   histories

in the third-person singular form of regular verbs when the final *y* follows a consonant; the tense is formed by adding -*es*:

fry + es = fries   worry + es = worries

in the past tense of regular verbs when the final *y* follows a consonant; the tense is formed by adding -*ed*:

fry + ed = fried   worry + ed = worried

in the comparative and superlative of adjectives when the final *y* follows a consonant:

angry + er = angrier   sorry + est = sorriest

when adding any other suffix to words ending in *y* when the final *y* follows a consonant:

bounty + ful =   giddy + ness =
    bountiful   giddiness

Nouns of foreign origin

Nouns of foreign origin form the plural either in the regular English ways (by adding -*s* or -*es*) or by following the practice of the language in which the nouns originated. For some, both forms are acceptable. In the following brief list of such words, the preferred form is given first where two forms exist.

addendum: addenda
alumna: alumnae
alumnus: alumni
analysis: analyses
appendix: appendixes, appendices
beau: beaux, beaus
chateau: chateaus, chateaux
conquistador: conquistadores, conquistadors
curriculum: curriculums, curricula
datum: data
faux pas: faux pas
formula: formulas, formulae
hors d'oeuvre: hors d'oeuvres, hors d'oeuvre
index: indexes, indices
memorandum: memorandums, memoranda
medium: media

Words, letters, numbers used as words

Letters, numbers, and words used as words usually form the plural by adding -*'s*. (Military writing simply adds -*s*).

She made three A's last semester.

He left out all 0's in giving us the problem.

Do you know how many and's *you had in your last paper?*

The U.S. Navy bought one hundred CH-53s two years ago.

Irregular nouns

Some irregular nouns form the plural by altering the vowel.

goose: geese   mouse: mice
man: men   woman: women

A few form the plural with the addition of letters other than -*s* or -*es*.

ox: oxen   child: children

Compound nouns

Most compound nouns form the plural by adding -*s* or -*es* at the end of the last element of the compound.

stretcher bearers   vice-admirals

But when the significant element of the compound noun occurs earlier, the plural is formed on it.

brothers-in-law   sergeants-at-arms

Nouns ending in -*ful*

In nouns formed by the addition of the suffix
-*ful*, it is preferable to add the plural-forming -*s* at
the very end.

*He struggled out to the clothesline several times,
dragging armfuls of wet laundry.* (Also *armsful.*)

*By the time she collapsed, she had already lifted
twenty-eight shovelfuls of snow.* (Also *shovelsful.*)

Writing *i* before *e* except after *c*

The well-known jingle gives us a great deal of
help:

Use i *before* e
Except after c
Or when sounded as a
As in neighbor *and* sleigh.

The *ie-ei* confusion troubles even good spellers.
If the only exceptions had to do with the *a* sound,
we would have less trouble. Unfortunately there
are others. It is useful first to list a few of the
words that do follow the jingle.

i before *e*

achieve	grieve	reprieve
belief	mischief	retrieve
brief	pierce	shield
chief	priest	siege
field	relief	wield

Words that do not follow the rule, of course,
immediately come to mind. The *i* before *e* rule, for
example, is found in such words as *achieve, field,
priest, retrieve,* and *wield.* Just as quickly, however, we can think of words (admittedly, fewer)

where *e* precedes *i* even though no *c* precedes and the diphthong is not pronounced as *a*: *height*, and *seize* are merely two of them.

Exceptions to the rule that *e* comes before *i* after *c* (demonstrated in such words as *ceiling* and *receive*) also occur, chiefly in three situations: when *ie* is pronounced *ee* (*financier*); when *ie* is sounded as two syllables (*society*); and when *c* is sounded as *sh* (*ancient, proficient*).

Exceptions.

i before *e* after *c* sounded as *ee*

financier

i before *e* after *c* sounded as two syllables

societal	society

i before *e* when the *c* is sounded as *sh*

ancient	proficient
conscience	specie
deficient	species
efficient	sufficient
omniscient	

e before *i* after *c*

ceiling	deceive
conceit	perceive
conceive	receipt
deceit	receive

e before *i* when sounded as *a*

deign	heinous	rein
eight	inveigh	sleigh
feign	neigh	vein
freight	neighbor	weight
	reign	

Other exceptions

either	neither	their
height	seize	weird
leisure	sheik	

250 Words often misspelled

absence	attendance	conferred
accidentally	balancing	conscience
accommodate	battalion	conscientious
accumulate	beginning	consistent
achievement	believe	controlled
acknowledge	beneficial	controversy
acquaintance	benefited	criticize
acquitted	boundaries	decision
advice	business	deferred
advise	calendar	definite
affect	candidate	description
among	category	desperate
analysis	cemetery	dictionary
analyze	changeable	dining
apartment	changing	disappearance
apparatus	choose	disappoint
apparent	chose	disastrous
appearance	chosen	disciplinary
arctic	commission	dissatisfied
arguing	committee	dormitory
argument	comparative	effect
arithmetic	coming	eighth
ascend	compelling	eligible
athletic	conceivable	eliminate

embarrass	intelligence	perspiration
eminent	interestingly	physical
encouraging	interpretation	picnicking
environmental	irresistible	possession
equipment	its	possessive
equipping	it's	possibility
especially	knowledgeable	immediately
exaggerating	laboratory	practically
excellence	laid	precede
exhilarating	led	preference
existence	lightning	preferred
experiences	loneliness	prejudice
explanation	losing	preparatory
explanatory	maintenance	prevalent
familiarize	maneuver	principal
fascination	manufacturing	principle
fiery	marriage	probably
foreign	mathematics	procedure
formerly	maybe	proceed
fortieth	miniature	professor
forty	mischievous	pronunciation
fourth	mysterious	prophecy
frantically	necessary	prophesy
generally	ninetieth	psychological
government	ninety	psychology
grammar	noticeable	quantity
grievous	noticing	quiet
height	occasionally	quite
heroic	occurred	quizzes
hindrance	omitted	realize
hoping	opportunity	really
hypocrisies	optimistic	recede
hypocrite	originality	recognition
imaginary	parallel	recognize
imaginative	paralysis	recommend
imagine	paralyze	reference
incidentally	pastime	referring
incredible	performance	repetition
independence	permissible	repetitive
inevitable	personal	restaurant
intellectual	personnel	rhythm

ridiculous	statue	tries
sacrifice	studying	tyranny
sacrilege	succeed	unanimous
sacrilegious	successful	undoubtedly
salary	successive	unnecessarily
schedule	supersede	unnecessary
secretary	surprise	until
seize	studying	useful
separate	temperamental	usually
sergeant	tendency	vilify
severely	than	village
shining	their	villainous
siege	then	weather
similarity	thorough	weird
sophomore	receive	whether
specifically	to	writing
specimen	too	your
stationary	tragedy	you're
stationery		

Overcoming Spelling Problems

Even after you have learned to apply all the rules given in this book, you may still have trouble spelling certain words. *You have learned to write them incorrectly.* Now it is time to learn to write them correctly. If you will establish a system for learning to spell these words correctly and *do the work your system demands*, you will finally overcome your spelling problems.

A system that has helped many poor spellers employs a personal collection of troublesome words and an eleven-step procedure. The only tools required are a good dictionary and a pack of index cards. Each card you create and master represents a single important step toward good spelling.

Here is the way to proceed.

1. Consult a dictionary to find any word that gives you trouble. Look at the word long enough to

say it *correctly* in your mind, letter by letter, without looking at it.

2. Write the word on a card *from memory*.
3. Check the dictionary to make certain you have spelled the word correctly.
4. On the back of the card, write the first two or three letters of the word in large letters.
5. Close your eyes and picture the spelling of the word.
6. Check the front of the card to see whether you have remembered the word *correctly*.
7. Cover the word and write it again *correctly* from memory.
8. Check to see whether you have written it correctly. By now you have correctly written the word twice. You have also pictured the word in your mind *correctly*.
9. Once a week—more often if you have time— review each card in your collection. *Look only at the back of the card*, the side on which you wrote the first few letters of the word. Picture the entire word in your mind.
10. Check the front of the card to see whether you have remembered the word *correctly*.
11. Cover your earlier spelling and write the word on the card *correctly from memory*.

When your card shows five correct spellings of the word, remove it from your collection and put it in an inactive file. Check through that file from time to time—once a month or so. If you find that you have forgotten the spelling of a word, write a new card for that word and start the process all over again. You will not have to do this often.

All of us—poor spellers in particular—should check our papers and reports for spelling before and after final typing.

SPELLING REVIEW CHECKLIST

1. *Consistency.* Not only must all words be spelled correctly, they must also be spelled consistently where more than one spelling is correct. If, for example, you decide to use the form *ensure*, use it always except when writing about *insurance underwriting.* If you are not a born speller, a check for consistency can take a good deal of time. For this reason you might consider adopting the spelling improvement program described previously.
2. *Applying Experience.* Pay particular attention to misspellings in previous papers. Unless you make a conscious effort to memorize correct spellings, you will probably repeat your errors.
3. *Applying the Rules.* If you find yourself wondering whether you have misspelled certain words, check your dictionary and give serious thought to memorizing the spelling rules supplied in this chapter. Poor spellers spend a great deal of time looking up the same words, or the same types of words, again and again. Memorization of some rules is worth the time. When you reach the point at which those rules are part of you, you will not have to spend time on endless checking and rechecking.

CAPITALIZATION

Capitalization practices can almost be summed up in a few simple rules.

Sentences

The first letter of every sentence is always capitalized.

I began the conversation by saying, "She called this morning."

    "Who?" He stared at me.

    "Ellen."

    "And what did she have to say?" He clearly was curious.

Quotations

The first word of a quotation is capitalized when the quotation is a complete sentence.

> *An otherwise forgotten man, Thomas Riley Marshall, secured his place in history when he said, "What this country needs is a good five-cent cigar."*

The first word is not ordinarily capitalized when the quoted material is not a full sentence.

> *We can do without Marshall's "good five-cent cigar" if we can find an acceptable one-dollar six-pack.*

When a quotation is interrupted, the second part of the quotation is not capitalized unless it is a sentence.

> *"Things they do not understand," said de Musset, "always cause a sensation among the English."*

> *"Death has its own way of embittering victory, and it causes glory to be followed by pestilence," wrote Victor Hugo. "Typhus is the successor of triumph."*

Lines of Poetry

Most poets capitalize the first word of every line of verse. In quoting a poem, the poet's usage should be followed. When you write your own poetry, capitalize in the way you find most meaningful.

The sunshine is a glorious birth;
But yet I know, where'er I go,
That there hath passed away a glory from the earth.
William Wordsworth

I and *O*

The pronoun *I* and the interjection *O* are always capitalized.

They wanted to know whether I was ready.
The trumpet of a prophecy! O wind,
If Winter comes, can Spring be far behind?
Percy Bysshe Shelley

Note. Shelley capitalizes *Wind*, *Winter*, and *Spring* because he is employing personification—a figure of speech in which inanimate objects, forces, or abstractions are treated as animate forces. Such words may be treated as proper nouns.

Proper Nouns and Adjectives

A proper noun is the name of a particular person, place, or thing. Proper nouns are capitalized.

My youngest son, Jon, will escort Maria Jones to the dance.

The capital of Connecticut is Hartford.

Bostonians are proud of their Museum of Fine Arts, which has an excellent collection of paintings.

A proper adjective is an adjective derived from a proper noun. Proper adjectives are capitalized.

I learned to think clearly when I studied Euclidean geometry. (The proper adjective *Euclidean* is derived from Euclid, the name of an ancient Greek mathematician.)

The Security Council agreed to hear the repre-
sentatives of the Palestinian forces. (The proper
adjective *Palestinian* is derived from the place
name Palestine.)

When a proper noun consists of two or more
words, local practice is followed in capitalizing.

Stratford-on- Avon	Dien Bien Phu	Atlas Mountains
Lake Superior	Rio Grande River	Sierra Leone

Proper nouns are capitalized in the following
sentences.

Richard's ambition was to explore the Altamira
and Wyandotte caves. (The last word is not capitalized, because it is not part of any particular
name.)

Richard's ambition was to explore Altamira Cave
and Wyandotte Cave.

Dictionaries usually indicate whether a noun is
proper or common.

Particles

Many foreign names and names that once were
foreign begin with particles, such as *van* and *di*.
Anglicized names call for different treatment from
that given to foreign names.

Anglicized names.   When particles are treated as
separate parts of a name, they are capitalized.

Agnes De Mille   Carl Van Doren   Alfred Du Pont

When a particle is joined with a name, the
name is capitalized only when a family retains the
original capital letter.

Joe DiMaggio   *Kurt Vonnegut*

Foreign names. The particles *van* and *von* are never capitalized.

Paul von Hindenburg   *Vincent van Gogh*

The particles *de*, *du*, *di*, and *da* are capitalized only when first names and titles are omitted:

Pietro di Donato, but *Di Donato*

Vicomte de Lesseps, but *De Lesseps*

Europeans write these names as *Donato* and *Lesseps* when first names and titles are not included.

Places and Directions

Compass directions

Points of the compass are usually capitalized when they are part of the names of specific regions or places.

Have you ever visited East Corinth, Vermont?

Believe it or not, West New York is in New Jersey.

In my parents' recent trip to the United States, they especially enjoyed touring the Northwest.

The South voted solidly for Jimmy Carter in 1976.

When points of the compass indicate directions, they are not capitalized.

Go north on this road for two miles.

They sailed west-northwest all afternoon and ended up in Gloucester.

Names and nicknames of regions

Regional names and geographic nicknames are always capitalized.

> *The Sun Belt attracts men and women eager to spend their retirement years in a mild climate.*
>
> *Massachusetts is still referred to as the Bay State.*
>
> *Marco Polo spent several years in the Orient.*
>
> *Will the Middle East ever achieve lasting peace?*

Streets, buildings, parks, companies, and the like

The proper names of locations and institutions, as well as their nicknames, are always capitalized. Notice that when common words such as *street* and *park* form part of the name, they are also capitalized.

> *Much of the advertising in the United States is conceived in agencies located on Madison Avenue.*
>
> *Thousands of visitors are still willing to pay to go to the top of the Empire State Building, even though the World Trade Center is taller.*
>
> *Yellowstone Park is noted for its geysers.*
>
> *The International Business Machines Company has a large share of the computer market all over the world.*
>
> *Children in need benefit from the activities of UNICEF, the United Nations International Children's Emergency Fund.*
>
> *The Bank of England is affectionately known as The Old Lady of Threadneedle Street.*

Other Instances

Names in religion

The names of gods and titles of sacred writings are always capitalized.

> *Muslims hold the Koran sacred, believing it to be the work of Muhammad as dictated to Gabriel.*
>
> *Anyone who believes in God may be said to be a deist.*
>
> *They pray to Allah several times a day.*
>
> *The Morgan Library has several Gutenberg Bibles.*
>
> *One of the first things many children learn is the Lord's Prayer.*

Pronouns that refer to God are sometimes capitalized.

> *I pray to Him in His wisdom.*

Nationalities, races, and languages

Nouns and adjectives formed from geographic and ethnic proper nouns are capitalized.

> *During her recent trip to Europe, Mary Ann found the Italians friendlier than the French.*
>
> *Mary Ann spoke fluent Italian, but her French was rusty.*
>
> *I particularly like Russian soups, but Russian bread is too sour for the taste of an Englishman.*
>
> *The so-called Bantu homelands have created a new South African nightmare.*

Scientific names of races are capitalized, but not colors.

Members of the so-called white race are generally Caucasoids.

Days of the week, months, holidays

Specific designations of time are capitalized.

Monday, February 14, is St. Valentine's Day.

I will see you at the polls on Election Day, Tuesday, November 5.

Documents, eras, prizes, and events

The names of special awards, occurrences, documents and eras are capitalized.

When I visited Washington, D.C., I had a chance to read the full text of the Declaration of Independence.

The Paleozoic includes the Cambrian, Ordovician, Silurian, Devonian, Mississippian, Pennsylvanian, and Permian periods.

Saul Bellow won the Nobel Prize for Literature in 1976.

Who can forget the 1985 World Series?

Titles

Titles of high rank are capitalized when they accompany a name or when they refer to a specific person. A title that merely names an office and does not refer to a specific individual is not capitalized.

Thousands of pilgrims received the blessing of Pope John Paul II.

Henry VIII needed a male heir, so advisers to the King sought a divorce for him.

*The President holds televised press conferences,
a practice followed by all presidents since Eisen-
hower.*

Other titles are capitalized only when they precede a name.

*We asked Secretary-Treasurer Betty Furst to de-
liver her report in person.*

*Did you know that Richard Melville, vice presi-
dent for marketing, will retire next year?*

*I know that Hans Andersen, her country's min-
ister of defense, favors the treaty.*

Some writers and editors—particularly those
who work for newspapers and magazines—prefer to
capitalize all titles of high rank under every circum-
stance.

Vatican City has been the residence of all Popes.

*The highest office in the United States is that of
President.*

Academic degrees

All titles of learning are always capitalized.

*She earned her Associate in Arts degree last
year and is now working toward a Bachelor of
Science degree.*

*Albert Lehner, M.D., will speak tonight on the
treatment of allergies in children.*

Titles of books, plays, ships, paintings, songs, and the like

The first word in a title and all the other words
except articles, conjunctions, and prepositions of
fewer than five letters are capitalized.

For Whom the Bell Tolls   *As You Like It*

The S.S. *Queen of Heaven*   *Washington Crossing the Delaware*

The Gulf Between Us

Course titles

School subjects are capitalized when they are actual course titles, but not when they are general subjects.

> *I suffered through Sociology 1133 last semester.*
>
> *All pre-med students take Chemistry 45 and 46.*
>
> *He is taking sociology, organic chemistry, and economics.*

Family relations

Family relations are capitalized only when they are used as substitutes for names.

> *I remember Father bent over his work far into the night while Mother managed all of us, her household chores, and a part-time job as proofreader.*
>
> *I asked my brother for his help many times.*

CAPITALIZATION REVIEW CHECKLIST

1. *Consistency.* Have you settled all questions of capitalization consistently? Examine every use of capital letters in your paper to make certain.
2. *Amount of Capitalization.* Most writing requires little use of capital letters beyond the first letters of the first words of sentences. If you find yourself using many capital letters, you may need to review every use in your paper to see whether

you have invented some new rules. Perhaps you have fallen into the trap of using capital letters to achieve emphasis.

3. *Applying Experience*. Have you been criticized for mistakes in capitalization in earlier papers? Check out your past errors and do not repeat them.

4. *Applying the Rules*. When you are uncertain whether a word or phrase should be capitalized, leave nothing to chance. Check the rules, and consult the dictionary.

PART III

WRITING PAPERS AND REPORTS

CHAPTER 11

The Library Research Paper

The work put into a solid library research paper of the kind assigned in schools and colleges builds skills that prove valuable in later professional and business careers. Any good researcher has mastered the art of systematic investigation, has learned to evaluate the results, and has developed the ability to report the findings clearly and concisely. The best way to begin to develop these useful skills is to go through the complete process that ends with submittal of a first-class library research paper.

The required work can either be put off until the week before the paper is due—with disappointing results and a tired writer—or it can be scheduled carefully, planned effectively, and accomplished efficiently. This chapter outlines everything that must be done to achieve a good research paper, from selecting a subject to typing the final draft.

PRELIMINARIES

Working to Schedule

A semester cannot be stretched. From the day a paper is assigned, only a fixed period of time remains in which to accomplish a great deal of work. Some instructors, especially in freshman courses, establish a series of checkpoints. By requiring students to keep on schedule, the instructor can supply guidance all along the way.

Typical Research Paper Schedule

- Subject approval: March 4
- Preliminary bibliography: March 18
- Outline approval: April 2
- Paper due: May 4

If the instructor does not establish such a schedule, it is important that you set up some kind of timetable for yourself. By breaking the job down into separate tasks and by keeping to a realistic schedule, you will be able to do your best. But if you let the work slip, you will be too hurried at the end to do your best. Especially if you must write several papers in a single semester, you need to be well organized. It is disastrous to let the work pile up at the end of a semester.

Choosing a Subject

Many students have difficulty deciding on a suitable subject for a research paper. Instructors are usually ready to help and will schedule a conference with each student for this purpose.

Of course the topic finally agreed upon has to be related to the contents of the course. The instructor can be helpful with advice about whether a topic is worth pursuing, whether you have the necessary background to handle it, and whether the college library will be able to offer sufficient information. The instructor will steer you away from topics that are too narrow or too broad for a paper or are inappropriate for your particular abilities and interests. As you develop your ability to do research, you will be able to judge these matters for yourself.

Choosing a Topic: Answer These Questions

- Does the topic interest you?
- Can you find enough research material in the library to cover the topic?
- Do you have adequate background to do the research?
- Does your instructor approve?

An ideal topic for any research paper is one that interests you so much that you can hardly wait to get started. But what if there does not seem to be any subject appropriate to the course material that makes you want to work? A meeting with your instructor and an hour or two spent reading general articles in encyclopedias will soon reveal a topic you can sink your teeth into. Suddenly something in an article will connect with something in your own background, and ideas for a paper will begin to flow.

RESEARCH

Building a Bibliography

Once you think you have found an area that interests you, you are ready to discover whether the library has sufficient material. You must establish a list of books and articles that deal with the topic. There are a number of sources for this information.

Major articles in encyclopedias end with general bibliographies that lead to additional information. The library card catalogue indicates whether your library has the books cited in those bibliographies.

The card catalogue also lists everything the library owns on any subject. The card catalogue, which is arranged alphabetically, has at least three cards for every book the library owns; the book is listed by author, title, and subject.

As a first step you will want to look under the subject heading or headings that relate to your area of interest. For each book in the catalogue that appears promising—it is best not to overlook anything at this stage of your research—record the information needed to locate the book, preferably using a separate 3 × 5 card for each book. Write down the author, title, and call number. (Some people prefer to list the title first; the method you use may depend somewhat on your topic.) The information is supplied in the card catalogue, along with additional information, such as place and date of publication.

Other research guides in your library will lead you to some other books, and especially to magazine articles. For example, *The Reader's Guide to Periodical Literature* indexes more than 100 nontechnical magazines. To help readers locate articles of interest on a variety of subjects, it is arranged alphabetically by topic. There are also many bibliographies for particular subjects; for these, consult *The Bibliographic Index* or a reference librarian.

Bibliographies in special subjects include the following:

Art: *How to Find Out About the Arts*. Neville Carrick, Oxford, 1965.
Business: *Business Periodicals Index*. New York, revised annually.

Economics: *Dictionary of Economics*. Harold S. Sloan
and Arnold J. Zurcher, New York, 1970.
Education: *The New York University List of Books
in Education*. Barbara S. Marks, New
York, 1968.
History: *Guide to Historical Literature*. American
Historical Association, New York, 1961.
Literature: *A Reference Guide to English Studies*.
Donald F. Bond, Chicago, 1971.
Science and Engineering: *Science and Engineering
Reference Sources*. Harold R. Malinowsky,
Rochester, New York, 1967.

You are sure to find one or more that will prove
helpful in your research.

Reading for General Information

Once you have made a list of books on your
subject—compiled from encyclopedia articles, the
card catalogue, and special bibliographies—you are
ready to get down to real work. Your reading should
begin in the most generalized books, because they
give broad coverage, and it is most useful to begin
with an overview. As you gain general knowledge
on your topic, you will proceed to specialized articles and books to complete your survey of available
information. In the books you consult you may well
find bibliographies that take you still deeper into
your subject.

An Experienced Researcher Always

- follows every lead
- keeps a record of call numbers for every book
  used for a paper
- works mostly in the library, where everything needed is available—encyclopedias,
  dictionaries, specialized reference works, photocopying and microfilm equipment

Once you have collected index cards for general books that appear promising, look over the books and use their tables of contents and indexes to see whether the books will be useful to you. You can tell in minutes what a book contains and which parts pertain to your subject. As you find entries that appear interesting, go to the pages referred to and skim as quickly as you can. If enough books show promise, you are on to something worthwhile. If the books themselves have bibliographies, make index cards for the titles that deal directly with your topic. Later you will check the card catalogue to see whether the books are available or whether they are obtainable through interlibrary loan. If they are in your library, add the call numbers to the appropriate index cards. Once you have decided that a book is useful to your purpose, add to the card the name of the publisher, place of publication, and date the book was published; you eventually will have to include this information in your bibliography. The call number is important because it indicates where the book is shelved in the library; once you have finished using the book, this number has no further significance for your paper. (See pages 233–37 and 237–39 for requirements of footnotes and bibliographies.)

Narrowing the Topic

What to do if too much information turns up for you to research thoroughly in the time you have? If your search turns up so much material that you would be foolish to undertake the subject in a single research paper, you need not abandon the topic altogether. You may be able to reduce it to manageable size—and the time to do so is before you become involved in careful reading and note taking. For a paper in literature, for instance, you can narrow a subject from an entire group of writers to a particular writer; or from all the works of a writer to one novel in particular, or even a single character in that work. Practically any subject can be subdivided logically until it is suitable for a worthwhile paper.

If, on the other hand, you find there is too little information on a subject that interests you, you may be able to expand it. For example, you may want to write on current uses of windmills but cannot find enough material. (This is not surprising; when a subject is truly new, there has not been time enough for scholars to write books on it.) But two or more subjects within the same field may provide the material you need; in the case of windmills, one possibility is to include current applications of other devices, such as those exploiting geothermal energy and tidal energy. Alternatively, the use of windmills throughout history is a sizable topic that allows you to include your interest in current uses.

The rule of the experienced researcher is simple: *When a single subject is too small, combine two or more to create a subject worthy of a research paper*. Without discarding the few useful sources you have already located, go back to the card catalogue and to the bibliographies you have found. Sooner or later your search will uncover the sources needed for a suitable and interesting research paper.

Taking Notes

You will soon find that you do not have time to read every word in all the books that pertain to your subject. Minutes spent with the table of contents and the index of each book you use will lead you to the appropriate pages. Read these thoroughly—and *thoroughly means slowly*. Read again and again if necessary, and think carefully about what you read. When you have identified what you want and have understood it clearly, you are ready to take notes.

Experienced researchers prefer to take reading notes on cards, rather than in notebooks. Many prefer large cards, which are easy to handle and can accommodate several notes from the same book or article. Others prefer 3 × 5 cards, one for each note. A topic heading at the top of each card allows you to sort your cards by topic and arrange them in the desired order once the paper is outlined.

Primary
source: *the work, event, or person under study. Primary sources in history, for example, are accounts of events written by participants or eyewitnesses.*

Secondary
source: *interpretations or critical commentary by scholars reflecting on but not participating in the subject of the primary source.*

As you read each source, you make a note whenever you come across a fact or insight or opinion you want to record. If you think there is a chance you will want to quote the writer's information verbatim in your finished paper, you will need to copy it down precisely; otherwise, you need only make your record in your own note-taking form. Each note should include the source (book or article), in some short form that will identify it enough to lead you back to your bibliography card when the time comes, and the page number on which you found the information.

As your paper begins to take shape in your mind, you will be able to assign a subtopic to each card; this goes at the top of the card. For example, in the paper on windmills, one subtopic might be *Holland*; another might be *in Literature*; still a third, *U.S.— 20th Century*. The specific subtopics depend both on the subject of the paper and your particular interest. It is best not to make these categories too broad, or you will find that all cards fit under the same heading. It is not useful, however, to set the terms so narrowly that there is a different topic for each card. Think ahead; the subtopics should broadly parallel the topics of the subsections of your finished paper. But do not worry; you can always cross out a topic listed on a card and change the wording—this is one area where neatness does not count for much.

As your reading gives you insights of your own, you may want to record these on cards as well, under the appropriate heading. When you write your paper, these will remind you of directions you want to take. As your reading continues, you will also identify of new subtopics.

In Summary

Include in each note all the information needed for use in the paper. Make doubly sure that you record the page number where the information is found in the source book or article.

Quote directly when a source puts something so well—which usually means in few words—that you cannot say it any better. To change the words in any way would make the expression longer and the thinking less striking. Obviously, few texts are worthy of lengthy quotation. When you quote, use quotation marks. If you neglect to indicate in your notes that you are quoting, you may forget to do so in your paper and lay yourself open to charges of plagiarism.

Summarize when you wish to express a thought you have found and can do so in fewer words than the source. Again, remember that the thought is not your own. When you come to write the paper, your notes will remind you of where you found the thought so that you can write an appropriate footnote or other citation.

Comment when you wish to record a thought of your own in response to something you are reading. Though you will want to refer to the material you have read when you write your paper, you will also make it clear that you have done some thinking on your own.

WRITING

Theme Statement and Outline

Like any researcher, you start your library search with a vague idea of what your reading will reveal. Like any good researcher, all through your library search you are prepared to examine each of your findings to see whether it supports your original idea. With this open attitude toward what you read, you know what all that reading adds up to by the time you complete your research. What began as a broad *subject* for investigation developed into several *topics* related to the subject, which now point toward a central *theme* to be stated, analyzed, and developed in a *paper*. You will find it helpful at this point to write an outline of what you may write. The outline will indicate a theme, summarizing briefly what the paper is about, as well as the main and minor ideas supporting that theme.

The outline will be the road map for the organization of the final paper, and that paper will state the theme, expand it, explain it, give examples, and cite sources for information introduced to support the thinking and conclusions.

A *theme statement* gives the gist of what library research reveals and provides a focus for the final paper. The theme statement also organizes the paper, because once a theme statement has been made, you can go on to establish how your main ideas and minor ideas should be arranged to support that statement.

An outline is the best and quickest means of developing that organization. (Outlines help to order a writer's thinking, but if you cannot write an outline—or a theme statement—until you have gone through a first draft, work without one. After all, the paper itself is what counts.)

The type of outline used is not important here. A good paper can be assembled merely from a page of assorted words and phrases if those words and phrases mean something to you. An elaborate sentence outline, at the other extreme, guides you section by section and paragraph by paragraph while you write your paper. Most writers use something between these two extremes.

The best way to learn to write an outline is to compile one from a paper you have already completed. You will see that the outline guides writer and reader through the entire paper. No matter how carefully an outline is constructed, however, it usually undergoes revision while the paper is being written. The act of writing stimulates thinking and usually leads to improved structure. In the example that follows, the outline includes sentences for sections, phrases for paragraphs and for groups of paragraphs.

You have completed your library research on the Tonkin Gulf Incident, which played an important part in increasing United States participation in the Vietnam War. Since the paper to be written deals with historical events, *chronological organization* is appropriate.

Theme Statement. The August 1964 Tonkin Gulf Incident, which appears to have been instigated by the United States, turned lack of support for involvement in Vietnam into overwhelming backing for President Lyndon B. Johnson's leadership and made possible greatly increased military action.

I. The Vietnam War was going well for the North Vietnamese and Viet Cong by August 1, 1964, and President Johnson had far less than a majority of public support for increasing United States involvement.

   A. Conditions in North Vietnam
   B. Conditions in the Republic of Vietnam
   C. Political and military situation in the United States

II. The U.S.S. *Maddox* and *C. Turner Joy* became involved in naval actions with North Vietnamese PT boats in the Gulf of Tonkin off North Vietnam.

    A. Provocative mission of the *Maddox* and *Joy*—July 30 and 31

    B. The first encounter—August 2

    C. The second encounter—August 3

    D. Deliberations of the President and his advisers

    E. Air attack by United States warplanes on North Vietnam PT-boat bases—August 5—an escalation of the war

III. Congressional response and public reaction in the United States overwhelmingly supported military action, establishing the basis for increased involvement by the United States.

    A. Role of the Senate in events leading to Tonkin Gulf Resolution

    B. Passage of resolution by the Senate—August 7

    C. Shift in public opinion to strong support of increased military action

IV. Using the Resolution as a basis for troop and plane deployment, President Johnson multiplied United States effort in the months following.

The logic of a subject suggests the order for an outline and for the paper written from it. The sample outline above is chronological because it deals with historical events. Other subjects call for other arrangements. A paper comparing the customs of three different cultures, for example, might call for four sections. The first, second, and third would each describe the customs of one of the groups, and the fourth would explain the similarities and differences. There would also, of course, be introductory and concluding sections. The introduction would describe the framework of the paper and state the theme. The conclusion would restate the theme and summarize the findings that validate that theme. A paper proposing a solution to a problem might be in three main sections—the first to describe the problem and state the theme; the second to deal with proposed solutions that are rejected on appropriate grounds; and the third to explain fully the recommended solution, show its advantages over the other solutions, and restate the theme of the paper. A paper evaluating a literary or artistic figure might be written in two main sections—one devoted to an account of the career and contribution of the figure under study, the other to major works, with detailed support for the writer's evaluation of the figure under study.

The First Draft

Nothing is gained from racing through the first draft of a research paper. You have done your research; you have your outline and notes; your theme statement is in front of you throughout your writing, to tell you what you are setting out to establish. Nothing will slip your mind if you work carefully and slowly, writing every sentence in the most polished fashion you can manage. If you work in this manner, you will only have to correct the completed first draft and go on to final typing. If you hurry your first draft, you probably will have to do a second draft before getting to the final one.

In writing a first draft, leave generous margins and ample spacing between lines. This method will give you the room you need when you are reworking the draft. Cramped copy makes revision awkward.

Work through your card file to stimulate your thinking and writing, but be aware that an unweeded file does not produce strong and convincing papers. The first notes made during a research project often prove less than useful when you get down to writing. (As you worked through all the sources your library provided, your understanding of your subject grew and changed. What first appeared pertinent may have turned out to be trivial or wrong.)

Put everything into your paper that you want in it: *quotations, reference sources, footnotes, references to footnotes*—everything the finished paper will require. If you want to include lengthy quotations, tape them into the paper instead of taking the time to type them. As you get all you want from a note card, put it aside. A shrinking pile of cards gives you courage by indicating progress. Complete one section before going on to the next, working from the first one to the last. In this way you will have a clear idea of what you have said earlier and need not say again. You will also have an understanding of the logical flow of the paper. You will be listening to your thinking. Do your thoughts make sense? If you were your reader, would you accept the reasoning expressed and the conclusions reached? Play the reader's role, looking over your own shoulder as you write. Discard the vague. Strengthen the weak. Make sense. Convince.

Just as the entire paper requires a logical beginning, middle, and end, each section and paragraph within the paper should have a logical structure. The length of a unit of writing is not determined by formula: so many lines make a paragraph, so many paragraphs a section, so many sentences a paper. A paragraph develops to completion the thought expressed in the *topic sentence,* which introduces or states the main idea. When you feel satisfied, end the paragraph. When you have met all the requirements of a section you have planned, end the section. When you have brought all the sections of a paper together in a concluding section, end the paper.

Remember

* Use direct quotation to support your thinking in language better than you can write.

* Do not use direct quotation merely to pad your paper.
* Do not use direct quotation to borrow someone else's ideas.

Finish your first draft and give yourself time to recover. If you have scheduled your work properly, you have time to put some distance between yourself and your paper. When you come back to the paper, with the perspective time gives, you will ask yourself the crucial questions: What does the paper state? Is it worth stating? Is it stated well? Does the paper support the theme statement? Does the theme statement need polishing? Is the writing as clear as it can be? Are all the footnotes in place? Is every footnote reference in the text? Is the bibliography consistent and correct?

Footnotes

The majority of writers follow the form for footnotes and bibliographies established in the *MLA Style Sheet* (second edition), published by the Modern Language Association; the *Manual of Style*, published by University of Chicago Press; or the *Style Manual of the United States Government Printing Office*, available from the Superintendent of Documents, Washington, D.C. These three sources, available in most libraries, provide guidance in all situations requiring footnotes and bibliography for general writing. Other styles are more common in scientific writing and in some social science areas.[1]

Footnotes may be grouped together as endnotes in numerical order at the end of a research paper, but readers usually prefer footnotes typed on the pages to which they refer, either between solid

[1] A helpful book for the student's use is Ehrlich and Murphy's *Writing and Researching Term Papers and Reports*, published by Bantam Books.

lines within the text[2] or at the bottom of the page.[3] If you are uncertain how much space a footnote will take up, type it out first on a separate sheet of paper. Type each footnote single space, indent the beginning as though it were a paragraph, and type the appropriate number slightly above the line and just before the first word.

---

[2]This footnote shows how to type a footnote within the text of a paper. The footnote is set off by solid lines above and below and is double-spaced before and after each of the solid lines.

If you have included the information that normally goes in a footnote in the text, no further reference is necessary. If, for example, the text states, *"It is interesting that Flaubert does not mention Emma until the third chapter of* Madame Bovary," all the necessary documentary material is given, making a footnote superfluous.

Footnotes are numbered consecutively; the same number is inserted in the text at the point where the footnote applies that is given to the footnote itself. In the text, the number is typed directly after and above the word to which the footnote applies. If any mark of punctuation (except a dash) appears after that word, place the footnote number after it.[4] Do not punctuate the number.

All information from other sources must be documented. If it is not, you are open to charges of plagiarism.

Standard requirements for common footnotes follow. (See the *MLA Style Sheet* [second edition] for a complete listing of forms of footnotes and internal documentation.)

---

[3]Before the first footnote at the bottom of a page, leave a double space or type a line ten spaces long, beginning at the left margin. The footnote number is indented three or five spaces from the margin. The other lines begin flush with the left margin.

Books

Author (first name first), title (italicized in print, underscored in typewriting), place of publication, publisher, and date of publication (place and publisher separated by a colon), page or pages referred to.

[5]Bruce Wetterau, *Concise Dictionary of World History* (New York: Macmillan, 1983) 46.

The entry ends in a period. Place, publisher, and date of publication are enclosed in parentheses.

[6]Stephen H. Spurr and Burton V. Barnes, *Forest Ecology* (New York: Wiley, 1980) 224–26.

There are two differences between this footnote and the previous one. Here the work has two authors, both listed by first name first, and the reference covers several pages.

[4]This footnote appears merely to remind you to number footnotes consecutively.

In typing a footnote, indent three or five spaces before typing the footnote number. All other lines are typed flush left.

Articles printed in periodicals

Author (first name first), article title (enclosed in quotation marks), periodical title (italicized in print, underscored in typewriting), periodical volume number, date of publication, page or pages referred to.

[7]Albert B. Smith, "Improving College Teaching," *Teaching-Learning Journal* 1 (Spring 1975): 30.

Note that no comma is used within the date of publication.

Articles reprinted in a book

⁸Melvin Backman, " 'The Bear' and *Go Down Moses*," original title "The Wilderness and the Negro in Faulkner's 'The Bear,' " *PMLA* LXXVI (December 1961), reprinted in *William Faulkner*, ed. Dean Morgan Schmitter (New York: McGraw-Hill, 1973) 137.

The above illustrates a complex footnote. The article cited had a different title when it first appeared in *PMLA (Proceedings of the Modern Language Association)*. Both dates of publication are supplied. The writer of the paper who supplied this footnote wants to make certain that the reader knows that the reference is to the article found in the book *William Faulkner*, rather than to *PMLA*. Italics are used for the book title and quotation marks for the article titles.

Second references to books or articles

The sample footnotes shown above are appropriate for the *first mention* of a book or article. If the same sources are cited a second or third time or more, the entries are abbreviated.

⁹Smith 32.
¹⁰Backman 145–46.

These footnotes tell the reader that an earlier footnote gives a full citation of these sources. Such abbreviation is appropriate only when the authors cited appear in a single book or article citation. If more than one book or article by the same author is mentioned, the footnote would have to supply enough information to tell the reader which specific book or article is referenced.

¹¹Smith, "Improving College Teaching," 32.

If more than one author has the same name, the first name needs to be included.

[12]Anne Smith 32.
[13]Charles Smith 83–92.

Including the title makes it clear which of Smith's articles, among several that have been cited, is being referred to. Including the first name makes it clear which Smith is meant.

Footnotes, as you know, do not exclusively cite sources used in research. They may also be used to permit the writer to make comments worth including but removed from the central discussion of the paper. The footnote on this page appeared in a student's paper on the ineffectual leadership of a certain political figure early in this century.[14]

Bibliographies

A bibliography lists alphabetically by authors' last names every work cited in the text of a paper or in footnotes to the paper. It also includes all the sources the writer used in formulating ideas, even when the works were not cited in the paper. A bibliography should not, however, be padded by the inclusion of every title located during research. A bibliography is intended to list sources that proved helpful; it is not meant to impress.

While all bibliographies are arranged alphabetically, there is more than one way to proceed. Some bibliographies list all works used in a single alphabet, by author's last name, whether a work cited is a book or an article. Other bibliographies distinguish among books (listed first), magazine articles (listed second), and others (newspaper articles, encyclopedia articles, letters, and the like; listed last). Still others make a distinction between primary sources and secondary sources or between works actually used in footnotes and others that have sup-

[14]We can easily understand the reluctance of the Mayor to answer Steffens's questions, since the Mayor was under indictment at the time for embezzlement of municipal funds.

plied certain insights or that can serve as further reading.

In whatever system is used, the work is listed by author (last name first). But there are situations in which the author is not known or the author is unimportant. In such instances the name of the publication serves as the name of the author. For such works as pamphlets that are issued anonymously, the sponsoring institution is listed first. When a work is an anthology, the name of the editor is listed first. If the authorship of an old work is not known, the title takes precedence.

The abbreviated bibliography that follows gives examples of each of the forms you are most likely to encounter. Note that all the authors, titles, and so forth are freely invented; the purpose of the example is to demonstrate style, not to lead you to actual works.

Note also the punctuation and indentation. Though more than one system of punctuation is acceptable, the one given here is easy to apply. It works as follows.

Author's last name is given first (though a second author is given first name first).

Parts of an entry are separated by periods.

Place and date of publication for a book are not enclosed in parentheses.

No page references are given. The bibliography is a listing of works used, not a reference to specific portions of the works.

Inclusive page numbers are supplied for articles. If an article is broken up within a periodical, the inclusive page numbers are given for each part.

The word *pages* is not used before giving the page numbers of an article. If an author is listed consecutively in a bibliography for more than one book or more than one article, the name of the author is replaced by a short solid line in the second and following references; a period follows such a line.

Bibliography

Books

Andrews, Charles. *Four Years of College—And More*. New York: Harper & Row, 1962.

———. *Graduate School*. New York: Harper & Row, 1963.

Chapin, Mary, and Harry Adams, eds. *Twenty Views of Colleges*. Livermore, Calif.: The Oddball Press, 1980.

Educational Testing Service. *Guidelines for Applying to Colleges*. Princeton, N.J.: Educational Testing Service, 1977.

My Years in Ye Olde Harvard Yard. Boston, 1778.

Taylor, James. Personal communication (letter to the writer, March 17, 1984).

Articles

Astor, Muffie. "How I Got Through Smith." *Cosmopolitan*, XL (February 1982), 263–279.

"Higher Education." *Encyclopaedia Britannica*, 11th ed., Vol. 8, 937ff.

Reston, James. "Reform in Our Colleges." *The New York Times*, April 29, 1984, p. 47, col. 3.

The most important considerations are completeness and consistency.

The Final Draft

Two readings of the first draft are essential. First, read the entire paper slowly and thoughtfully to examine the flow of ideas. As you read, ask yourself: Is the structure clear? Does the reasoning hold up? Does the argument convince? If you find weak points in your paper, mark them but do not stop at that point to make changes. Lack of clarity and poor arrangement of elements are what you mark. When you have finished this careful reading, go back to the marked places and do whatever repair is necessary. Do not retype. Merely write in the new version and cross out the old. Rearrange material that needs rearrangement, using whatever symbols work for you to indicate where material properly belongs.

When you are satisfied that you have corrected all major weaknesses of expression, when you have eliminated unnecessary repetitions, and when you have added the needed clarification and transitions, read the paper again. Now you must search out every error, no matter how small: sentence structure, spelling, punctuation—everything. You may be weary of your paper, but close editing pays off in improved writing.

Finally you are ready to type your final draft. Besides the original for submittal to your instructor, you should make a carbon or photocopy for yourself. This second copy protects against lost papers. Clean your typewriter keys and change the ribbon, if necessary. Use white, unlined 8½ × 11 bond paper. Instructors must read many papers in a brief period. They appreciate papers that show pride of authorship.

Type the title page first. Do not number the title page or the first page of text. Beginning with the second page of text, number every page at the right margin about half an inch from the top of the page. On the first page of text, which is page one but does not carry a number, begin typing three to four inches from the top. On all other pages of text, begin typing one and a half inches from the top. Leave one-inch margins at left, right, and bottom.

Indent the first line of each paragraph three, five, or ten spaces, using the selected indentation for every paragraph of text. Double-space all text matter.

Single-space within footnotes. Double-space before and between footnotes. Single-space within entries in the bibliography. Double-space between entries.

THE LONELY EARLY YEARS
A Study of the Young Hawthorne

Emma Dalton

English 3102
Professor Kronish
May 21, 1985

Triple-space before and after a quotation in the text when the quotation is long enough to be an extract (see pages 176–177). Indent the entire quotation an additional few spaces. Use the same one-inch right margin for quotations that is used for text. Add additional indentation to indicate a paragraph in the original of a quotation. Single-space the quotation.

Erase and retype all errors. But do not hesitate to make last-minute corrections in ink if no time is left for retyping. Your instructor would rather see mistakes corrected in your own handwriting than read a paper containing errors.

Check to see that all pages are in correct order, and clip or staple your paper together in the upper left corner.

You are responsible for everything in the paper, even if you do not do your own typing. From the first footnote to the last, from the first entry in a bibliography to the last, from the first word on the title page to the last word in the text—everything is yours, and you have the responsibility of seeing that it is correct.

A BRIEF WARNING

A student who improperly uses someone else's words or ideas is guilty of plagiarism. Such intellectual dishonesty is usually detected, and the plagiarist becomes subject to academic discipline. The plagiarist risks suspension or dismissal.

In research writing, the plagiarist may copy actual words used in a research source without identifying the source. This is the easiest kind of plagiarism to detect. You must supply footnotes or other documentation for all sources of information you use, whether in quotation or summary.

Borrowing someone else's ideas and expressing those ideas in your own words is also plagiarism unless you supply the source of the ideas. Stealing ideas is a more subtle kind of intellectual dishonesty than stealing words, but an experienced instructor will recognize ideas that are not your own.

Your best safeguard against plagiarism is to do your own thinking. While you are expected to be influenced by information, ideas, reasoning, and language you find in your sources, you must preserve your independence and originality in organizing and writing your paper. Whenever you borrow a thought or idea, identify the source; then you will never have to fear charges of plagiarism.

CHAPTER 12

Business Writing

A generation ago business writing was elaborate, complex, and formal. Today business writing is above all clear, compact, and complete.

Clear because business people must be able to understand information exactly as the writer intends.

Compact because business people have so much to do each day that they quickly lose patience with rambling, long-winded presentations.

Complete because business people have no time to search out necessary information missing from a report or letter they are reading.

Business people do not read correspondence and reports for enjoyment or diversion. They read to acquire information necessary for making decisions and taking action.

Business writing includes many types of letters and reports, but it begins with employment résumés and letters of introduction.

JOB APPLICATIONS

Résumés

A résumé relates the pertinent work and allied experience, education, and personal information by which employers judge an applicant's qualifications for employment. No résumé alone will guarantee a job. But it can do a great deal to get the applicant a favorable hearing. A good résumé opens doors to interviews; a poor one closes them.

Employers conduct personal interviews before anyone is hired for a position of real substance. They want to learn everything they can about an applicant. They want to make certain that the applicant's personal qualities match the requirements of the position that is open. Not least, they want to see the kind of impression the applicant makes in person.

Both when you look for your first opportunity and as you advance in your career, you may have to apply in writing for every new job. You will find it helpful, therefore, to learn how to write a résumé that opens doors for you and that represents you in the best possible light, so that employers will be eager to meet you—and to hire you.

There are various ways to set up an effective résumé, but all should meet the requirements of clarity, compactness, and completeness. This is also one area where neatness counts for a great deal. Some people go to great lengths to have their résumés set in type, making the end result look like an attractive and professional offering. Such an effort, however, is not necessary—in fact, it is not even appropriate except for some extremely experienced and high-priced managers. For all other résumés, a perfectly typed and intelligently arranged listing of qualifications is sufficient. Note that the typing should be perfect—no handwritten corrections or insertions of any kind. Once you have achieved a perfect master copy, however, the tedious work is done: You will simply make photocopies, and these are what you mail out. You keep the master (do not fold it or let it get soiled) in case more copies have to be made. Should you apply for another position a year or two later, this master can easily be updated and retyped.

Depending on whether the résumé is being prepared for an entry-level or a more advanced position, the weight given to the separate elements will vary. All résumés, however, will include the following.

1. Applicant's name, mailing address, and phone number where the applicant can be reached during working hours.
2. Applicant's work experience. This category will, of course, list any jobs in the same field in which the applicant is now seeking employment. But any related work experience should also be cited.
3. Applicant's educational background, including any college and advanced degrees and fields of specialization.
4. Any volunteer experience, hobbies, or special skills that are pertinent to the job being applied for.
5. References.
6. In addition, some résumés carry a line indicating the type of job being sought.

In the past many people included personal statistics on their résumés—age, height and weight, marital status, and physical condition. This information is no longer considered relevant; in fact, legislation forbidding discrimination against women, against the handicapped, and so forth makes it inadvisable to include such data.

The two principal ways of setting up the information in the résumé are *chronological* (samples 1 and 2) and *functional* (sample 3). (See pages 250–255.) In the chronological résumé the separate categories of education and work experience are listed *backward* in the order of occurrence—most recent job first, then the one preceding it, and so forth; latest degree earned or latest school attended first, and so on. In the functional résumé, work experience is divided not by time but by the kind of work performed—administrative, for example, or work requiring the operation of particular machinery, and the like. The other categories (such as hobbies) follow the same pattern for each type of résumé.

The résumé will also vary somewhat depending on whether the applicant is seeking work for the first time or has a background of related work experience to offer. In the first case, the educational background will be listed first and in the greatest detail. In the latter instance, the list of previous work experience should come first and be most specific. The educational background then may be summarized in a few lines.

Name and Address

It is important that anyone who receives your résumé be able to get in touch with you easily. You will, of course, give your permanent address, but you may also need to include a temporary address (such as a school dormitory). You may also wish to include your home telephone number and your number at work. Make certain that each is clearly labeled. This information generally appears at the top of the résumé, either centered or to one side. When there are two addresses and phone numbers, it works well to center the name, then place the addresses below it, one on each side.

Work Experience

In the chronological résumé, begin the listing of each previous job with the dates of employment, followed by the job title and then the name and address (city only) of the firm. In the functional résumé, the job title will come first, and the dates will be the final item in the entry, following the name and address of the firm. The listing may also include a brief description of the work performed, skills involved, and responsibilities assigned. Part-time and summer jobs also have their place in this section. The salary you received has no place in a résumé.

Education

If you attended more than one college and university, or any trade school, there should be a separate listing for each. Besides mentioning the degree or certificate obtained and the major field, minor fields and related course work may usefully be listed. If you have just been graduated and have little or no work experience, you may wish to include your grade-point average.

Include high-school attendance only if it is relevant or if it calls attention to outstanding achievement. Any potential employer can assume that someone who has been accepted by a college has successfully completed earlier educational requirements.

Special Abilities

This category will include all knowledge of languages—foreign languages as well as computer languages (current practice treats them equally). Skill on any machinery also belongs here; this includes office machines (such as computers) and heavy machinery if any of these are within your experience and are applicable to the kind of work you are now looking for.

Volunteer work, club associations, and participation in charity drives should be listed if they relate to the kind of work you are seeking. Ringing doorbells to collect contributions to the March of Dimes, for example, gives some preliminary training for all kinds of sales work. Experience as president of a glee club or Campus Young Republicans or Democrats means that you have already demonstrated ability in organizing and motivating others for a common purpose—a requirement for any job in which you will be supervising a work force of any size.

Hobbies should be chosen with equal care. The fact that you love to bake, for instance, and have won your local 4-H Bake-Off cannot impress an employer who is looking for someone to coordinate a large payroll, but it may give you the edge you need if you are applying for a restaurant-management position.

References

Before you begin to compile your résumé, you would do well to let a few people know that you are looking for a new position and ask them if they would be willing to give you a good reference, should any prospective employer get in touch with them. If they are willing to write letters of recommendation for you, you are free to make copies for further use.

On the résumé itself, however, it is current practice not to list the names and addresses of people willing to supply references for you. On the résumé there is a line reading *"References supplied on request," "References available upon request,"* or similar wording.

To illustrate all these points, some sample résumés follow. The first is for a young woman trying to improve her present situation; the second represents a recent college graduate; and the third is the résumé of an older woman returning to the work force after some years of inactivity.

Joan Murphy
783 Elm Street
Treebrook, New Jersey 07771
(201) 555-1234

Previous Work Experience

July 1982 to present: Animal Health Technician, Treebrook Veterinary Group. Assisting in three-person mixed practice. Duties include laboratory work, surgical assistance, emergency treatment, and medical records. Practice limited to small animals.

Summer 1981: Animal Health Technician, Downe County Animal Hospital, Downe, Pennsylvania. Full range of duties, especially client contact and inventory control. Large animal practice, specializing in brood mares.

September 1981 to May 1982 (part time): Animal Health Technician, County Emergency Clinic for Animals, Downe, Pennsylvania. All emergency services, including client contact and telephone advice.

Education

M.A., 1985, Erie University, Microbiology.
B.S., 1982, Pennsylvania State University. Biology major, anthropology minor. Graduated with honors.

Professional Qualifications

Member, American Academy of Veterinary Technicians

Licensed, Pennsylvania

Certified, New Jersey

Additional Skills

Speaking and writing knowledge of Spanish

Basic accounting (payroll, inventory)

References

Available on request

James Murphy

Current Address

1607 Harris Hall
Community University
Seaside, NJ 07070
(201) 497-8749

Permanent Address

783 Elm Street
Treebrook, NJ 07771
(201) 555-1234

Position Desired

An entry-level position in the field of business
administration.

Education

Seaside Community College, Seaside, NJ, B.A.,
1985
Major: accounting; minor: retailing.
Grade point average: 3.5 in major; 3.0 overall.

Central High School, Treebrook, NJ, 1981.
Scholastic Honor Society. National Merit
Scholar.

Other Skills

Languages: Spanish; Polish; Fortran.
Pilot, licensed for small aircraft.

Extracurricular Activities

Campus Correspondent, Newark Star-Ledger,
1982–1985.
Regularly reported on sports events, other
newsworthy events as they occurred.

President, Student Political Union, 1984–1985. Organized monthly lecture series open to all students; ran Board of Directors' meetings; instituted faculty-student debates in conjunction with 1984 elections.

Work Experience

Summer 1984—Office floater, Worldwide Electronics Conglomerate, Inc., Trenton, NJ. Handled various bookkeeping and accounting duties in payroll department for 27 branch offices.

Sept. 1983–June 1984—Bookkeeper, Garden State Realty, Trenton, NJ. (part time). Responsible for all books of two-person real-estate firm.

Summer 1983—Sales clerk, Gentlemen's Emporium, Treebrook, NJ. Retail sales in men's clothing store.

References—Furnished on request.

Willing to relocate.

Mary Joan Murphy

783 Elm Street
Treebrook, NJ 07771
(201) 555-1234

OBJECTIVE   Administrative/supervisory position, preferably in art-related field

SKILLS   Administrative
                 Managed art gallery, supervised staff of seven, installed exhibitions.

                 Organized yearly arts fairs for community.

<u>Personal and Written
Communication</u>
Fund raising by mail and telephone.

Interviewed applicants for arts grants.

Worked with teenagers on specific projects.

<u>Other</u>
Fluent in French and Italian, both spoken and written.

Word processing, stenography, dictaphone.

EDUCATION   Wellesley College, Wellesley, MA,
                   B.A. Art-history major; mathematics minor.
                   June 1957

                   Trenton Community College,
                   Trenton, NJ,
                   M.A. Business administration.
                   December 1985

EXPERIENCE
                   City Art Gallery, New York, NY,
                   1957–1959. Manager. Arranged
                   for exhibitions, supervised
                   opening parties, dealt with staff
                   and clients.

                   Art Department, Wellesley College, 1955–1957. Research assistant. Worked with professor on
                   funded monograph, checking references, organizing footnotes
                   and bibliography, arranging for
                   permissions (elaborate correspondence).

Treebrook Arts Fair, Treebrook, NJ, 1965–1984. Originated, established, and ran a yearly fair to raise funds for Treebrook Library. Artists included painters, musicians, craftspeople.

Mary Joan Murphy   page 2

New Jersey Arts Council, 1978–1980. Interviewed applicants for arts grants in the Trenton area. Wrote detailed opinions and reviews for state agency.

Northern New Jersey Women's Clubs, 1980–1983. Local representative for yearly fund drive. Raised money through letter campaign and follow-up phone calls and personal appeals.

Treebrook Public School System, Volunteer Arts Program, 1980–1982. Worked with seventh-graders to paint murals on walls of new school building; with high-school sophomores on originating and carrying through a poster contest to celebrate Treebrook Centennial.

HONORS AND AFFILIATIONS

Graduated from college summa cum laude.

Corresponding secretary, Treebrook Women's Club.

Member, New Jersey Art Association.

Member, Alpha Rho Tau (professional fraternity in art field).

CREDENTIALS AND REFERENCES UPON REQUEST

Letters of Application

With your résumé you will send a covering letter, introducing yourself as a person. Such a letter usually begins by explaining why you are getting in touch with the particular company—whether you have heard of a specific job opening (through a newspaper advertisement, for example) or whether you are initiating a contact in the hope that a position will become available soon.

Your second paragraph might be used to say something specific about the particular company and indicate the contribution you feel you could make to its operation. If you are answering an advertisement, for example, you might point out that in a previous position you gained experience in the skills being sought.

Finally, indicate that you hope for a personal interview. If you are applying for a position that will require you to travel to the interview, you might suggest a time when it will be convenient for you to be there and volunteer to telephone for an appointment.

Like the résumé, the letter of application should reflect your seriousness and your ability to do a good job. Such a letter, however, can be more personal, and it can show some confidence and warmth. There are many ways of wording and organizing a letter of application. The following sample is only one of them.

1105 Plane Avenue
Chicago, Illinois 60614
May 7, 1985

Ms. Barbara Dutton, Employment Supervisor
Baker, McCormick, and Drake
Certified Public Accountants
409 Third Avenue
New York, New York 10017

Dear Ms. Dutton:

I would like to apply for the position of junior accountant specializing in retail practice you advertised in today's <u>New York Times</u>. The enclosed résumé gives details of my background and experience, showing my qualifications for the position you describe. I can think of nothing better than launching my career with a firm as fine as Baker, McCormick, and Drake.

My two years in the accounting department of a large retail chain have given me complete familiarity with accounting requirements of retail businesses, and I have written many letters and reports of the types you mention in your advertisement. I also played an active role in assisting our auditors in performing two annual audits, so I am familiar with audit procedure.

I have enjoyed my work during the past two years and intend to make my career in accounting. I am leaving my present position because opportunities are limited in so small an office. In addition I wish to broaden my knowledge of accounting practice and qualify as a CPA, so I can move ahead in the field as far as my talents permit.

If you wish, I shall ask Prairie State to forward my undergraduate transcript as soon as I

complete my final semester's work ten days
from now. I believe it will show that I have taken
all the accounting courses offered at Prairie
State and have never received any grade but "A"
in all 32 credits. If you wish to write to any
of my employers or teachers for personal evalu-
ations, please do so.

Sincerely yours,

Janet Marquith

BUSINESS LETTERS

People who work in offices find that letters
occupy much of their work time, both writing and
reading them. As a reader, you will appreciate letters that get directly to the point. As a writer,
therefore, you must learn to please your own readers, who want you to come to the point.

There are many types of business letters: in-
quiries, orders, responses, remittances, acknowledg-
ments; personal letters to employees, personal letters
to clients; form letters for personnel matters and
public relations; customer service letters, sales promotion letters, sales letters; letters asking for credit,
letters extending credit, letters refusing credit; letters offering payment, letters asking for payment,
letters explaining why payments are late. All these
share certain characteristics: They are polite, direct, clear, correct, and as brief as possible.

Since many chapters of this book deal with good
writing, the remainder of this chapter will not repeat any of the suggestions presented elsewhere.
Instead, some examples of good business letters are
provided. Each example presents only the salutation, body, and complimentary close. The correct

spacing and punctuation of the inside addresses, date, and name of the writer are shown in the sample letter of application provided above.

Letter of Inquiry

Dear Mr. Cauthen:

I am conducting a study for the National Insurance Association of current underwriting practices of its members. This study will be reported in a volume scheduled for publication early next year. Because your company for many years has led the New England area in underwriting volume, I would not consider my study complete without consulting one or more members of your Underwriting Department.

I plan to be in Hartford during the first two weeks of October and would appreciate the opportunity to spend two days with anyone you designate from Providence Mutual to talk with me on underwriting practices. I anticipate that I will need at least that amount of time to cover all the items I am planning to include in my study.

For the convenience of your staff, I am enclosing a list of the topics I plan to cover during my stay with you.

I know I am asking for a great deal of time with your staff, but I hope the information developed in this industry-wide study will compensate you for the expenditure of time.

The report will be distributed to you, of course, as a member of the NIA, and your cooperation will be recognized in the foreword.

I look for an affirmative reply at your convenience.

Sincerely yours,

Response to an Inquiry

Dear Mr. Caldwell:

We at Providence Mutual are always eager to do our share in any program sponsored by your organization. We recognize the benefit we all receive from active cooperation in studies such as the one you describe in your recent letter.

We will, therefore, make available to you during the first two weeks in October several senior underwriters on our staff, who will be requested to supply you with any information you require. The information you sent with your letter has been distributed for study by our underwriting staff.

To help us in scheduling, I would appreciate a telephone call as soon as you have selected the days you will actually spend with us. My secretary knows of your request, of course, and will be ready to set firm dates with you if you call while I am away from my office.

I hope you will find time to lunch with me and members of my staff on the days you spend with us.

Please let me know if I can be of further assistance.

Cordially,

Complaint

Gentlemen:

I am not writing this letter to complain about the promptness or efficiency of your customer service. In the past two months we have

had to make nine emergency requests for repair of your 6620 photocopying machine. In each
case your staff responded promptly and accomplished the needed repair within a few hours.

What I am complaining about is that we had
to call on you so many times within so short
a period for assistance with a machine only
three months old. You know as well as I that
a machine we depend on for reliable service
should not require such frequent repair.

You also know as well as I that we do not
own the machine but are merely leasing it. The
terms of the lease call for automatic renewal
of the lease unless we notify you of our intention to terminate our agreement at least one
month before the end of the lease.

Since the current lease period ends six weeks
from today, I hereby notify you that we will
not renew unless your machine suddenly shows
signs of giving better service than it has so far.

Sincerely yours,

Reply to Complaint

Dear Mrs. Pastor:

Your letter arrived at my desk half an hour
ago and left me red-faced with embarrassment
but eager to help with the service problem you
describe. You are entirely justified in feeling
the way you do, and I am eager to do everything I can to see that the problem is resolved
as promptly as possible. Eagle Industries does
not want to lose your valuable business.

I have initiated the following actions in hope
of returning you to our list of satisfied customers.

1. By now you have had a telephone call from me, asking permission to inspect and overhaul your present 6620 photocopier on your premises. This work will be performed at no cost to your company, and our service personnel will be directed to accomplish all necessary work over the weekend or after the close of your business day, so there will be no interruption of your work.

2. I have instructed the head of our service department to conduct a component-by-component study of the machine you are leasing to determine whether we have delivered to you a machine that fails to meet our quality requirements. This is especially important to us, since we have experienced great customer satisfaction with the 6620 line. Of more than 2000 machines now in use, yours is the only one that has required anything but routine maintenance.

3. If we discover any fundamental flaws in the machine you now are using, we will replace it with a new machine from our assembly line and credit you in full for the time you have had the present machine.

I hope this reply is satisfactory. I will be calling you on the telephone as soon as our actions are complete to determine whether everything we have done meets with your approval.

Please accept my apology for any inconvenience we have caused and my assurance that we will remedy the situation quickly and completely.

                                    Sincerely,

Sales Letter

Dear Dr. Sammis:

You are one of many physicians in the Dallas–Fort Worth area who were interested enough in new developments in automated diagnosis to stop at our booth during the recent Texas Medical Society Convention. At that time you indicated you might profit from subscription to our computerized diagnostic laboratory service, now used by more than 34,000 California physicians.

We are preparing to offer our service to physicians in your area within the next 60 days and would appreciate the opportunity to call on you and explain the low cost and high reliability of our automatic diagnosis.

Our presentation will take only 15 minutes of your time, and we would be glad to schedule the presentation to meet your convenience.

I shall be telephoning your office on Wednesday, October 14, to set up an appointment. On conclusion of the meeting, I shall leave with you the necessary agreements to be completed if you wish to subscribe to our service. Be assured there will be no obligation on your part to make any commitment at the time of the presentation.

Sincerely yours,

Collection

Dear Mr. Townes:

I am writing to remind you that your account with us shows an unpaid balance of $204 for merchandise shipped to you on January 5, almost three months ago.

The summer buying season is about to begin and, before going on to Chicago to show our new designs, we are eager to clear up outstanding accounts. If there is some reason why you cannot make the payment, please don't hesitate to call me. If your payment is late because of some oversight, please oblige by putting the payment in the mail.

I look forward to receiving your check and to doing business with you, as we have done over the years.

Sincerely,

Recommendation

Dear Mrs. Duffy:

Nothing can give me more pleasure than having the opportunity to reply to your letter requesting information about James Lockner, an applicant for employment with your firm.

James worked for us for five years while he was a student, and in all that time he was punctual, reliable, courteous, and efficient. No part-time employee we have had in all my years with our company has been quicker to learn or more willing to work.

I hope you will see fit to offer James employment. All of us at Acme are rooting for him.

Sincerely yours,

Employment Offer

Dear Mr. Lockner:

We have completed our evaluation of your interviews and our study of your excellent qualifications and outstanding references. It is my pleasure to offer you a position as sales representative in our heavy equipment division at an annual salary of $17,500, as explained in our discussion on June 28.

If your interest in the position is firm, we would like to have you report here at the Personnel Office by 8:30 a.m. on the first of August. You will be assigned to headquarters for three months of training. On satisfactory conclusion of training, you will work out of our Minneapolis office, as you requested.

Please complete the enclosed Acceptance of Employment form and return it to us as soon as possible. In addition I would appreciate your taking the time to telephone me collect today to say whether you are going to join us.

The sales manager, Mr. R. J. Holness, joins me in extending congratulations to you at the start of what we hope will be a highly successful career with Farm Equipment, Inc.

Cordially,

As all these examples show, good business letters are polite, direct, clear, correct, and as brief as possible. Since careers in business usually include the writing of many letters, it is never a waste of time to practice the skill. Letters are written by people and read by people. The good letters you write will help you make good impressions on others. Any poor letters you write may have the opposite effect.

BUSINESS REPORTS

Business reports may be brief replies—less than a page long—to questions that can be answered easily. What are the company's sales in the Northeast in the current quarter, broken down by states, and how do they compare with the previous year's results in the corresponding period? How does the company's wage scale for secretaries compare with wages paid by other firms in the area?

Business reports may also be elaborate—covering many pages and supplying answers to questions that require a great deal of research. Why are the company's sales dropping in the Northeast? What are the company's principal product deficiencies, as reported by customers and sales staff? Can you recommend a program to improve the company's product line and recapture market leadership? What internal changes will be necessary to upgrade the company's sales effort? What changes in promotion and marketing do you recommend to support the sales campaign?

Each of these questions may be the subject of a brief, individual report. Together they become the subject of a long report.

No matter how simple or complex, a business report is intended to answer a specific question or set of questions. The company sales manager or president needs information for long-range planning. The marketing or accounting department needs information before establishing new procedures. The company must supply information to stockholders in an annual report. Whatever the need, a report will be written and submitted.

Business reports resemble college research papers except that the subject of the report is usually spelled out clearly and assigned to the writer. An exception to this is a report you may wish to write on your own initiative, recommending changes of some kind or pointing out the need for action in a certain area of the company's operations. Based on observations made during your day-to-day work, you decide to write a special report: *Our department can improve efficiency by computerizing our billing procedures . . .* or *Incoming orders can be processed within 24 hours if we . . .* Most companies encourage this kind of initiative by employees but before you begin to write, you would do well to find out whether your manager looks with favor on such writing.

Acquiring Information

When a report is assigned to you, your first decision will concern the best way to collect the necessary information. The principal sources of business information are

- observation
- interviews
- questionnaires
- library research

All these sources can yield the data that form the basis of a report.

Observation. If your report deals with a subject you have been considering for some time, you have probably observed enough so that you need only organize your thoughts, outline a report, and begin to write. Most often, however, you will have to make firsthand observations to find the information you need. For example, you may initiate a time-motion study of office procedures, shipping procedures, or production methods in order to gather data for a report on company operations. You may accompany sales representatives or customer-service personnel on their field trips if you are studying sales or service problems. Whatever the subject, whatever the type of observation you intend to make, you will need to keep careful records of what you learn.

If you know in advance what you are looking for, you will find it helpful to establish a format for your observations, so that the process of note-taking will be as easy as possible. If you have prepared a checklist of items to be observed, your notes will consist of check marks or number ratings corresponding to the qualities of the activities under observation; this method is less time-consuming than narrative writing. To avoid disturbing the people you are observing, you may decide to write your notes after each observation is complete; if you do, be sure to make your notes promptly after each observation so as not to overlook important information.

Interviews. Interviews are an excellent method of collecting information. Your company employs many people who, together, know a great deal about the company's business. Such people are usually pleased to help you collect the information you need. All that is necessary to get their cooperation is a polite request along with an explanation of what you are seeking and why. If you give people ample notice before approaching them for the information, and if your attitude makes it clear that you are seeking help from a knowledgeable source, you will have no trouble getting the facts you need. If you interrupt people while they are doing their own work, or if your attitude is less than open and respectful, you may get little from them.

Just as you will find it useful to develop a format for observations, you should have a list of specific items to cover in interviews. Make the final item in your checklist an invitation to the persons interviewed to speak on any topic related to your subject. You may find that a person you are interviewing on ways to improve office procedures, for example, has given much thought to the subject and has ideas you would never hear anything about if you relied only on a fixed series of questions you design yourself. By offering people the chance to speak freely, and by being a good listener, you may gain much more than you ever thought possible. You may also make friends with people who can assist you further in other work assignments.

Questionnaires. Questionnaires are most useful when you cannot speak directly with people who have information you need for a report. There are a few requirements to keep in mind when preparing a questionnaire.

- Make your inquiry personal and warm, so that the people you write to will be inclined to answer willingly.
- Limit the number of questions you ask, and make the questions brief and clear. People have work to do and will show no sympathy for a researcher who makes excessive or vague demands.
- Explain exactly why you are asking for information and how the people you are polling will benefit from answering your request.
- Supply a self-addressed, stamped envelope, so as to make replies easier for your respondents.
- Just as in planning an interview, make the last item in the questionnaire an invitation to respond freely on topics you may have overlooked.
- Express your thanks in advance.

Library Research. Library research on business topics often begins with a request to a company librarian to perform a search for printed sources of information. If your company does not have its own library, you will have to conduct your own search. Follow the procedures described in Chapter 11, using such helpful reference works as *Business Periodicals Index* and *Encyclopedia of Business Information Sources*. The *Index* guides the reader to approximately 165 periodicals in all fields of business. The *Encyclopedia* covers books and reports as well as periodicals.

Compiling the Report

Once you have collected all the information you need—whether through observation, interviews, questionnaires, library research, or a combination of several methods—you are ready to plan and write your report. The form of a technical report given in Chapter 13 is often applicable to business reports. You may also find it useful to follow the outlining procedures described in Chapter 11.

As you begin writing, keep in mind the assigned question that is the focus of the report. Remember that you are writing for a busy reader, and while that reader may want to know every important bit of information you have found, no reader has unlimited reading time. You must write your report in such fashion that if the reader stops at any point, the most important information up to that point has been covered. In this sense, a good business report is much like a well-written newspaper article, putting the most important information first. If possible—and good business writers always find it possible—abstract the entire report in the opening sentences of the report. Here are three examples of such openers.

Our sales in every state of the Northeast declined in the current quarter, the largest decline being 38% in New York, the smallest 2% in Vermont.

The company's median secretarial pay falls 3% above the median wage reported by ten compa-

nies of our size in our geographic labor market; only among clerk-typists, for whom our scale is 10% below the median, are we experiencing abnormally high personnel turnover.

Interviews conducted with all six members of our economic analysis section and responses to questionnaires distributed among our principal customers in the Southwest region indicate that our sales decline during the past six months resulted from our decision to defer redesign of our product line despite increased competition from McAndrew, Inc. and from D'Arcy Bros.

Such opening comments tell the reader exactly what a report will document, and the reader can expect the report to back up the opening statement completely.

Following the opening sentence, which you may think of as an *abstract*, you may want to write an *introduction*, citing the reasons for conducting the study and supplying other information that prepares the reader to understand the report fully. You may then write various sections with such titles as *Data Sources*, *Study Procedures*, *Findings*, *Analysis*, and *Conclusions and Recommendations*. You will usually reserve charts, tables, and other detailed information for an *appendix*, knowing that only the most careful reader will want to read such information. When a graph or other form of easily interpreted visual display can be used to summarize the central findings of your report, you may wish to make it part of your abstract. Business readers are accustomed to interpreting visuals.

A brief report need not include actual titles for the various sections, but the arrangement of material would remain the same. Whether you write a long report or a short one, however, your objective is to present your thinking directly, clearly, compactly, and completely.

CHAPTER 13

Technical Writing

Scientists and engineers do not spend all their time bent over laboratory equipment or sitting comfortably before computer consoles, conducting exciting experiments and tests, designing complex equipment, and developing grand new ideas. Before any technical or scientific project can get under way, an explanation of why and how the work should be done must be written. As a project is carried out, progress reports must be compiled. When a project comes to an end, the results must be reported. Someone has to do all this writing. That someone is usually a scientist or engineer. In some cases, one member of a working team reports on a team project. Large companies may also employ writers to prepare the proposals and reports on projects undertaken by the technical and scientific staff.

PRINCIPAL TYPES OF TECHNICAL WRITING

A *technical report* is the final task in a research, development, or test program. The writer has information the reader needs: what was found, how it was found, what the findings mean. If the reader grasps that information quickly and easily, the writer has done a good job. If the reader must struggle through trivial information in order to locate important ideas and facts, or if the desired information is presented in unclear language, the writer has done a poor job.

A *technical proposal* is submitted before a project can be authorized. It explains why and how the project should be carried out. The reader—either the head of the writer's own organization or a client of that organization—must be persuaded that the project is a good one. The reader wants to know the expected outcome of the project and the resulting benefits. If the proposal convinces the reader that the project is worthwhile, funds will be provided. If the writer fails to supply all needed information in a convincing manner, the work will not be authorized. Skilled proposal writers are highly valued in a technical organization.

A *technical manual* gives readers a clear understanding of a procedure, equipment, or system. It presents information logically, completely, and accurately. If the writer has collected all needed information and written clearly, the manual will ensure proper understanding and use of the procedure, equipment, or system. If the writer fails in any detail—no matter how small—the manual will not do its intended job.

Technical letters, *memorandums*, and *articles* keep scientists and engineers up to date on what is going on in their professions. These documents may be informal or formal, depending on whether they are distributed within an organization or published in a journal. They may be a few sentences long or cover many pages. Without injecting personal bias (as is true for all good technical writing) the writer tells what there is to tell, and tells only that. Of these various types of documents, scientists and engineers take greatest pride in writing articles for publication in journals.

The rest of this chapter presents general requirements for all technical writing before discussing specific requirements for reports and proposals, the most demanding form of technical writing.

GENERAL REQUIREMENTS

Your training in technical writing began when you wrote your first laboratory report for a course in science. Your training will end when you retire from technical work. From the moment you get your first job in a technical organization, you will find that everything you write is given close attention. Good scientists and engineers are as interested in the quality of their writing—and the writing of those who work for them—as they are in other aspects of their work. They know that technical effort counts for little if the written reports of that work do not convey information adequately.

Readers' Needs

When writing for members of your own organization, you know who your readers are, and you write to meet their needs. The head of your organization, for example, wants to know about the progress you have made toward the goals of the organization or the goals set for a particular project. Executives will usually read only enough of what you write to know the highlights of your work. Your co-workers are much more interested in the specific project and want to know everything you have found and exactly how you found it. They are more likely to read the entire report closely.

When you write for publication in a journal, you are addressing members of your profession and allied fields. Such readers may not know as much as your co-workers about the background of your work, but they will be able to understand everything you report, as long as your writing is complete and clear. Such readers can also be counted on to notice errors of fact or interpretation.

Aware of who your readers are, and what they want to know, you write to answer the specific questions they ask of anything they read: What work was done? What were the findings? What conclusions can be drawn? What recommendations are being made? What evidence exists for every claim? If you think of your readers as people of a particular background, asking particular questions, you can plan and write to meet their needs.

For the executive, you provide a tightly written abstract that hits the highlights of your work. For readers who want to know the background of your study, you write an introduction. For the close reader, you supply all the detailed information that makes your story complete. For someone who wants to go on to additional reading in your field, you compile a bibliography that leads readers to principal sources of information.

Objectivity

Technical writing must present facts exactly as the writer sees them, not as one might wish them to be. Your readers want to know

- what earlier studies have found
- what you have found
- what you logically conclude
- what you recommend

When information you uncover does not agree fully with your central findings, you present that information. By doing so, you give readers the opportunity to consider the disagreement and resolve it through further research. If you omit such information, you do a disservice to your profession.

A report of failure to solve a problem, for example, can be as valuable as a report of success, since it prevents other workers from repeating your errors. Technical writing has a responsibility to be objective, to report all findings fully.

Clarity and Conciseness

The elements of good writing are discussed in other parts of this book. If you are to do your job well, you must learn all the conventions of good style, so that you can write clearly and concisely. But technical reports offer two advantages not generally found in other writing. First, readers of technical material are accustomed to well-constructed charts, tables, and graphs. By presenting information in these forms, you cut down on the number of words to be written and improve clarity. Secondly, moving detailed information from the body of a report to an appendix enables readers to follow the flow of thoughts without getting bogged down, for example, in mathematical proofs or fine details of experimental procedure. A ten-page text may be followed by many times that number of pages of appendices. As long as your report refers readers to the information found in each appendix, all readers are satisfied.

Completeness

Any technical document must be complete. Readers will not go to the library to look up references needed to make sense of the text before them. Some reports, for example, cannot be read intelligently without a good deal of background information. If the writer is to satisfy the readers' needs, that information must be included in the report. While your readers will want to have bibliographic references for their own future study, you must give them the gist of what those references discuss. A brief summary will usually be enough, but sometimes you may want to include a reprint of an important article in an appendix. (This method is used for company reports, but it is not possible in journal articles.)

Tone

Technical writers try for a factual, objective, restrained tone: no hysterical enthusiasm, no self-congratulation, no certainty that what is being presented is the greatest news since the invention of the wheel. Technical writers do not advertise, they inform. Technical writers are respectful of their readers' intelligence, training, and education. They do not talk down to their readers. They do not preach to their readers. Your readers will expect you to make all your points clear, but they will resent being spoon-fed.

REPORTS

Readers of technical reports expect to find them arranged in logical order. Most organizations that employ scientists or engineers have standard formats and editorial practices. So do most technical and scientific journals. The following format is followed by most organizations and journals.

Title

A good title suggests to the reader no more and no less than the report actually delivers. This requirement is the only one you must consider when you are writing a title. Some writers prefer short titles to long ones, and some believe that titles should be catchy. While it is true that short titles are better than long titles, it is even more important for titles to be informative, rather than clever. If after noting the title a reader decides against reading your report because the subject is not of interest to that reader, you have written a good title. If a reader gets from your report exactly what the title promises, you have written a good title. If a reader is tricked by your title into reading a report that is not of interest to that reader, you have written a poor title.

A good title tells readers exactly what the report covers.

- Have you designed something? Your title may be "Design of . . ."
- Have you developed an automated procedure for doing something? Your title may be "Automated Procedure for . . ."
- Have you field-tested something? Your title may be "Field Tests of . . ."
- Have you devised a computer program for processing information? Your title may be "Computer Program for . . ."

Abstract

An abstract is a miniature report that condenses the most important information included in the rest of the report. An abstract usually runs no more than a page. Though part of a longer report, an abstract is sometimes distributed separately to inform an audience that will not normally read complete reports or to alert potential readers to the existence and contents of a report. To accomplish its purpose, an abstract quickly tells the reader

- *what* has been accomplished and *why*
- *how* the work was done (in general terms)
- *conclusions* and *recommendations* (in general terms)

The abstract can help a reader decide whether to read the full report. Yet even if readers go no further than the abstract, they learn a good deal about what has been accomplished. If they do go on, they can read with fuller understanding. Even a one-paragraph abstract can be highly informative.

> *Several minor changes in the layout of the 6230 circuit have been found in laboratory and field tests to increase power output by 10%. Manufacturing procedures are recommended for incorporating these changes in future production, and new production kit drawings are provided. Cost of manufacture is not expected to change.*

The reader of the above paragraph knows *what* has been accomplished and *why*; what general procedures were followed to arrive at conclusions; and principal conclusions and recommendations.

Introduction

A good introduction presents all the background information needed to understand the body of the report. If readers already know a great deal, or if the subject needs no background explanation, the introduction may be eliminated or presented briefly. Complex reports may require introductions of several pages. When readers turn to an introduction, they want to know

- of earlier attempts to accomplish the aims of your work

- information developed by previous researchers studying the field
- the specific goals of your work
- the relationship between your work and other current work
- what is contained in the rest of the report

An introduction therefore helps readers prepare to continue with fuller understanding. It does not present findings, since the abstract has already given a foretaste of these.

Body

The body of a report consists of those sections that state—in logical order—exactly what has been done in the particular project. The body may consist of a single section or of many. *Materials, Procedures, Analysis,* and *Results* are typical subdivisions of the body. To choose the best order for the sections that make up the body of a report, ask yourself: What will readers want to know first? What will they want to know next? And so on.

Each section represents a unit that can stand on its own. As you edit for final typing, ask yourself whether you are supplying everything readers want to know about the details of the work.

- Are the sections arranged in logical order?
- Are all procedures described accurately and fully?
- Are all materials identified specifically and accurately?
- Is the mathematical and logical reasoning correct and complete?

Valid technical work is reproducible—every finding can be duplicated by any other qualified person who uses the same materials and procedures described in the report of that work. The body of any report you write, then, must give readers all the information they need to perform your study themselves and arrive at the same results. When you edit your writing, put yourself in the position of a reader: Will you be able to duplicate your findings if you are given only what your report states? If the answer is yes, the body of the report has done its job.

Summary

The summary section, which restates the main accomplishments described in a report, differs from an abstract in acknowledging readers' ability to understand in more detail the information they have read in the body of the report. What was stated generally and qualitatively in the abstract may now be made more specific and quantitative. The following summary belongs to the same report for which an abstract was given above. A comparison of the two will illustrate the different approach.

> *Power losses in the 6230 circuit have been reduced from 16 watts to 14.6 watts by replacing terminals 31, 44, and 72 in the input stage with a single multiplex connection, to be designated connection 60. Tests conducted at extremes of temperature under laboratory conditions as well as field tests in the actual operating environment have established that six prototype circuits meet all applicable OSHA requirements and all performance criteria.*

> *Production Kit 3212A, now being stockpiled in Crib C, will replace the present Kit 3212, beginning with the next full production run, February 14. No change in tooling is required, and production time and cost are not affected. All interested departments have been notified in Production Change Notice 36, dated January 10.*

This summary gives the reader a good review of the principal information covered in the report.

Conclusions and Recommendations

Some reports have only a *Conclusions* section or a *Recommendations* section. Many reports have neither, while others combine the two in one section. The writer decides whether a report justifies inclusion of such sections.

Conclusions and recommendations reflect the writer's best judgment. It is possible for two or more investigators to conduct the same study, arrive at the same findings, and yet draw different conclusions. Recommendations resulting from any study may also differ. When you write conclusions and recommendations for a report to be read only within your own organization, your readers will understand that you are reporting your own thinking. Conclusions and recommendations of a report that will be published in a journal, however, will be seen by readers as representing the thinking of your entire organization; it is necessary, therefore, to obtain the approval of your superiors before publication.

The reasons underlying any stated conclusions and recommendations appear earlier in your report. The following example of *Conclusions and Recommendations* is from a report on seal materials for autoclaves (pressurized vessels used in many laboratories and in industrial processing). The first paragraph presents conclusions, while the second presents recommendations.

Neoprene seals, as currently fabricated, have reached their ultimate strength in our autoclave applications. Current design of the 2300 series autoclaves cannot be improved further unless all neoprene seals are replaced with seals less susceptible to deformation under high pressure.

A materials investigation should be conducted to select replacements for the neoprene seals now used in the 2300 series. The literature is now reporting creep-resistant materials that appear

promising for our application. Study of the liter-
ature, procurement of test specimens, and com-
plete laboratory testing up to the desired pressure
levels can be accomplished within three months
by personnel of our Materials Laboratory. Rede-
sign of the 2300 series can then proceed as planned
earlier to achieve significant uprating of pres-
sures for these autoclaves.

The reader now knows what the writer believes as a result of the study. If the rest of the report supports this thinking, the conclusions and recommendations come as no surprise. From the abstract on, the entire report leads to these statements.

Bibliography

Some reports include a list of publications referred to in the various sections. Journals follow a variety of editorial practices. Recommended forms are also presented in Chapter 11, above. The organization for which you work may, of course, have its own preferred style.

Appendix

An appendix presents material too detailed to interest most readers or material somewhat removed from the logical flow of the report. Such subjects as mathematical proofs, details of experimental readings, and lists of parts of complex apparatus are often detailed in an appendix. Each subject is treated in a separate appendix, so that a report may conclude with *Appendix A*, *Appendix B*, and so forth. The writer must supply a title for each appendix in addition to its letter designation.

Appendix C. Temperature-Pressure Readings

Some organizations prefer that all charts, tables, photographs, and graphs pertaining to a report be presented in appendices rather than in the text at the point where they are discussed. Typists prefer the former arrangement, and most scientists and engineers are accustomed to it.

PROPOSALS

A technical proposal differs from a technical report in that it seeks to convince the reader to adopt a course of action recommended by the writer. While a technical report is intended to inform, a technical proposal is intended to persuade. It says to the reader: Authorize a study I want to perform. Authorize purchase of equipment. Authorize construction of a building, bridge, or other structure. Buy something my organization sells. Hire my organization to perform a study for you. Supply funding for the project here described.

The specific purpose of a proposal may be any of these requests—and more—but all proposals ask someone to authorize the writer to do something the writer wants done. The reasoning supporting a proposal must be just as sound as that of a report. The facts presented must be able to withstand the same close inspection. The information must be just as complete. The approach to the subject is what makes the difference: From beginning to end, a good technical proposal presents clear and compelling reasons for the person to whom it is addressed to take the action suggested by the writer.

Proposals are of two types. Internal proposals request action within the writer's own organization; proposals to other organizations request action by clients, customers, government agencies, or other technical organizations.

Internal Proposals

Most organizations will not authorize their own staff to undertake technical or scientific projects without a written proposal stating the goals of the project, reasons why the project will benefit the organization, the time it will consume, the number of employees and consultants it will require, and its probable costs. Any project uses time, space, equipment, and personnel. If the project has a reasonable chance of success, and if the goal of the project fits in with the larger plans of the organization, the project can be justified. If the project seems less attractive than other possible projects, it will not be authorized on the grounds that the resources of the organization can be used better in other work. Thus, without the information presented in a proposal, managers cannot make sound decisions on whether to go ahead.

In writing a proposal to your own managers, you are arguing for your share of your organization's resources. It is essential, therefore, that you present all information pertinent to a favorable decision. The most important point to remember while you are writing is that managers think in terms of benefits to the organization. What can you write to sway them? Remember that you must be factual; nothing is gained from exaggerating possible benefits. Be as straightforward as possible, but present all the persuasive reasons for funding the study you are recommending. The work may increase the technical capabilities of your organization, or the work may improve your organization's products, increase its profits, lead to expansion of its product line. Whatever is the truth—and whatever is recognized as important within your organization—must be brought out fully.

If there are drawbacks—the project cannot be completed quickly, for example; or another division is engaged on a similar study—be frank. Indicate your awareness of any problems, but explain persuasively why the project, in your opinion, is nevertheless worth doing. Do not exaggerate the eventual benefits, but convey your conviction.

Proposals to Other Organizations

Engineers and scientists in industry often turn out to be their companies' best sales force. This is particularly true in industries that emphasize advanced technology. Competition for funding of research projects and for sale of large and complex systems requires the attention of the best technical minds. Proposals written to attract outside funding or sales may involve projects costing huge sums, and it is not too much to say that the business health of an organization may depend on the quality of its technical proposals. It is for this reason that engineers and scientists skilled in writing proposals are in demand.

How does one convince someone to fund a project or buy a product that may cost millions, even billions of dollars? The most persuasive method is to demonstrate that the anticipated benefits are too great to pass up. A convincing technical proposal opens by explaining exactly what is being proposed and why the person or agency addressed will benefit from it. In the case of a proposal for a large system, for example, the system is described in a sentence or two, and the specific benefits are immediately highlighted. This information appears in the abstract, which generally is no longer than a single page. Once the reader has digested this brief presentation, the stage is set for proving every point made in the abstract.

The remainder of the proposal—introduction, body, summary, appendices—carefully explains how the system is put together, how the system operates, how it is maintained, and how it is repaired, as well as everything else that is pertinent concerning the system. If you present this information clearly, you gain the reader's confidence in the quality of your system and the quality of your organization. Throughout the proposal the reader is persuaded again and again that much is to be gained by buying the system.

A proposal requesting funding for research work follows much the same procedure. The abstract tells exactly what you are offering to do and why the project will benefit either the funding source or an aspect of life important to the funding source. The rest of the report spells out the steps to be taken, supplies the schedule, and details the qualifications of the engineers, scientists, and others who will perform the work. The reader gains confidence in your grasp of your subject, your attention to detail, your experience in similar work. Above all, the reader clearly sees the benefits resulting from the proposed activity.

Yet you must remain as objective in writing for outsiders as in addressing proposals to your own organization. Everything you promise in a proposal must eventually be delivered. In technical proposals, as in all technical writing, complete objectivity is essential.

PART IV

APPENDICES

Dictionary of Usage

Usage is defined as the manner in which a language is commonly written or spoken. The suggestions and preferences offered here deal with problems most often encountered in academic, business, and technical writing.

A

a, an.   The article *a* is used before words beginning with a consonant sound: *a part; a heart.* The article *an* is used before words beginning with a vowel sound: *an elephant; an hour.* The rule is based on sound. The word *hour* begins with a vowel sound, as though it were spelled *our.* The word *heart* begins with the consonant sound *h.* Write *a history*, not *an history. History* begins with a consonant sound. Write *an historical novel* and *an historic event* because the consonant sound *h* is almost completely lost in these phrases.

absolute, absolutely.   These words are often misused as strengtheners (intensifiers) of terms that need no strengthening. *She is absolutely the most beautiful woman I know* is no stronger than *She is the most beautiful woman I know. Absolute* means perfect, complete, pure, unconditional. Save *absolute* for such expressions as *absolute monarch* and *absolute zero*, which do not have the same meanings as *monarch* and *zero*. Use *absolutely* only when the word it modifies needs strengthening and there is no chance you are wrong: *"I will show that the accused absolutely was not in the room when the shot was fired,"* the defense attorney said. See also *definitely; very.*

accept, except. The verb *accept* means receive: *I will accept your resignation. Except* appears most often as a preposition meaning excluding: *Everyone will be welcome except John.* The verb *except*, used far less often, means exclude: *Late papers are excepted* (excluded) *from consideration.*

adapt, adopt. *Adapt* means become accustomed: *Amy quickly adapted to her new school. Adapt* also means make suitable to conditions or requirements: *After considerable effort the engineers were able to adapt the old engine to meet requirements for increased torque. Adopt* means take up or practice, choose to take: *The sisters adopted a style of dress that displeased their parents.*

adverse, averse. Unfavorable situations and conditions are adverse: *An adverse school environment may make learning difficult for all but the most gifted students.* People who are opposed to a course of action are averse to it: *I am not averse to your suggestion but I need more time to make up my mind.*

advice, advise. *Advice* is a noun: *I cannot act on your advice.* *Advise* is a verb: *The physician advised me to stop smoking.*

affect, effect. The verb *affect* means influence: *Your eloquent words affected me deeply.* The verb *effect* means cause: *The prison sentence effected a welcome change in his habits.* The noun *affect* is reserved for use by psychologists and students of psychology. It means feeling: *My client showed strong affect during her early months of therapy.* The noun *effect* means result: *Your loss had no effect on me.*

aggravate. The verb *aggravate* means worsen: *Rough play late in the season aggravated his old knee injury.* The meaning of annoy or exasperate—as in *You are aggravating me, Fred*—is considered colloquial by many teachers and editors.

agree to, agree with. One agrees to a proposal. One agrees with a person.

ain't is used only, if it is used at all, in highly informal speech. It is best to avoid it in all writing. See also *contractions*.

all, all of. *All* is all that is needed except when a pronoun is the object of the preposition *of*: *Les wasted all his energy. Judith knew all her clients by name. All of us agreed to join the club. Judith knew all of them by name.*

allusion, illusion, delusion. An allusion is an indirect reference, one in which the object referred to is not named: *His poem on the seasons makes many allusions to life and death that go unnoticed by careless readers. The chairman made an allusion to (or alluded to) your absence when he said, "Some of our most talkative members are not here today."* An illusion is a false impression created by wishful thinking or by faulty perception: *The love he saw in her eyes proved to be an illusion. The children were fascinated by the magician's optical illusions.* A delusion is a mistaken belief resulting from self-deception: *Psychopaths frequently exhibit delusions of persecution.*

already, all ready. *Already* means previously or before: *She was already showing signs of suffocation.* All ready means completely prepared: *Are you all ready to have dinner?*

alright is an incorrect spelling of *all right.*

also should not be used in place of the conjunction *and: John, Jane, and* (not *also*) *Dick attended the book fair.* Do use *also* as an adverb: *Milton wrote, "They also serve who only stand and wait."*

alternately, alternatively. *Alternately* means in turn: *The pianist and the violinist played alternately through the evening; while one rested, the other was on stage. Alternatively* means instead: *You may study physics now; alternatively, you may defer your science requirement until next semester.* The noun *alternative* means choice: *You have two alternatives: accept the transfer or resign from the company.*

altogether, all together.   *Altogether* means entirely: *We were altogether disgusted by her lack of team spirit. All together* means in a group: *When we are all together, we manage to have a good time.*

among, between.   *Among* is most often used for three or more, *between* for two: *among all the contenders for the nomination; between the two brothers. Between* is also used to indicate a relationship of any two members of a group of three or more: *Agreements began to arise between the nations of the Middle East.*

amount, number.   *Amount* refers to things that cannot be counted: *Even a small amount of debris is unacceptable. Number* refers to things and people that can be counted: *There are a number of errors in the report. We expected a large number of people to attend. Amount* is always singular. *Number* is singular when it refers to a particular quantity, plural when it means several or many: *That number is too great for most people to grasp. A large number of diners become ill every time I cook.*

A.M., P.M., a.m., p.m.   These abbreviations are never used as nouns. *See me at 6 p.m.* (not *6 in the p.m.*). *See me at six in the morning* (not *six in the a.m.*). Capitals and small letters are equally correct in typing these abbreviations, but be consistent within a paper, report, or other writing.

an, a.   See *a, an.*

and etc.   is an example of saying the same thing twice. The *et* in *etc.* means and. The entire Latin expression for which *etc.* is the abbreviation is *et cetera*, meaning and the rest. *Etc.* applies only to things, not people. Except where space is a limitation, *etc.* should not be used. Substitute such expressions as *and so forth*, *and the like*, and *and others*. See also *et al*.

and/or. In most instances, either *and* or *or* expresses the intended meaning. It is worth rephrasing a sentence to avoid the awkward *and / or*.

angry at, angry with. If you must be angry, be *angry with* people, *angry at* anything else: *I am angry with my sister. I am angry at the way you were treated.* See also *mad*, *angry*.

ante-, anti-. The prefix *ante-* means before and appears in such words as *antecedent* and *antebellum*. The prefix *anti-* means against and appears in such words as *antipathy* and *antihistamine*. Never say or write that you are *anti* anything; say you are opposed to it.

anxious, eager. *Anxious* means fearful, apprehensive, concerned: *I became increasingly anxious as the operation dragged on and the surgeons sent no reassuring word. Eager* is used when an anticipation is joyous: *I am eager to attend the concert with you.*

anybody, anyone, everybody, everyone, nobody, somebody, someone. As pronouns all these are single words: *Anyone can learn to spell correctly. Everyone is welcome.* All these pronouns are singular: *Somebody has stolen my driver's license. Someone has to pay for the tickets.* When written as two words, the resulting phrases have different meanings: *There is no body of knowledge I like more. Every body in the temporary morgue has now been identified.*

anyways   is incorrect. Use *anyway: I am not being paid, but I will do the work anyway. Anyway* and *any way* have different meanings: *I will do the work any way you want me to.*

appraise, apprise.   *Appraise* means estimate the value of: *I am certain the jeweler will appraise your ring without charge. Apprise* means inform: *Have you apprised your parents of our plans?*

around   is an inadequate substitute for *about* or *near: I will see you about* (not *around*) *nine o'clock. Play near* (not *around*) *the school until I get home from work.* Use *around* to mean on all sides: *He walked around the block twice to cool off.*

as   is an awkward substitute for *because, since, for: They asked not to be disturbed because* (not *as*) *they were studying for their examinations. As* can be understood to relate to time; in the example, *as* can be misread to mean *while.*

as best, as best as   are incorrect replacements for *as well as: I am doing as well as* (not *as best as*) *I can. I am doing my best* (not *as best I can*).

as good or better than.   Insert *as* after *good: I want one as good as or better than hers.* The second *as* is needed in any comparative expression of this type: *She had done as well as or better than any man in the class.*

as regards   is a bad substitute for *about* or *concerning: I am writing about* (not *as regards*) *the radio I ordered.* See also *regarding.*

as well as   does not have the same meaning as *and*; it does not make a singular subject plural: *The bicycle, as well as the other toys you ordered, is not appropriate for Sonja. The bicycle and the other toys you ordered are not appropriate for Sonja.*

at about   is one word too many: *about* or *at* is enough: *They will be here about noon. They will be here at noon.*

at the same time that   means no more than *while: I entered while* (not *at the same time that*) *he was speaking.* Though we expect speech to have a certain amount of extra verbiage, writing should be as tight as possible.

at this point in time   means no more than *now. At that point in time* means no more than *then.* One meaning of *point* is a particular time. As an alternative to *then*, you may write *at that point: I decided at that point to leave the company. By then* (not *At that point in time*) *we knew the Senate would not be willing to take part in a whitewash.* See also *point in time.*

awful   is a weak substitute for *bad* or more descriptive terms: *How disappointed* (not *awful*) *I felt! It was a disappointment* (not *an awful disappointment*). Do not use *awful* as a vague intensifier (strengthener): *I felt cheated* is better than *It was an awful shame.* Use *awful* when you want to describe something that is extremely disagreeable. *The execution was awful. The smell of death after the earthquake was awful.* Loose use of *awful* will rob the word of its meaning of inspiring dread, terror. Use *awesome* to describe something that inspires awe—a feeling of overwhelming reverence, admiration, or fear: *Her grasp of linguistics was awesome.* See also *very.*

author   is always a noun, never a verb. *Thackeray authored many novels* is unacceptable. Instead: *Thackeray was a prolific author. Thackeray wrote many novels.* Resist the urge to make verbs of such nouns as *critique* and *gift.* See also *critique.*

averse, adverse.   See *adverse, averse.*

B

badly,   an adverb, is often misused as a complement of the linking verb *feel.* Correct: *I feel bad* (not *badly*) *about her loss.* Adverbs cannot complement (complete) linking verbs. Nor is *badly* a proper synonym for *very much: Huck wanted very much* (not *badly*) *to do what was right for Jim. Badly* is properly used to mean improperly or excessively: *We found that the children had been treated badly. The testing service found the radio to be badly defective.* See also *feel bad, feel badly . . .*

basic   has become an overworked adjective: *The basic truth is evident.* Truth is truth; what does *basic* add? *Essential* is also overworked, as are the adverbs *basically* and *essentially*. These words often appear to be sly attempts to support questionable claims: *Essentially, Ron is a decent fellow.* Is Ron decent or isn't he? Adding *essentially* makes the reader wonder whether the writer is being snide. *Basically, their position is valid.* Is it valid or isn't it?

beautiful   is another overworked adjective. The meaning of *beautiful* is well understood, but the word has been applied indiscriminately in speech and writing: *He is a beautiful person.* There is nothing wrong with seeing beauty in persons and ideas, but constant repetition of *beautiful* robs the word of meaning and marks the user as a lazy or imprecise writer. *He thinks only of others* (not *He is a beautiful person*). *I admire Fred and Mary because they treat their children well.* See also *meaningful; viable.*

because   is sometimes misused as a replacement for *that* in introducing noun clauses: *The excuse they gave for being late was that* (not *because*) *their train was delayed.* The noun clause *their train was delayed* serves as the complement of the linking verb *was.* The conjunction *that* introduces the noun clause. *They were late because their train was delayed.* The clause *their train was delayed* serves as modifier of the main clause *They were late.* The conjunction *because* introduces the modifying clause. See also *fact that; being as, being that; as.*

being as, being that   are incorrect replacements for *because* or *since: I am leaving because* (not *being as* or *being that*) *you refuse to cooperate.* See also *as.*

beside, besides. *Beside* is a preposition meaning by the side of: *She knelt beside me to pray.* *Besides* is an adverb meaning in addition: *Besides, they were unaware of the effect of their words.*

best. See *as best as.*

better can be used with *hd* to mean ought: *You had better* (not *You better*) *learn to listen to reason.*

better than is not used to mean more than: *We took more than* (not *better than*) *an hour to dress. Better than* is correct only in comparisons: *She is better than her sister in many ways. Your dish tastes better than mine.*

between, among. See *among, between.*

between you and I is incorrect for *between you and me. Between* is a preposition requiring the objective case, *you* and *me* are objects of the preposition *between.*

burst should not be confused with *bust: The pipes will burst* (not *bust*) *if they are not drained completely. Our pipes have burst* (not *bursted*)*. The verb *bust* is colloquial; the noun *bust* has entirely different meanings.

but, hardly. Because both these words are negative in meaning, they must not be used with other negatives. Instead of *I didn't have but one* or *I didn't hardly have any time,* write: *I had but one. I hardly had any time.* Watch out as well for *only* and *scarcely,* which can also have negative meanings. See also *hardly; scarcely; only.*

but what   is a regional (colloquial) spoken substitute for *that: I cannot believe that* (not *but what*) *he will not make the team. I believe he will make the team.*

buy   is a good verb: *I want to buy some.* As a noun, *buy* is limited to slang and business writing: *It was a good buy.*

C

can, may.   *Can* implies the ability to do something: *I can climb that hill. May* implies permission or intention: *You may leave the room. I may return tomorrow if the weather is good.*

cannot but   is an awkward phrasing. *You must* (not *cannot but*) *admire her.* See also *but what.*

cannot, can not.   *Cannot* is commonly used except when it is advantageous to place special emphasis on *not: I cannot find my keys. You really can not expect your friends to put up with such behavior.*

capitol, capital.   A capitol is a building that serves as the seat of government: *We filed our papers at the Capitol. Capital* is the spelling used for all other meanings, including money and a city that contains the seat of government: *He could recite the capitals of all fifty states. They lack sufficient capital to start a business of that size. Capital* is also used as an adjective with several meanings: *That is a capital crime in South Carolina. He is a capital fellow.*

censor, censure.   As verbs, *censor* and *censure* have different meanings. *Censor* means examine and remove objectionable parts of a work: *The mayor censors all films shown in our city. Censure* means criticize strongly: *After his improprieties were revealed, the Senate censured him.*

childish, childlike. *Childish* carries a negative connotation of immaturity: *Oscar's wife accused him of being childish. Childlike* has the approving connotation of innocence, purity—all that is good in children: *We all admired the childlike trust young Mary showed.*

climactic, climatic. *Climactic,* related to *climax,* refers to decisive acts or events: *The trial was approaching its climactic phase. Climatic* is related to *climate: We are told we can anticipate major climatic changes in the next decade.*

close proximity. This phrase says the same thing twice. One or the other word will do. *The stars appeared close to one another. Its proximity to the beach made the property desirable.* Even better: *The property was desirable because it was only twenty feet from the beach.*

compare to, compare with, contrast with. To show that one thing is like another in an unreal, or metaphoric, sense, *compare to* is used: *Shall I compare thee to a summer's day?* To analyze real, or literal, likenesses or differences between people, objects, and ideas, *compare with* is used: *Why compare the boy with his older brother?* To emphasize differences, *contrast with* is used: *Mother was always contrasting my erratic behavior with his steady habits.* Avoid comparing or contrasting anything or anybody with anything or anybody inappropriate: *I compared him with her* (not *with her manners*). *I contrasted her novel with his* (not *with his ability as a writer*).

complement, compliment. The verb *complement* means fill out or complete: *Her hat complemented her dress perfectly. A bottle of fine wine complemented the meal.* The verb *compliment* means praise: *I wonder why he complimented me on my work? As* nouns, *these words retain the difference in meanings: A complement is needed after a linking verb. His exaggerated compliments made me uncomfortable.*

consensus of opinion. *Of opinion* is superfluous. *Consensus* means general agreement in belief or opinion: *The class was unable to reach a consensus.* (Notice the spelling: *consensus* has nothing to do with a census.)

contact is an overused verb in the sense of *communicate*. It is best replaced with a more precise verb: *ask, inform, speak, write, telephone,* and so forth. When the form of communication cannot be specified, it is better to use *get in touch with* or *communicate with*.

contemptible, contemptuous. Acts worthy of contempt or scorn are contemptible: *I find cheating contemptible.* People showing contempt are contemptuous: *Why is he always contemptuous of me?*

continual, continuing, continuous. *Continual* means repeated but frequently interrupted: *We were annoyed by his continual sneezing. Continuing* means existing over a long period: *The architect said he had a continuing interest in the design of small homes.*

Continuous means uninterrupted and ongoing: *The continuous action of the waves enables shellfish to find the food they need.*

contractions. Such everyday contractions as *don't* (for *do not*), *let's* (for *let us*), and *you're* (for *you are*) should be avoided in formal reports and papers: *We are* (not *We're*) *convinced that it is* (not *it's*) *crucial to run further tests before going into production.*

contrast with. See *compare to, compare with, contrast with.*

could of is a colloquial spoken variant of *could have: We could have* (not *could of*) *danced all night.* See also *of.*

council, counsel, consul. *Council* means governing board: *Take your petition to the City Council. Counsel* means attorney: *I suggest you retain counsel. Counsel* also means advice: *Have you had the advantage of her counsel?* The verb *counsel* means advise: *He counseled caution.* A *consul* is a foreign-service officer: *Burton served England as consul in several African countries.*

counterproductive is an overused bureaucratic word meaning tending to hinder attainment of a desired end: *Their self-defeating* (not *counterproductive*) *protests brought even greater repression. Their fruitless protests were finally abandoned.*

credible, credulous. *Credible* means believable: *The jury thought her testimony credible. Credulous* means easily deceived, gullible: *How can anyone with that much experi-*

ence be so credulous? Similarly, *incredible* and *incredulous* also have different meanings: *I find his account incredible* (unbelievable). *Why is he always incredulous* (skeptical)?

criteria, criterion.   The plural noun *criteria* means standards of judgment: *Have you met all the criteria for admission? The organization does not reveal its criteria for selecting members.* The singular noun *criterion* means standard of judgment: *I do not understand the first criterion you established for selecting administrative assistants. Age may not be applied as a criterion in judging applicants.* There must always be noun-verb agreement when either the singular or the plural noun is used.

critique   is a good noun but a poor verb: *I agreed with the critique* (or *criticism* or *review*) *printed in the newspaper. Now we will have a chance to criticize* (not *critique*) *her latest poem.*

D

data   is a plural noun, the plural form of *datum* (though the singular is almost never seen except as a modifier in, for example, *datum point*). Careful writers use a plural verb with *data. His data were convincing.*

deduce, deduct.   *Deduce* means draw a conclusion: *Sherlock Holmes deduced that the crime had been committed by a monkey. Deduct* means subtract: *Social security payments were deducted from our salaries for seven months.* Notice that the noun *deduction* has both the above meanings: *Holmes made many clever deductions. Social Security deductions unfairly affect poorly paid workers.*

definitely   is an empty and overworked modifier. *She was interested* means just as much as *She was definitely interested.* See also *absolute, absolutely.*

delusion.   See *allusion, illusion, delusion.*

dependent, dependant.   *Dependent* is the preponderant spelling. It is the only acceptable one when the word is used as an adjective: *My children are dependent* (not *dependant*) *on me.* It is also the preferred spelling for the noun: *My only dependent is my mother.* While *dependant* is an acceptable spelling for the noun, it is rarely used and best avoided.

desirable, desirous.   Desirable objects or people are sought after: *I find her desirable.* Desirous people yearn for something: *Tillie was desirous of achieving wealth.* Even better: *Tillie desired wealth.*

device, devise.   *Device* is a noun: *She has every kitchen device a chef can want. Devise* is a verb: *Try to devise a good solution.*

differ from, differ with.   *Differ from* is used to express dissimilarity: *Your painting differs from his in treatment of color. Differ with* is used to express disagreement: *I may occasionally differ with you on small matters, but we always agree on important affairs.*

discreet, discrete.   *Discreet* means prudent in speech or behavior: *Be discreet about our plans* *if you want to succeed. Discrete* means separate: *Do you know that there are seven discrete steps in the solution to that problem?*

disinterested, uninterested. Though these words may sometimes be listed as synonyms, careful writers give them different meanings. They use *disinterested* to mean impartial: *A good referee is always disinterested. Uninterested* means showing lack of interest: *You are uninterested in mathematics, and I know why.*

dissemble, disassemble. *Dissemble* means pretend: *A successful poker player must be prepared to dissemble now and then during a game. Disassemble* means take apart: *Once you have disassembled the motor, test each part.*

distinctive, distinguished. *Distinctive* means readily identifying: *Lord Fawn's distinctive lisp marked him as an idle aristocrat. Distinguished* means eminent or marked by excellence: *His distinguished sister was promoted to company president only five years after she joined our company.*

don't is the correct contraction of *do not,* but incorrect for *does not: He doesn't* (not *don't*) *know the way home.* In writing, contractions are best avoided except for informal letters, notes, and the like.

due to the fact that. Why this lengthy expression when *because, due to,* and *since* carry the same meaning? *Her success was due to her perseverance* (not *due to the fact that she persevered*). See also *fact that.*

E

eager. See *anxious, eager*.

early on seems to be a fad expression, meaning no more than *early* or *soon*.

ecology, environment are frequently confused nouns. *Environment* means conditions surrounding a living organism: *Pollution can damage our environment. Ecology* means the study of the interactions of plants or animals with their environments: *Many college students take courses in ecology*.

effect. See *affect, effect*.

e.g. This Latin abbreviation for *exempli gratia* (for the sake of example) is used in scholarly footnotes, charts, and the like. In straight text, it should always be replaced with *for example* or *for instance*. See also *i.e.*

either, neither. These words refer to one of two items or groups of items, never to more than one of two: *Either you play a strong role in our community organization, or I resign. Neither the magazines nor the newspapers reported the incident accurately. Joan, Alice, or Fred* (not *Either Joan, Alice, or Fred*) *must be home in time to prepare dinner.* See also *neither*.

elicit, illicit. *Elicit* is a verb meaning draw forth: *The chairman decided to remain silent in order to elicit helpful suggestions from the group. Illicit* is an adjective meaning unlawful: *Illicit drugs soon disappeared from the campus.*

emigrate, immigrate. The prefixes *e-* (out of) and *im-* (into) are the keys to these verbs. *Emigrate* means leave a country to settle elsewhere: *Large numbers of young men and women emigrated from Ireland during the nineteenth century.* *Immigrate* means enter a country to make one's home: *She immigrated to Canada to find a peaceful life.* Emigrants emigrate; once they have immigrated, they become immigrants. Migrants and migratory workers travel from place to place, seeking work or a place to settle down. When they do settle down, they are no longer migrants or migratory workers.

eminent. See *imminent, eminent*.

enormity. The primary meaning of *enormity* is excessive wickedness: *Who can grasp the enormity of genocide?* It should not be used to indicate a large quantity or high level: *The degree* (not *enormity*) *of her generosity was never forgotten by the town.*

enthuse is a colloquial usage, to be avoided in papers and reports. More formal wordings are *be enthusiastic* and *show enthusiasm for: Once he had seen the campus, he was enthusiastic about everything connected with the college.*

environment. See *ecology, environment*.

epithet, epitaph. An *epithet* is an expression that characterizes a person or object—for example, *first lady* for the wife of a president, *the Oval Office* for presidential power. *Epithet* also means a contemptuous expression: *I have never heard epithets that match the ones she uses when* *she loses her temper.* An *epitaph* is a tombstone inscription: *Here lies an honest man.*

equally as.   Such expressions as *equally good*, *equally bad*, and *equally wrong* do not need *as: Your proofs are equally* (not *equally as*) *time-consuming.*

essential   is an overworked and usually unnecessary adjective. *The essential truth* means no more than *the truth*. See also *basic*.

et al.   is the Latin abbreviation for *et alii*, meaning and others. It is generally found only in scholarly bibliographies to indicate multiple authorship: Jones, Arthur, *et al., A History of Nepal*. In straight text it should always be replaced with *and others* or a similar phrase. Notice that *et* in *et al.* is not an abbreviation and therefore is not followed by a period. *Et* means and.

etc.   is the abbreviation for *et cetera*, a Latin phrase meaning *and the rest*. It is appropriately used in lists, charts, and the like. In straight text it should always be replaced with *and others, and so forth*, or a similar phrase. See also *et al.*

everybody, everyone.   See *anybody, anyone . . .*

every day, everyday.   *Every day* is a phrase that functions as an adverb: *We do certain chores every day. Everyday* is an adjective: *Everyday affairs can be boring.*

every so often   can profitably be replaced with *often, infrequently, occasionally*, or the like. If these single words do not adequately convey the intended meaning, more specific wording—such as *every two days, weekly, once a month*—can be used.

except.   See *accept, except.*

expect   means anticipate. It does not mean suppose: *We expect you for lunch. I suppose* (not *expect*) *she knows the way to your house.*

F

fact that.   This phrase is frequently misused in claiming as fact something that is unworthy of such claim: *The fact that the Yankees may not win has not crossed Billy's mind.* Such a slight thought is too obvious to be classified as fact. Rewrite: *That the Yankees may not win has not crossed Billy's mind.* Again: *That* (not *the fact that*) *she may be pregnant seems a possibility.* This thought has not been established as fact. But: *The fact that Napoleon was born in Corsica has never left Frenchmen's memories.* Napoleon's birthplace is a fact that can be verified. See also *due to the fact that.*

farther, further.   The distinction between these two words, though smudged, is nevertheless still observed. *Farther* applies to distance: *You will travel farther in a day if you start early in the morning. Further* is more often used to mean more or additionally: *I have no further interest in your career. She will question me further tomorrow morning.*

feel bad, feel badly, feel good, feel well.   Of these four common expressions, only the second is inappropriate. The linking verb *feel* takes a predicate adjective as its complement—for example, *bad, good, well, strong, weak. I felt bad* (sad) *about her failure. I felt good* (happy) *about her success. I felt well* (healthy) *all day.* (*Well* is also an adverb: *He dances well.*) *Feel badly* is a misguided attempt to find an adverb for a linking verb, since linking verbs cannot be modified.

fewer, less. *Fewer* refers to things that can be counted: *Fewer people attended than we had anticipated. Less* refers to things that cannot be counted: *This cereal contains fewer* (not *less*) *calories. He eats less than he once did. This cereal contains less sugar than most.* See also *more, less.*

finalize. See *-ize words.*

financial, monetary. *Financial* refers to money matters: *He had no financial skill. We used to have a financial interest in that business. All of us should manage our own financial interests. Monetary* refers to banking and to management of money by governments: *The Federal Reserve Board establishes monetary policy in the United States. No ordinary individual plays a role in monetary affairs.*

fine is a vague and overused modifier. A more descriptive modifier can usually be found: *Sam is a generous* (not *fine*) *man. The weather was clear* (not *fine*). *I like you* (not *like you fine*).

flaunt, flout. *Flaunt* means show off: *My dentist appeared eager to flaunt his skills. Flout* means show contempt for: *Too many*

> *members of this administration flout the laws of our country.*

flunk is slang and therefore inappropriate in papers and reports. *I am afraid I will fail (not flunk) the final examination.*

foot, feet. *Foot* is singular, *feet* is plural. In such phrases as *a six-foot rule, foot* correctly functions as an adjective. *Feet* is always a noun: *The shelf measures three feet.*

for example. See *such as.*

for real. *For real* and the countless other *for* expressions waiting to be coined should be avoided. *No one will be admitted free (not for free). No one will be admitted without charge.* The slang expression *Is he for real?* has its charm but means no more than the slang expression *Is he real?*

former, latter are words used to indicate one of two. When referring to one of more than two, *first* and *last* are used. *After examining the ranch house and the Tudor, I wanted to buy the latter. After examining the ranch house, the Tudor, and the Cape Cod, I selected the first (not the former).* See also *later, latter.*

forthcoming is incorrectly considered a substitute for *forthright* or *candid. He was forthright (or candid, not forthcoming) in his testimony. Forthcoming* means approaching or available when promised: *The forthcoming debate is attracting great interest. Will the necessary funds be forthcoming?*

fortuitous, fortunate. These two good adjectives are in danger of losing their separate identities. *Fortunate* means lucky: *We are fortunate in having an interesting speaker with us. Fortuitous* means unplanned, accidental: *The bombing of the hospital was fortuitous; the bomb was intended for another target. A fortuitous encounter sometimes gives more pleasure than a thoroughly planned date.*

fulsome. This adjective has nothing to do with *full.* It means disgustingly insincere: *I found his fulsome praise unflattering and unworthy of the man.*

funny is used only to mean amusing: *I find few comedians funny. Funny* is not a synonym for such words as *odd, strange, queer,* and *unusual: His behavior at the party was strange* (not *funny*), *since he claims that he did not have a drink.*

further. See *farther, further.*

G

good is an adjective, not an adverb: *The car runs well* (not *good*). As a predicate adjective, *good* serves as a complement of linking verbs: *seem good; be good; feel good.* A person who helps other people *does good; do-gooder* is a twentieth-century coinage that has gained many advocates. See also *feel bad, feel badly, feel good, feel well.*

got to is an inappropriate substitute for *have to, has to, had to: I have to* (not *got to*) *leave now.*

graduate. More and more the intransitive use—as in *she graduated from college*—is used in place of the older *she was graduated from college*. However, the form that omits *from*—as in *I graduated high school*—is still frowned upon.

graffiti is a plural (the singular is *graffito*). *Subway graffiti are so colorful that I envy the artists' skill.*

grievous presents a spelling and pronunciation problem. The word has only one *i*. There is no word that is spelled or pronounced *grievious*.

H

had of, had ought. *Had* should be used instead of the colloquial *had of: I wish I had* (not *had of*) *bought that car. Should* or *ought* takes the place of *had ought: You should* (not *had ought to*) *be more careful in the future. You ought to* (not *had ought to*) *practice more.* See also *of*.

hanged, hung. *Hanged* is used for executions, *hung* for everything else. *They hanged the poor man. They hung all their paintings. The sides of beef hung for a month.*

hardly should not be used with a negative expression, since *hardly* itself carries a negative meaning: *You can* (not *can't*) *hardly blame him. They hardly* (not *don't hardly*) *ever go to see her anymore.* See also *but, hardly; only; scarcely*.

healthful, healthy. Food and climate can be healthful; people are healthy. *When asked why he was so healthy, he replied that he ate only healthful dishes.*

himself.   See *myself, yourself* . . .

historic, historical.   *Historic* means history-making: *The historic attack on Pearl Harbor is commemorated each year in the United States. Historical* means relating to history or pertaining to history: *She is best known for her exciting historical novels.*

hopefully.   This good adverb is changing. Again and again it is appearing in sentences in which *hopefully* has nothing to modify. *Hopefully, you will be home by ten* is intended to mean *I hope you will be home by ten. Hopefully* is traditional in such constructions as *she said hopefully* and *they peered hopefully*, where *hopefully* has verbs to modify. "*My life is over,*" *he said hopelessly.* "*My life is just beginning,*" *she said hopefully.*

hung.   See *hanged, hung.*

I

i.e.   is the abbreviation for the Latin phrase *id est*, that is (not to be confused with *e.g.*, for example). It is appropriately used in scholarly works, lists, charts, and the like. In straight text it should always be replaced with *that is.*

if and when   means no more than either *if* or *when* alone: *I shall see him when* (not *if and when*) *he is ready to see me. If* (not *If and when*) *you hear any news, please call me at once.*

illicit.   See *elicit, illicit.*

illusion.   See *allusion, illusion, delusion.*

imaginary, imaginative. These adjectives are frequently confused. *Imaginary* means unreal: *My daughter has an imaginary playmate she describes as a blue boy with wings. Imaginative* means showing powers of imagination: *Imaginative literature, particularly stories for children, was her principal interest.*

immigrate. See *emigrate, immigrate.*

imminent, eminent. *Imminent* means about to occur: *We have been told the birth of the child is imminent. Eminent* means outstanding, distinguished: *They were unable to find an eminent scientist willing to sponsor the research.*

implement is a favorite verb of bureaucrats, who use it as a replacement for *do, carry out, authorize, conduct, accomplish, apply, perform,* and many other verbs. *The engineers wanted to do* (not *implement*) *the work as quickly as possible. They decided that they would carry out* (not *implement*) *the plan as soon as they found the money for it.*

imply, infer. *Imply* means suggest: *The witness implied in her testimony that the company books had been kept dishonestly, but the prosecutor could not get her to say so directly. Infer* means conclude from evidence: *From what Beatrice said, we inferred that her marriage was far from happy.* Speakers and writers imply; listeners and readers infer. The nouns associated with *imply* and *infer* are *implication* and *inference.*

in all probability   means nothing more than *probably: Juan will probably* (not *in all probability*) *be elected.*

in case   usually means nothing more than *if: Go to the library if* (not *in case*) *you have time.*

incidence, incidents.   *Incidence* means rate of occurrence: *The incidence of crime is growing in some rural areas. Incidents* are events: *Two incidents of that type were reported last night.*

incredible, incredulous.   See *credible, credulous.*

infer.   See *imply, infer.*

ingenious, ingenuous.   *Ingenious* means clever: *Edison was an ingenious inventor. Ingenuous* means naive, frank: *Aware that Emily was ingenuous, her brother and sister-in-law never confided in her or expected her to understand the subtleties of their relationship. Disingenuous*, the antonym of *ingenuous*, means lacking in candor.

in, into.   *In* refers to position or location: *He was put in charge of the department. The child is in her crib. Into* refers to motion from outside to inside: *The patient was moved into the intensive care unit.*

innumerable, numerous.   *Innumerable* means too many to be counted: *We found innumerable insects inside the closet. Numerous* means many: *Numerous guests left before the party ended.*

in regards.   The *s* must be deleted. *In regard to* or *with regard to* will serve the purpose.

Better yet, write *about: I am writing about my unfilled order, which I placed with your company two months ago.* See also *as regards.*

inside of means nothing more than *inside* or *within: They remained inside* (not *inside of*) *the house. I shall be there within* (not *inside of*) *two hours.*

in terms of. This phrase is overused and misapplied. *He considered the plan in terms of its merits and its risks* means nothing more than *He weighed the merits and risks of the plan. In terms of* has become a grand expression, a darling of pretentious speakers and writers. *In terms* might best be restricted to such uses as *in loving terms* and *in terms of endearment,* in which *terms* has the meaning of *words. He spoke in terms too difficult for me to understand. The terms of employment* (conditions of employment) *were never made clear. Prison terms* (periods of confinement) bear some relation to the nature of the crimes committed by felons.

interpersonal. This word, used by some social scientists as an elaborate substitute for *personal,* has inevitably become a favorite of many laymen. To make matters worse, *interpersonal* almost always appears with *relationship,* which is already implicit in the word *interpersonal. They enjoyed a close interpersonal relationship* means nothing more than *They enjoyed a close relationship* or *They were good friends.*

in the event that means nothing more than *if: If* (not *In the event that*) *he attends the meet-*

ing, we can expect complete disruption.
If it rains (not In the event that it rains),
the game will be postponed.

in the not too distant future. See *near future.*

in view of the fact that means nothing more than
because and probably misrepresents as
fact a statement that is unproven or trivial. See also *fact that.*

irregardless is incorrect for *regardless: They will*
continue their struggle regardless (not *ir-*
regardless) of the consequences.

it is, there is, there are are indirect, word-wasting
ways to open sentences. Such sentences
waste the subject position on the empty
expletive *it* or *there.* The linking verbs
that follow—*is, are, were, was, will be*—
add nothing. We end up with *It is child-*
ish of you to behave in such a manner
instead of the forceful and direct *Your*
behavior makes you appear childish. By
avoiding *it is* we have six words in place
of eleven. See also *there is, there are.*

it's I, it's me. Who now will answer *It's I* when
asked *Who's there?* Even though *It's I*
has grammatical correctness on its side,
It's me is universally acceptable.

its, it's. The possessive of *it* is *its: Its battery*
should be replaced. The contraction of *it*
is is *it's: I assure you it's beyond me.* See
also *contractions.*

-ize words. The suffix *-ize* allows almost unlimited
possibilities for new verbs—*criticize, os-*
tracize, plagiarize, and so on—but it does
not give license to create verbal mon-

sters. Some *-ize* coinages are welcome, enabling us to express in a single word thoughts that might otherwise require a phrase. Other *-ize* verbs are pretentious replacements for existing verbs that convey the same meaning—*finalize* for *complete, optimize* for *perfect, conceptualize* for *conceive* or *think, formularize* for *formulate.*

J

judicial, judicious.   *Judicial* refers to matters of law: *The judicial process must not be disrupted. Judicious* refers to careful judgment: *Be judicious in choosing a partner.*

just   is a weak replacement for *completely, simply, quite, only, merely: The boredom of household duties completely* (not *just*) *exhausted her. I was simply* (not *just*) *incapable of studying last semester.* (Better yet: *The boredom of household duties exhausted her. I was incapable of studying last semester.*) *The book costs only* (not *just*) *eleven dollars.*

just exactly.   This gushing phrase appears in such sentences as *This is just exactly what I want.* Better: *This is exactly what I want. This is precisely what I want.* Best: *This is what I want.*

K

kind of, sort of   are poor substitutes for *somewhat* or *rather: I was somewhat* (not *kind of* or *sort of*) *disappointed.* Even *somewhat* and *rather* are vague modifiers, candidates for deletion: *I was disappointed. Kind of* and *sort of* apply to variety or type: *What* *sort of man is he? What kind of cereal do you prefer? A* is not used after *sort of* and *kind of: She is the sort of* (not *sort of a*) *person you should consider for the job.*

kind, type, both singular: *This kind* (not *these kind*) *of behavior; these kinds of behavior; that type of furniture; those types of furniture.* When using *kind* or *type,* the verb that follows must agree in number with its subject: *This kind of behavior is objectionable. Those types of furniture are suitable for any home.* (The word *such* can usually replace *type* and *kind: Such behavior wins you no friends.*)

L

lack. As a verb, *lack* does not need *for: We lack* (not *lack for*) *ambition.* As a noun, *lack* is followed by *of: They suffered from a lack of money.*

large part is a weak substitute for *many* or *most: Many* (not *A large part*) *of the books were damaged. Large part* can be used to mean *much* when referring to a structure: *A large part of the building was destroyed by fire. Large part* shares the disadvantages of vagueness with *much, many,* and *most.* What is *a large number, a large portion, a large proportion,* or *a large share?* Where possible, be specific. *All but three of the books were damaged. One wing of the building was destroyed. He has spent all but three hundred dollars of the money his mother left him.*

later, latter. *Later* is the comparative form of *late: He was habitually later than I. One of* *his later works was banned in Boston. Latter* means the second of two: *As for the problems of cost and time, the latter can easily be resolved, but not cost.* See also *former, latter.*

laudable, laudatory. *Laudable* means deserving of praise: *The critics said her early performances were laudable for their dramatic interpretation. Laudatory* means giving praise: *The laudatory speeches given during Edna's retirement dinner pleased everyone but Edna herself.*

lay, lie. The principal parts of *lay* are *lay, laying, laid.* The principal parts of *lie* are *lie, lying, lain. Lay* means place: *Lay the books on the table. He is laying bricks. He laid the linoleum. The hens have laid eggs all winter. Lie* means incline or rest. *Lie on the beach. She is lying on the couch. The books have lain there unread for a month.* (*Lie,* meaning to tell an untruth, has still other forms—*lie, lying, lied.*)

lead, led are the present and past forms of the verb *lead: General Patton led his troops across the Rhine. I think it is time to lead the fans in a cheer.* (The metal is *lead: Pewter is an alloy of tin and lead.*)

learn, teach. *Learn* means acquire knowledge: *Students learn. Teach* means impart knowledge: *Some college professors teach poorly.*

leave, let are frequently confused verbs. *Leave* means depart from: *Leave the room at once. Let* means permit: *Let me go.* Exception: *Let me* (equally correct, *Leave me*) *alone.* In papers and reports, *Let me alone* is preferred.

less. See *fewer, less; more, less.*

let's us in effect uses the same word twice. *Let's* is the contraction of *let us: Let's* (not *Let's us*) *go to the theater.* See also *contractions.*

liable is a weak substitute for *likely* in expressing probability: *Mike was likely* (not *liable*) *to lose his job because of his frequent absences. Liable* (with *for*) expresses legal responsibility: *Are you liable for damages? Liable* should not be confused with *libel*, a legal term meaning defamation of a person: *Libel is difficult to prove in United States courts.*

lie. See *lay, lie.*

lightning, lightening. *Lightning* is a natural phenomenon: *We sought shelter during the lightning storm. Lightening* is a reduction in weight or severity: *We ought to consider lightening our packs.* The verb *lighten* also has the meaning of to make lighter: *Joyce will not consider lightening her hair color.*

like is a preposition: *Anyone like Tom has a good chance of succeeding. Like* is not used as a conjunction: *Tom ran as though* (not *ran like*) *the law were after him.* The recent expression *tell it like* (instead of *as*) *it is* is a forceful misapplication of *like.*

likely. As an adjective, *likely* is appropriately used to say that something is probable or suitable: *A likely story! This is a likely book for for your research.* As an adverb, however, *probably* is more appropriate:

He will probably (not *likely*) *arrive before lunch.*

literally, figuratively. *Literally* means actually: *By the fifteenth we literally had no money left. Figuratively* means not actually: *We figuratively fell through the floor when the foreman made his announcement.* In this cliché no one actually (literally) fell through anything. The writer was exaggerating to show a degree of surprise. If he had written *We literally fell through the floor in surprise,* he either would have been wrong or we would know that termites had been hard at work.

loath, loathe. *Loath* (also spelled *loth*) is an adjective that means reluctant: *He was loath to show his cards, since he had such a poor hand. Loathe* is a verb that means to despise: *One cannot help but loathe a bully.*

look good, look well. One can look good and one can look well. The former refers to appearance, the latter to health. See also *feel bad, feel badly, feel good, feel well.*

loose, lose. *Loose* is an adjective. *My collar is loose. Lose* is a verb: *I hope you do not lose your way.*

lot of, lots of are weak substitutes for *many* or *much*. See also *large part; innumerable, numerous.*

M

mad, angry. *Mad* means insane: *Ophelia went mad. I am angry with* (not *mad at*) *you.* See also *angry at, angry with.*

many, much, most. *Many* is used for things and people that can be counted: *Many dogs run loose.* *Much* is used for things that cannot be counted: *Much trouble can be avoided. Much sugar was used in her recipes. Most* is used for everything: *Most dogs eat well. Most trouble cannot be avoided. Most sugar is wasted.* See also *most.*

may. See *can, may.*

may be, maybe. *May be* is a verb form: *We may be there on time. Maybe* is an adverb: *Maybe she did not hear us.*

may of, might of, must of. See *of.*

mean for is a colloquialism for *mean that: We did not mean that you should stay home* (not *We did not mean for you to stay home*).

meaningful. This overworked adjective usually serves little purpose unless accompanied by an explanation: *We found his statement meaningful in that it clarified his beliefs and supported them logically.* Since the word *meaningful* is vague, the sentence is best reworded: *His statement clarified and supported his beliefs.* Expressions such as *meaningful relationship* and *meaningful discussion* tend to be empty. More specific terms will improve any sentence.

media. This word is plural (the singular is *medium*): *Many people feel the news media are* (not *is*) *creating stories instead of reporting and interpreting them. My favorite news medium is the newspaper. Medium* and *media* do not refer to newspapers, television, and the rest unless specified (*the news media*) or so understood in context. *Medium* means instrument or means; there are entertainment media, instructional media, and many other types of media.

might of. See *of.*

monetary. See *financial, monetary.*

moral, morale. The adjective *moral* refers to morality, the standards of human conduct: *You pose a moral question that only you may answer.* The noun *morale* means mental outlook or condition: *Team morale had never been lower before an important game.*

more, less are superfluous as modifiers of comparatives: *You are better* (not *more better*) *than I am in important ways. I am not as hungry as you are* (not *I am less hungrier than you are*). See also *fewer, less.*

most is not an appropriate substitute for *almost: We understood almost* (not *most*) *everything the speaker said. Most* may be used to mean the greater amount: *We understood most of what you said. More* and *most* cannot modify adjectives that do not allow modification. *Unique*, for example, cannot become *more unique* or *most unique*, since *unique* means one of a kind. See also *many, much, most.*

much. See *many, much, most.*

must of. See *of.*

myself, yourself, himself, ourselves, yourselves, themselves. The *-self, -selves* pronouns are used as intensifiers (strengtheners): *I myself bear no ill will*. They also serve as reflexives: *They act as though they hate themselves*. The most common misuses of these pronouns are corrected in the following examples. *She gave me* (not *myself*) *a box of cigars. I am no taller than she* (not *herself*). *My parents asked my sister and me* (not *myself*) *to go with them*. The correct form of the third person plural is *themselves*, not *theirself* or *theirselves*. See also *ourself*.

N

near future is a weak substitute for *soon*. Even weaker is *in the not too distant future*, which also means *soon*. Whenever possible, use specific expressions: *tomorrow; two days from now; next week*.

needless to say is merely a space-filler. Whatever is needless to say need not be said and should be left out.

neither is used for one of two: *He neither drinks nor smokes. I will recommend neither Joe nor Al*. Since *neither* is negative, *either* is used when the sentence already contains a negative: *I will not buy either* (not *neither*) *car. I will buy neither car*. See also *either, neither*.

nice is a weak substitute for adjectives that carry specific meanings: *starry sky* means more than *nice sky; generous person* means more than *nice person*. Vague modifiers are best avoided.

noisome, a rarely used word, has nothing to do with *noisy*; it means disgusting: *The chemistry experiment gave off noisome fumes that drove us from the laboratory.*

nowheres is a colloquialism for *nowhere: Nowhere we looked did we find land at a price we could afford.*

number. See *amount, number.*

numerous. The preposition *of* is not used after *numerous: Numerous* (not *Numerous of*) *manuscripts were sold at auction yesterday.* In most sentences, *many* conveys the same meaning as *numerous* and has the advantage of simplicity. See also *innumerable, numerous.*

O

obviate the necessity of. This expression uses unnecessary words. *Obviate* means make unnecessary: *By finishing his tables with fine steel wool and tung oil, he obviates* (not *obviates the necessity of*) *frequent polishing.*

of. Informal speech sometimes substitutes *of* for *have* in such expressions as *may have, might have, could have, should have, ought to have, would have,* and *will have.* But even informal writing always uses *have.*

of between is an awkward substitute for *of* in such expressions as *a crowd of between ten and fifteen thousand.* Better: *a crowd of ten to fifteen thousand.*

off of   uses one word too many. *He jumped off (not off of) the diving board. Stay off (not off of) the roof.*

on account of   is an inadequate substitute for *because* or *because of*: *He was rejected because (not on account of) his aptitude test scores were low. She was given a seat because of her age.*

only   should not be used with negatives: *I wanted only to avoid hurting her (not I wanted only not to hurt her).* See also *but, hardly; hardly; scarcely.*

opt for   is a bureaucratic and pretentious substitute for *choose* or *decide*: *They chose (not opted for) direct action. She decided on (not opted for) a policy of cordial co-operation.*

oral, verbal.   See *verbal, oral.*

ordinance, ordnance.   *Ordinance* refers to decrees or laws: *The city council establishes fire ordinances. Ordnance* refers to military weapons and ammunition: *The troops spent many hours making sure their ordnance— especially their 105mm howitzers—remained combat-ready.*

ought to   is never preceded by *had*: *They ought to (not had ought to) keep better records. They ought to (not had ought to) have kept better records.* See also *had of, had ought.*

ourself.   Only a monarch, judge, or editorial writer may use *ourself*: *We ourself find no error in the proposed application.* The rest of us must write *ourselves*: *We found our-*

selves encumbered with debts and respon-
sibilities we had never wanted. See also
myself . . .

out loud   is a colloquial substitute for *aloud: Mother*
read aloud (not *out loud*) *to us every*
evening during those harsh winters.

outside of.   *Of* is an unnecessary addition: *They*
remained outside (not *outside of*) *the house*
during the party. See also inside of.

owing to the fact that.   This phrase is a cumbersome
substitute for *because: Because* (not *Ow-*
ing to the fact that) *we had so little money,*
we were forced to do without everything
but the essentials. Owing to is another
unfortunate substitute for *because: Be-*
cause of (not *Owing to*) *her illness, she*
could not compete in the games. See also
fact that.

P

party.   This noun should not be used to refer to
an individual: *He* (not *That party*) *made a*
serious error. Such usage is acceptable
only in contracts and similar documents:
the party of the first part. The word is
also properly used in the sense of *partici-*
pant: I am not a party to (a participant in)
the dispute.

past.   Expressions containing words that refer
to the past do not need the additional
adjective *past: past experience* is no more
than *experience,* and *past history* is no
more than *history. His record* (not *past*
record) *hurts his chances for employment.*

per   is effective only in combination with Latin words: *per diem*, not *per day; per capita*, not *per person*. With English equivalents of these words, *a* sounds better: *Many consultants are paid $750 a day. The admission fee was $20 a person, $30 a couple. The price is 10 cents a hundred. Per se* is Latin for *by itself* and the like. *We do not oppose hard work per se, but we do reject meaningless work.* More effective: *We reject meaningless work, not hard work.*

percent, percentage.   *Percentage* is used when numbers are not specified: *a small percentage. Percent* is used after numbers: *15 percent; 20 percent.*

persecute, prosecute.   *Persecute* means harass: *Minority groups have often been persecuted. Prosecute* means pursue or—rarely—persist in: *District attorneys prosecute criminal cases. Governments prosecute wars.*

phenomena   is a plural noun: *These phenomena are* (not *This phenomena is*) *disturbing. Phenomenon* is the singular form: *Lightning is a natural phenomenon.*

plenty   is a colloquialism for *quite* or *very: The yellow one is quite* (not *plenty*) *good.* Both *quite* and *very* are vague and overused, however; omission is effective: *The yellow one is good.* See also *very*.

point in time   is an overworked expression that means no more than *point: By that point* (not *point in time*) *the plot had gone so far that nothing could stop it.* See also *at this point in time*.

poorly   is a colloquialism for *poor* in expressions dealing with health: *The cow is sick* (not *doing poorly* or *feeling poorly*).

practicable, practical.   *Practicable* means capable of being accomplished: *Your plan is practicable if you have enough capital to carry you through the first year of operations.* *Practical* means sensible or aware of results: *He is a practical person, always concerned with getting a job done as inexpensively as possible.* An impractical person is unconcerned with how much things cost. An impracticable plan should be discarded because it will not work.

pre-.   This prefix is unnecessary with such words as *recorded* and *planned*. *The preceding program was recorded* (not *prerecorded*). *A vacation is planned (not preplanned)*. *Pre-* is sensibly used, for example, in the word *precede*, which has a meaning entirely different from that of *cede*.

precipitate, precipitous.   *Precipitate* means overly hasty: *Guard against precipitate action.* *Precipitous* means steep: *The riverbank is precipitous near the falls.* *Precipitate* is also a verb meaning bring about prematurely: *Discovery of the embezzlement precipitated the bank officer's resignation.*

preclude.   *Preclude* means make impossible. Actions can be precluded: *Their poverty precluded buying a house* (not *precluded them from buying a house*) *even though the monthly payments would be low.* People cannot be precluded: *Her handicap grew steadily worse and finally precluded all physical activity* (not *precluded her from performing all physical activity*).

prefer   is followed by *to,* not *than: I prefer your ideas to* (not *than*) *mine. She prefers staying home to* (not *than*) *going to a bad movie.*

previous to, prior to   are weak, pompous substitutes for *before: She was appointed before* (not *prior to* or *previous to*) *earning her doctorate.*

principal, principle.   The adjective *principal* means chief: *My principal concern is your safety.* The noun *principal* usually refers to the head of a school or officer of an organization: *She was a principal in the engineering concern for many years. Principal* also means capital: *The bank demanded payment of the principal as well as all earned interest. Principle* is always a noun referring to truth or standards: *He was completely lacking in principles. In principle you are entirely correct, but you have neglected important considerations in assessing the problem.*

probably.   See *in all probability; likely.*

prophecy, prophesy.   *Prophecy* is a noun: *Her prophecies proved incorrect. Prophesy* is a verb: *The astrologer prophesied a marriage blessed with many children.*

prosecute.   See *persecute, prosecute.*

Q

questionable, questioning.   *Questionable* means open to doubt: *The Watergate investigation concerned itself primarily with questionable official acts. Questioning* means quizzical: *His questioning attitude made me so*

*uncomfortable that I decided to find an-
other therapist.*

question as to whether. *Question as to* adds nothing
to *whether* in such sentences as *The question as to whether the indictment was
properly drawn was raised by the grand
jury.* Better: *The grand jury did not question whether the indictment was properly
drawn. Whether the indictment was properly drawn was not discussed by the grand
jury.*

quite a. *Quite a bit, quite a few,* and other such
expressions are vague. Explicit expres-
sions are always more effective: *50 percent; more than half; majority; three;
fourteen. He took quite a bit of time to
answer* tells little. More informative: *He
took five minutes to answer.* See also *very.*

quote cannot function as a noun in formal speech
and writing. The noun is *quotation: Were
you able to find a suitable quotation* (not
a suitable quote)? *Quote* is an accepted
verb: *Did you quote enough from the Bi-
ble to make your sermon interesting?*

R

raise, rise. *Raise* is a transitive verb (it takes a
direct object): *I raise corn and alfalfa.
He raised his sisters and brothers. Each
year the landlady raises our rent. Rise* is
intransitive (does not take a direct object): *Can you actually see the cake rise?
The sun rose after eight. They have risen
early all their lives.*

rarely if ever is a lightweight substitute for *rarely.
Rarely ever* is just as pointless. *You will*

rarely (not *rarely if ever* or *rarely ever*) *find me in the library. Seldom* is close to *rarely* in meaning and can provide welcome variety: *I am seldom found in a library.*

rather. See *kind of, sort of.*

ravage, ravish. *Ravage* means destroy: *Fire ravaged our village. The poor child was ravaged by fever. Ravish* has several meanings, among them rape and carry off by force. Both meanings are directed at people rather than property: *All the young women of the village were ravished by the invaders.*

really. Like *very, really* is used too often as a vague strengthener (intensifier). While *really* means in reality or truly and can be applied to many thoughts, it can almost always be omitted without damaging meaning: *Cats are useless* (not *really useless*) *in a modern apartment.* Habitual use of *really* leads to such gushing sentences as *She did really well* and *I really like you.* Yet sentences do benefit from use of the word when it strengthens the intended meaning: *He really was at home when he said he was.* The distinction between *real* and *really* is important. *Real* is an adjective; *really* is an adverb: *real events,* not fiction; *really sick,* not pretending.

reason is because is not a logical formulation. The accepted form is *reason is that: The reason I am angry is that* (not *because*) *you neglected to call on time. Reason* may often be omitted: *I am angry because you neglected to call on time.* See also *because.*

refer   should not be followed by *back: Refer* (not
             Refer back) *to my first letter on this topic.*

regarding.   This word and all its cousins—*in regard
             to, in respect to, with respect to, relating
             to, relative to,* and the old-fashioned *as
             regards*—can be replaced by *about* or *con-
             cerning: I am writing concerning your
             advertisement for a computer program-
             mer. They have no doubt about her abil-
             ity to do good work.*

regretful, regrettable.   People can be regretful: *Since
             you clearly intended no harm, why be
             regretful over what happened?* Only ac-
             tions or the results of actions can be re-
             grettable: *The stockholders found your
             unprovoked outburst regrettable. The con-
             sumer attitude toward recent price rises
             is considered regrettable by large corpor-
             ations.*

relation, relationship.   *Relation* describes a connec-
             tion of things or abstractions: *No one fully
             understands the relation between unem-
             ployment and inflation. Relationship* de-
             scribes a connection based on friendship
             or association of people: *The business re-
             lationship they enjoyed was the envy of
             their competitors.* See also *meaningful.*

respectfully, respectively.   *Respectfully* means with
             respect: *They speak respectfully of you.
             Respectively* means singly in the order
             mentioned and usually appears in such
             awkward sentences as *John and Jim
             were eight and ten years old respectively.
             Respectively* is seldom needed. Such sen-
             tences can usually be rewritten: *John was
             eight years old and Jim was ten.*

right   is a colloquialism for *very, somewhat,* or *extremely: I am very* (not *right*) *proud of you.* Better: *I am proud of you.* See also *very.*

rise.   See *raise, rise.*

S

said.   This verb form is sometimes used as an adjective by lawyers and others who deal with legal matters: *The said contracts were deemed void.* Whenever *said* is used as an adjective, it conveys the impression of legality, usually inappropriately: *The said faulty part must be returned to the tool crib.* Better: *Return the faulty part to the tool crib.*

says.   As the past tense of *say, says* is a colloquialism: *She said* (not *says*) *yesterday that she would attend the meeting.*

scarcely   cannot be used with negatives: *I scarcely had time* (not *scarcely had no time*) *to finish the work.* See also *hardly, neither.*

seldom.   See *rarely if ever.*

-self, -selves.   See *myself . . .*

sensory, sensual, sensuous.   *Sensory* refers to the senses or sensation: *The experiment calls for isolating the subject so that all sensory stimuli are blocked. Sensual* usually refers to gratification of physical or sexual appetite: *He was interested in sensual pleasures rather than serious study. Sensuous* applies most often to aesthetic enjoyment: *The critic responded favorably to the sensuous music played that evening.*

set, sit. *Set* means place in position: *Set the vase on the table. Sit* means be seated: *Sit wherever you wish.* (To confuse matters, it must be noted that the moon, planets, stars, hens, and concrete—correctly—set.)

shall, will. At one time these words had separate meanings and uses, but the distinction is fast disappearing, with *will* winning for most uses. Traditionally, formal writing showed the future by: *I shall; we shall; you will; he, she, it,* and *they will.* Determination, necessity, and duty still are indicated by: *I will; we will; you shall; he, she, it,* and *they shall.*

should of. See *of.*

similar. This word means resembling, not same: *Joe's father's reaction was similar to mine, but I managed greater control.*

simple, simplified, simplistic. *Simple* means easy to understand: *She was able to solve simple problems without paper and pencil. Simplified* means made less complex: *Simplified concepts are useful in textbooks written for children. Simplistic* refers to oversimplification of complex matters by ignoring complexities: *Voters were frightened by the simplistic solutions the President proposed for complex economic problems. Simplistic* condemns; *simple* and *simplified* carry no judgments.

since. Although *since* may be used to mean because, such use requires care. This is because *since* can also refer to time past. Within a sentence, the meanings may be distinguished by use of a comma to indicate because. Time: *He has lived in New*

York since 1960. Cause: *He considers himself a New Yorker, since he moved here many years ago.*

sit. See *set, sit.*

so. *So* is an invaluable adverb in such formulations as *She was so intelligent I was in awe of her.* But when *so* is used as a conjunction—for example, *We were late, so we took a taxi*—a sagging sentence may result. Rewriting invariably produces a stronger construction: *Because we were late, we took a taxi. We took a taxi because we were late.*

someplace, some place. *Someplace* is a poor substitute for the adverb *somewhere: My dog is hiding somewhere* (not *someplace*) *between your house and mine. Some place* refers to an unspecified location: *Some places were still unfilled late in the competition.*

somewhat. See *kind of, sort of.*

sort of. See *kind of, sort of . . .*

specie. *Specie* refers to coined money: *Gold specie is highly valued.* It is not the singular of *species*, which has the same form in the singular and plural: *She wrote her thesis on a rare plant species. Those species are rapidly approaching extinction.*

stationary, stationery. *Stationary* means not moving: *A stationary target is easy to hit with a rifle. Stationery* means writing paper and related items: *My father's stationery store was known throughout the city.*

stayed, stood. *Stayed* is the past tense of *stay: They stayed at the reception long after they should have gone home. We stayed in bed. Stood* is the past tense of *stand: We stood at attention while the anthem was played. The building stood near the town green.*

stimulant, stimulus. A stimulant temporarily arouses organic activity: *According to the article I read, most stimulants are not addictive.* A stimulus causes a response: *Her remark provided the stimulus we needed to complete our project.*

stood. See *stayed, stood.*

such as. The phrase *such as* introduces the listing of a few examples or illustrations: *The children were given a variety of toys, such as dolls, jacks, and board games.* The phrase implies that what follows is an incomplete selection; it is misleading to add *and others* or *and so on* at the end. The same rule applies to any list following *for example.*

such that. Even when correctly used, *such that* leads to awkward and vague sentences: *Their position was such that we could not meet their demands.* Better: *They asked for so much money that we could not come to an agreement. They asked for more money than we could afford. Such that* is not used before a clause that indicates result: *They made a strong protest such that the city changed its policy.* Better: *They made such a strong protest that the city changed its policy. They made so strong a protest that the city changed its policy.*

sure.   *Sure* is an adjective, not an adverb: *One sure way to fail is to neglect your studies. Sure* is not a substitute for *certainly* or *surely: You surely* (not *sure*) *cannot mean that.*

sure and   is a colloquial substitute for *sure to: Be sure to* (not *sure and*) *sit in the bleachers if you want to meet baseball fans who know the game.*

suspicion   is a noun, not a verb: *They suspect* (not *suspicion*) *everything we do. He cannot overcome his suspicion that they want to ease him out of the company.*

swell   is not an acceptable substitute for *good* and similar words except in informal speech: *Johnson's dictionary had a good* (not *swell*) *initial sale. Since I met Lily, I have felt wonderful* (not *swell*).

T

talk to, talk with.   *Talk to* means inform: *Tomorrow I shall talk to the men and women on the assembly line about the new safety regulations. Talk with* means converse: *I want to talk with you about our plans for completing the project.*

teach, learn.   See *learn, teach.*

than, then.   *Than* is a conjunction: *Her work is no better than yours. Then* is an adverb: *I then decided to return to my office and finish some work.*

theirself, theirselves.   See *myself . . .*

their, there.   *Their* is the possessive form of *they: Their taxes were so high that they were* *forced to sell the house. There* is an adverb: *She went there on her own. There* is also an expletive: *There is no use in arguing further.* See also *there is, there are.*

themselves.   See *myself . . .*

there is, there are.   *There is* is followed by a singular: *There is only one shirt at the laundry. There are* is followed by a plural: *There are two shirts and four sheets at the laundry. There is* and *there are* should not be used habitually to start sentences. See also *it is, there is . . .*

these kind, those kind.   See *kind, type.*

thusly.   Since *thus* is an adverb, it does not need the *-ly* ending: *Thus, he was unable to finish the work he had started. Caruso sang the note thus* (not *thusly*).

to, too.   *To* is a preposition: *I gave the package to the receiving clerk. Too* is an adverb: *We found the book too difficult. She is too ill to perform tonight. Too* is not a good substitute for *very: He is not very* (not *too*) *ill.* See also *very.*

try and   is colloquial for *try to: Try to* (not *Try and*) *find the part quickly.*

type.   As a noun, *type* requires the addition of *of* in such expressions as *type of novel: That type of business* (not *type business*) *requires too much capital.* In technical expressions, *type* is often included unnecessarily. *An automatic transmission* (not *automatic-type*) *requires frequent inspec-*

tion. Type is singular, *types* plural: *this type; that type; these types; those types.* See also *kind, type.*

U

unbend, unbending.   The verb *unbend* means relax: *After a long flight, the crew would often unbend in the airport coffee shop before returning home. The crew was unbending in the airport coffee shop.* (In the second example, *was unbending* is in the past progressive tense of *unbend.*) The adjective *unbending* means incapable of compromise: *On questions of personal conduct, the minister was unbending. She was unbending in her insistence on high standards of scholarship.* (In these examples, *unbending* is the complement of *was.*)

underneath.   It is incorrect to follow *underneath* with *of: The beads were underneath* (not *underneath of*) *the table.*

uninterested.   See *disinterested, uninterested.*

unique   means one of a kind. It does not mean unusual. Since few things are unique, the word should be used with care, and modifiers should be used with utmost care: *The helicopter provides unique* (not *most unique* or *very unique*) *air transportation.* Some people or things may be *nearly unique, perhaps unique, probably unique, apparently unique,* and so on, but never *most unique, very unique,* or *entirely unique.*

unless and until.   These three words do no more than the single words *unless* or *until: I* *will not see you again unless* (or *until,* but not *unless and until*) *you send me a written apology.* See also *when, as,* and *if.*

usage. This word is properly used for matters involving customs and standards: *English usage is difficult for the foreign-born.* It is a poor substitute for *use: He noted the increasing use* (not *usage*) *of alcohol among high-school students.*

use, utilize. These words have the same meaning. Why not use the shorter word?

V

various. This word is not followed by *of: Various* (not *Various of*) *useful techniques are being developed. Various* (not *Various of*) *ideas were discussed before the final decision was taken.* Since *various* implies a number of different items, *some, several,* or *certain* may serve better in many sentences: *Several* (not *Various*) *engineers are being considered for promotion.*

verbal, oral. Though the difference between these words is disappearing, their original meanings can be useful. *Verbal* means in spoken or written words: *Her verbal skills are extraordinary in one who is deaf. Oral* means spoken or referring to the mouth: *Oral communication has been made easier by widespread use of the telephone. The dentist told me I would have to consult an oral surgeon.* The sentence *We reached a verbal agreement* unfortunately means only, *We used words to reach an agreement.* Better: *We reached an agreement. We reached a written agree-*

ment. *We reached an oral agreement.* Oral agreements are verbal agreements, but for careful writers and speakers verbal agreements are not necessarily oral.

very. The greatly overused adverb *very* can profitably be omitted as the modifier of an adjective or adverb. In innumerable cases, the word modified is just as strong without *very*. *A very special person* means nothing more than *a special person*. *A very beautiful woman* is no more attractive than *a beautiful woman*. *Tired*, for example, can stand without *very* unless *exhausted, sleepy*, or some other precise meaning—which can be stated—is intended. Though *very pleased* and *very interested* are commonly accepted, *very* should not be used to modify other past participles, such as *defeated* or *used*. *Very nearly defeated* and *very widely used* convey meaning (in these phrases, *very* modifies adverbs), but they can do as well without *very: nearly defeated; widely used*. *Very* is also an adjective: *He decided to visit her on the very day she was to leave for her new job.* See also *unique*.

viable is a currently favored adjective that is used when *practicable* or *workable* is more apt: *We consider the plan a workable* (not *viable*) *solution to our problems*. *Viable* has other meanings that make it appropriate for specialized uses: *A viable organism, for example, is one capable of surviving to maturity.* While *viable* has many applications, we risk overusing it by putting it to petty uses: *The menu you propose for the team dinner is viable*, means that we can afford pork and beans for eleven players and the coach.

W

wait up   is a colloquialism for *wait: She was running so swiftly that I had to ask her
to wait* (not *wait up*) *for me.* Anxious
parents may *wait up* for inconsiderate
children (that is, the parents do not go to
bed before their children come home). See
anxious, eager.

want for.   *Want for* means lack: *I hope we never
want for food and shelter again.* The
phrase is not an acceptable substitute for
want: I want (not *want for*) *you to do the
work right now.*

ways.   *Ways*, the plural of *way*, has many uses:
*She found faster ways of designing the
circuits. I do not like his ways.* It is not a
substitute for *way* in the sense of distance: *We were a long way* (not *ways*)
from home.

when, as, and if   is a useless phrase: *I will see her
when* (or *if*, but not *when, as, and if*) *she
returns.* See also *unless and until.*

where   should not be confused with *that: We read
that* (not *where*) *Italy is changing its monetary policy.*

where . . . at.   This phrase is popular slang in such
sentences as *I didn't know where I was
at*, meaning *It was confused.* This charm-
ing expression must be restricted to informal speech and writing.

whether or not.   *Whether* is usually enough: *I do not
know whether* (not *whether or not*) *he will
be there.* The longer expression can be
used to add emphasis: *I will do this*

whether or not he agrees. I will do this whether he agrees or not.

which.   *Which* refers to things in a nonrestrictive clause: *The coat, which I had worn for eight years, was too shabby to wear any longer. Which* does not refer to people: *Customers who* (not *which*) *pay their bills promptly are given good service. Which* should not be used in a vague sense. In the sentence *I decided to go to the game on the spur of the moment, which I did,* the antecedent of *which* is vague: it can refer to the decision or the trip to the game. Better: *I went to the game on the spur of the moment.*

who, whom.   *Who* is subjective and *whom* is objective, but it is often difficult to determine whether the subjective or objective case is correct. In the sentence *She is the manager (who* or *whom) spoke to us last week,* the correct pronoun is *who* because in the dependent clause *who spoke to us last week,* the pronoun *who* is the subject of the verb *spoke.* In the sentence *I know (who* or *whom) she spoke with yesterday,* the correct pronoun is *whom* because in the dependent clause *whom she spoke with yesterday,* the pronoun *she* is the subject of the verb *spoke,* while the object of the preposition *with* is *whom.* The same rule functions for the relative pronouns *whoever* and *whomever.*

whoever, whomever.   See *who, whom.*

who's, whose.   *Who's* is the contraction of *who is: Do you know who's missing? Guess who's coming to dinner. Whose* is the possessive of *who: Do you know whose book is missing? Whose little boy are you? Whose* refers usually to people: *The convict whose parole has been denied has vowed to fast until death.* See also *contractions.*

will. See *shall, will.*

-wise. Many awkward words are being coined by adding the suffix *-wise* to nouns—*money-wise, opinionwise,* and so on. This suffix does not mean *with respect to,* as such coinages imply. It does mean *in the manner of* or *in the direction of: otherwise, likewise, lengthwise.* In certain expressions the word *wise* is used with the meaning of *having wisdom: streetwise children; penny-wise and pound-foolish.* See also *-ize words:*

would like is a weak substitute for *want: I want* (not *would like*) *you to try milk instead of coffee. Would like for* and *want for* should not be used in place of *want: I want* (not *I would like for* or *want for*) *you to try milk.* See also *lack.*

would of. See *of.*

Y

you know. This expression is frequently used inappropriately as a space-filler in speech, indicating a lack of suitable words. See also *meaningful.*

yourself, yourselves. See *myself* . . .

Dictionary of Grammatical Terms

In constructing sentences, many professional writers tend to rely on their sense of what is right and what is wrong, without being able to explain their constructions in terms of grammar. Nevertheless, it is sometimes helpful to use grammatical terms in explaining the way a sentence works. For your convenience, therefore, the grammatical terms discussed in this text are collected and defined here, along with other terms used by composition teachers.

absolute.   See *comparison.*

absolute phrase.   Phrase closely related in meaning to the rest of a sentence in which it is found, but grammatically independent of it. Absolute phrases occur either before or after an independent clause.

Her marriage ended, Jessica set out for the city to start a new life.

Alfred went slowly toward his truck, the rain falling gently on his head and broad shoulders, scarcely wetting him, reminding him only of the approaching winter. (Three absolute phrases.)

abstract noun, concrete noun. Nouns are classified as abstract or concrete. An abstract noun names an abstraction—a quality, condition, or idea. A concrete noun names things that can be touched, seen, tasted, heard, or smelled.

I enjoy nature. (Abstract.)

I picked up a book and sat in my chair. (Concrete.)

accusative case. See *case; objective case.*

active voice, passive voice. Verbs may be active or passive. A verb in the active voice, also known as an active verb, has a subject that performs the action of the verb. A verb in the passive voice, also known as a passive verb, has a subject that receives the action of the verb.

Larry mailed his law school applications early. (Active.)

His applications were mailed yesterday. (Passive.)

adjective. Word used to modify a noun, pronoun, or verbal.

Fine wine is expensive. (Fine modifies a noun.)

I pity poor you. (Modifies a pronoun.)

She was given a prize for safe driving. (The adjective *safe* modifies a verbal.)

See also *demonstrative adjective; descriptive adjective; interrogative adjective; numerical adjective; possessive adjective; pronominal adjective; proper adjective; relative adjective.*

adjective clause. See *clause.*

adjective phrase. Phrase used as an adjective.

A hot dog in a fresh bun makes a tasty lunch.
(The adjective phrase *in a fresh bun* modifies the
noun phrase *A hot dog.*)

adverb. Word used to modify any part of speech
except a noun or pronoun. An adverb
may also modify an entire clause.

Leave immediately. (*Immediately* modifies a
verb.)

To wait patiently is more than I can manage.
(*Patiently* modifies a verbal.)

I like freshly baked bread. (*Freshly* modifies a
participle.)

The painting was bright red. (*Bright* modifies an
adjective.)

The prisoner sat quite passively. (*Quite* modifies
an adverb.)

Finally he left the room. (*Finally* modifies an
entire clause.)

Many adverbs end in *-ly,* but others do not. To
decide whether a word is an adjective or adverb,
identify the part of speech the word modifies. A
modifier that modifies anything but a noun or
pronoun is an adverb. See also *conjunctive adverb.*

adverb clause. See *clause.*

adverb phrase. Phrase used as an adverb.

Fred moved his car to the other side of the street.
(The adverb phrase *to the other side of the street*
modifies the verb *moved.*)

Before the test, I drank three cups of coffee.
(The adverb phrase *Before the test* modifies the
verb *drank.*)

agreement. A verb must be plural when its subject
is plural, singular when its subject is sin-

gular. When the verb meets this requirement, it is said to agree in number with its subject. A pronoun must be plural when its antecedent is plural, singular when its antecedent is singular. When a pronoun meets this requirement, it is said to agree in number with its antecedent. A pronoun must also agree with its antecedent in person and gender.

Boys and girls swim together in our pool. (Plural verb *swim* agrees in number with plural subject *Boys and girls*.)

A wise person exercises regularly. (Singular verb *exercises* agrees in number with singular subject *person*.)

The women said they would not strike. (Plural pronoun *they* agrees in number with plural antecedent *women*. It also agrees in person, since *women* is third person.)

The dog wagged its tail happily. (Singular pronoun *its* agrees in number with singular antecedent *dog*. It also agrees in person and gender, being third person and neuter.)

Sara said she would not go along with the scheme. (Singular pronoun *she* agrees with antecedent *Sara* in number, person, and gender.)

See also *gender; number; person.*

antecedent.   Word or words to which a pronoun refers.

After Alice finished writing her paper, she joined us for a pizza. (*Alice* is the antecedent of *her* and *she*.)

The tree died before the time the tree surgeon arrived to treat it. (The noun *tree* is the antecedent of *it*.)

See *agreement.*

appositive.   Noun or noun substitute—also known as noun repeater—placed next to another noun or noun substitute to explain or identify it. The appositive, or noun repeater, is said to be in apposition to the first noun or noun substitute.

Mr. Williams, my speech teacher, has helped me improve my diction. (The phrase *my speech teacher* is in apposition to *Mr. Williams.*)

The prosecutor called both of them, the child and her mother, to the stand to give testimony. (The phrase *the child and her mother* is in apposition to *them.*)

article.   Articles function as adjectives. The three articles are *a*, *an*, and *the*. *The* is the definite article; *a* and *an* are the indefinite articles.

auxiliary verb.   Verb used with other verbs to form voice and tense.

Mrs. Jackson was admired by all of us. (Passive voice, *was admired.*)

Mr. Page was pruning his prize shrubs. (Past progressive tense, *was pruning.*)

Commonly used auxiliary verbs are *be*, *can*, *do*, *have*, *may*, *must*, and *should*.

case.   Form of a noun or pronoun that shows its function in a sentence. See *subjective case; possessive case; objective case; possessive case.*

clause.   Group of words containing a subject and verb. Clauses are either independent (main, principal) or dependent (subordinate). An independent clause may stand alone as a complete sentence, but a dependent clause may not. (Dependent clauses stand as complete sentences in formal writing only when an experienced writer chooses to violate the rule in order to achieve a particular effect.) Dependent clauses function as nouns, adjectives, or adverbs. They are also called noun clauses, adjective clauses, and adverb clauses, depending on their use within the sentence.

Dogs make good companions, but many people prefer cats as house pets. (Independent clauses, connected by *but*.)

Whoever is elected will face difficult problems. (*Whoever is elected* is a dependent clause used as noun.)

The cow that dropped its calf last night is out in the high pasture. (*That dropped its calf last night* is a dependent clause used as adjective.)

Gisele does her work when she finds time for it. (*When she finds time for it* is a dependent clause used as adverb.)

collective noun. Noun singular in form but referring to a group. A collective noun is treated as singular when the group is thought of as a unit; it is treated as plural when the members of the group are considered individually.

The minority is too small to make its voice heard. (Collective noun *minority*, thought of as a unit, is treated as singular.)

The majority in our shop are dissatisfied with their working conditions. (Collective noun *majority*, thought of as meaning *more than half the number of individuals*, is treated as plural.)

common noun, proper noun. Nouns are classified as common or proper. A common noun is any member of a class of persons, places, or things. A proper noun is a specific person, place, or thing.

fireman; beach; stone. (Common nouns.)

John McNulty; Ashtabula; Eiffel Tower. (Proper nouns.)

See *abstract noun, concrete noun.*

comparison. Changes in adjectives or adverbs to indicate degrees of quality or amount. Comparison has three degrees: absolute, comparative, and superlative. The comparative degree expresses a greater amount than the absolute when comparing two persons, things, or qualities. The superlative degree expresses the greatest amount when comparing three or more persons, things, or qualities.

Anne is a good sister. She treats her brothers well. (Absolute.)

Fred is a better swimmer than Irv. He strokes better. (Comparative).

Dalmatians make the best firedogs. They run fastest of all breeds. (Superlative.)

complement. Adjective or noun used to complete the meaning of a linking (copulative) verb. Complements are referred to as predicate adjectives or predicate nouns.

My mother felt sick. (Predicate adjective complementing linking verb *felt.*)

Lucy was an accomplished flutist. (Predicate noun complementing linking verb *was.*)

Adjectives or nouns that complement (complete the meaning of) a noun or pronoun are called objective complements.

We find him objectionable. (Adjective acting as objective complement of pronoun *him.*)

They named the secretary chairman as well. (*Chairman* is a noun acting as objective complement of noun *secretary.*)

complex sentence. Sentence consisting of one independent clause plus one or more dependent clauses.

Even though most of the people in our neighborhood are poor, very few are receiving welfare benefits. (Dependent clause followed by independent clause.)

compound sentence. Sentence consisting of two or more independent clauses.

We will do our best to see the film, but I cannot say when. (Two independent clauses connected by *but.*)

compound-complex sentence. Sentence consisting of two or more independent clauses plus one or more dependent clauses.

Companies in our city are discharging their employees, and our people are finding it harder than ever to find work that pays well. (Two independent clauses connected by *and* and followed by the dependent clause *that pays well.*)

concrete noun See *abstract noun.*

conjugation. Change in verb form to indicate person, number, tense, and voice.

conjunction. Word or words that join words, phrases, or clauses.

Coordinating conjunctions join elements of equal value. The most common are *and, or, but, for,* and *yet.*

The boy and girl went home together. (Coordinating conjunction joining two nouns.)

Blue flowers and red flowers often are grouped in striking arrangements. (Coordinating conjunction joining two noun phrases.)

Schools are poorly staffed in some cities, but municipal budgets do not permit aggressive hiring. (Coordinating conjunction joining two independent clauses.)

Subordinating conjunctions join dependent clauses with independent clauses. The most common are *although, as, because, since, when,* and *where.*

We no longer see much of our neighbors, because we are so busy. (Independent clause followed by dependent clause and joined by subordinating conjunction.)

All we get are squirrels, although we put out excellent bird food. (Independent clause followed by dependent clause and joined by subordinating conjunction.)

conjunctive adverb.   Adverb used as a conjunction to connect independent clauses. The most common conjunctive adverbs are *however, therefore,* and *thus.*

Their proposal contained sufficient information to satisfy even the most demanding; however, many other companies submitted more detailed documents.

coordinating conjunction.   See *conjunction.*

copulative verb.   See *linking verb.*

declension.   Change in the form of a noun or pronoun to show number, gender, and case.

definite article.   See *article.*

demonstrative adjective. Adjective that modifies and identifies a specific noun or pronoun.

this theme; that opera; these companies; those rivers.

For further examples of demonstrative adjectives, see *demonstrative pronoun.*

demonstrative pronoun. Pronoun that refers to a specific antecedent. The demonstrative pronouns have the same form as the demonstrative adjectives but, unlike the adjectives, do not modify.

This is just what I want. (The antecedent of *This* is a noun understood by the writer and the reader of the sentence.)

That will no longer be available in all colors.

The demonstrative pronouns (and adjectives) are *this, that, these, those, the former, the latter, the first, the second,* and so on.

dependent clause. See *clause.*

descriptive adjective. Adjective that names a condition or quality of the noun it modifies.

purple prose; gray skies; disheveled dress; torn shirt.

direct address. Construction in which a writer addresses the reader directly, using the listener or the reader's name or an appropriate pronoun.

George, please forget the past.

If you will fold your papers and sign your names, you may leave the examination hall.

Stop working now. (*You* is understood.)

direct object.   Word or words that receive the action of a verb.

> *They found their wallets.* (*Wallets* is the direct object of *found*.)

> *The cat ate its food.* (*Food* is the direct object of *ate*.)

See also *indirect object*.

direct quotation.   Word-for-word quotation of a written or spoken message.

> *"Give me one more chance," the boy pleaded.*

Even when words are omitted, a quotation is considered direct as long as the omission is indicated and the words supplied are those of the original.

> *"Fourscore and seven years ago, our fathers brought forth . . . a new nation. . . ."*

See also *indirect quotation*.

ellipsis.   Incomplete expression readily completed by a reader. Also called elliptical expression.

> War and Peace *is much longer than most other novels.* (The missing word is *are*, which is understood after *novels*.)

Ellipsis is also a mark of punctuation (. . .) used to indicate that material has been omitted deliberately from a direct quotation.

> *"In the beginning there was. . . ."*

expletive.   The grammatical term designating *it* and *there* when these words function only to open sentences. Expletives have no meaning; they are merely introductory words.

It is later than you think. (*It is* is merely a convenient way to open the sentence.)

There are too many unanswered questions in this investigation.

finite verb. Verb that can serve as the predicate of a clause or sentence. In this book, *verb* is used in place of *finite verb.* See also *verb; verbals; verb phrase.*

gender. Masculine, feminine, and neuter. The gender of pronouns is shown in the third person singular—*he, she, it; him, her, it; his, hers, its.* A few nouns also have gender—for example *host, hostess; actor, actress.* Ships and airplanes are often treated as feminine.

The ship lost her (or *its*) *mast twenty miles out.*

The cat licked its paws.

A boy who loves his mother tries to be kind to her.

See also *agreement.*

genitive case. See *case; possessive case.*

gerund. Verb form ending in *-ing* and functioning as a noun, not as a verb. Gerunds are classified as verbals.

Loafing can be productive. (Gerund as subject.)

Eunice loved skiing. (Gerund as object.)

I am no longer interested in cooking. (Gerund as object of preposition.)

Gerunds have the same form as present participles but are distinguished from them by function. See also *participle; verbal.*

gerund phrase. Phrase containing a gerund and functioning as a noun.

> *Antihistamines are generally the best remedy for summer sneezing.*

> *In selecting a new automobile, the couple paid careful attention to fuel economy.*

imperative mood. Verb form used in giving commands.

> *Stop now and think.*

See also *mood.*

indefinite article. See *article.*

indefinite pronoun. Pronoun without a specific antecedent.

> *Anyone can learn to swim.*

> *Everyone wants a secure life.*

independent clause. See *clause.*

indicative mood. Verb form used to make a statement or ask a question.

> *Antoinette swims every day.*

> *Is Sven working this winter?*

See also *mood.*

indirect object. Noun or pronoun receiving the direct object of a verb.

> *They told me tall stories.* (The indirect object *me* receives the direct object *stories.*)

> *They gave their car good care.* (The indirect object *car* receives the direct object *care.*)

See also *direct object.*

indirect quotation. Quotations summarized or paraphrased, not given word for word.

> *The secretary said that he was not interested in working for us any longer.*

See also *direct quotation.*

infinitive. Form of a verb that functions as noun, adjective, or adverb. An infinitive, which is a verbal, does not function as a verb. An infinitive is usually preceded by *to.*

> *She loves to study.* (Infinitive functioning as noun, object of *loves.*)

> *The actress has many lines to memorize.* (Infinitive functioning as adjective, modifying *lines.*)

> *Arnold has come here to help.* (Infinitive functioning as adverb, modifying *has come.*)

See also *infinitive phrase; verbal.*

infinitive phrase. Infinitive plus its modifiers and object. Infinitive phrases have the same functions as infinitives.

> *He refused to read a book during lunch.* (Infinitive phrase functioning as noun, object of *refused.*)

> *He wants a magazine to look at on the train.* (Infinitive phrase functioning as adjective, modifying *magazine.*)

> *Her mother traveled to pass time.* (Infinitive phrase functioning as adverb, modifying *traveled.*)

inflection. Change in the form of a word to indicate grammatical relation. Inflections include declension, conjugation, and comparison. Declension is the inflection of nouns and pronouns. Conjugation is the inflection of verbs. Comparison is the inflection of adverbs and adjectives. See *comparison; conjugation; declension.*

intensive pronoun. Pronoun that strengthens a noun or pronoun.

The adviser himself did not know the benefits I could obtain.

The cat itself caused the accident.

They themselves are to blame for the confusion.

The intensive pronouns are formed by adding *-self* or *-selves* to the appropriate personal pronoun.

interjection. Exclamatory expression with no grammatical relation to a sentence in which it occurs.

Gosh, is she really that sick?

My, I had no idea.

interrogative adjective. Adjective used in asking a question.

Whose hat was taken? (Whose modifies hat.)

Which way should we proceed? (Which modifies way.)

interrogative pronoun. Pronoun used in asking a question. Many interrogative pronouns are the same words that are used as interrogative adjectives, for example, *whose, which,* and *what,* but function as pronouns rather than as adjectives.

Whose was taken? (Whose is the subject of was taken.)

Which is correct? (Which is the subject of is.)

intransitive verb.   Verb that does not take an object.

> *They worried all through the night.*
>
> *Thomas ran as fast as he could.*

See also *linking verb; transitive verb.*

irregular verb   (also called *strong verb*). Verb that forms past tense and past participle by a change of vowel—for example, *begin, began, begun.*

linking verb   (also called *copulative verb*). Verb that links its subject and complement.

> *She is ill.* (Verb *is* links subject *She* with complement *ill.*)
>
> *Oscar was a butcher for many years.* (Verb *was* links subject *Oscar* with complement *butcher.*)

An adjective serving as complement of a linking verb is called a predicate adjective. A noun serving as complement of a linking verb is called a predicate noun. See also *complement; predicate.*

main clause.   See *clause.*

modifier.   Word or words that limit, describe, or make more precise the meaning of the word or words modified.

> *A new pair of shoes can be uncomfortable for days.* (The adjective *new* modifies *pair.*)
>
> *Alice wept silently.* (The adverb *silently* modifies *wept.*)

See also *nonrestrictive modifier; restrictive modifier.*

mood.   Form of a verb that shows whether a statement is thought of as fact, command, wish, or condition contrary to fact. See also *imperative mood; indicative mood; subjunctive mood.*

nominative case. See *case; subjective case.*

nonrestrictive modifier. Modifier of word or words already limited (restricted) to a single member of a group or class. Nonrestrictive modifiers can be omitted from a sentence without substantially altering meaning, because the reader already has sufficient information to understand who or what is being discussed.

My dog, which has been sick for weeks, is beginning to recover. (*My* is a restrictive modifier in this sentence. It limits all dogs one could possibly think of to the one dog I own. The nonrestrictive modifier *which . . . weeks* can be omitted from the sentence without substantially altering meaning.)

See also *restrictive modifier.*

noun. Person, place, thing, quality, action, or idea functioning as subject, object, object of a preposition, and so on. A noun substitute is any other word that can perform the functions of a noun in a sentence. Noun substitutes include pronouns, gerunds, and noun phrases and clauses. See also *abstract noun, concrete noun; collective noun; common noun, proper noun.*

noun clause. See *clause.*

noun phrase. Phrase functioning as noun.

Shuttle flights to Washington have become expensive. (Noun phrase functioning as subject of *have become.*)

noun repeater. See *appositive*.

noun substitute. See *noun*.

number. Characteristic of nouns, pronouns, and verbs that shows whether they are singular or plural.

She admires good books. (*She* is singular, *admires* is singular, *books* is plural.)

Elephants move slowly as they graze. (*Elephants* is plural, *move* is plural, *they* is plural, *graze* is plural.)

See also *agreement*.

numerical adjective. Adjective that assigns a number to the noun it modifies. Numerical adjectives may be cardinal (indicating quantity) or ordinal (indicating order).

Some homes have two fireplaces. (Cardinal.)

Can you remember your first love? (Ordinal.)

object. See *direct object; indirect object; object of a preposition*.

objective case (also called *accusative case*). Form of a pronoun showing that the pronoun is a direct object, indirect object, or object of a preposition.

The bat hurt me. (Direct object of *hurt*.)

Has the bursar given them the money? (Indirect object of *Has given*.)

The social worker found an apartment for her. (Object of preposition *for*.)

objective complement. See *complement*.

object of a preposition. Noun, pronoun, or noun substitute that follows a preposition.

We distributed the candy to them.

We looked at the painting.

parallel construction. Repetition of grammatical pattern to achieve coherence (logical relation) and emphasis.

Government of the people, by the people, and for the people. (Three prepositional phrases in which only the preposition changes.)

participle. Adjective form derived from a verb. Present participles end in *-ing—coughing, swimming,* and the like. Past participles usually end in *-ed* if the verb is regular—such as *exhausted, permitted.* The past participles of irregular verbs usually show changes in vowels in addition to changes in endings—for example, *catch, caught; spring, sprung; lose, lost; do, done.* Participles are verbals. They have the same form as gerunds, and only the difference in use distinguishes one from the other.

No one wears a smoking jacket in our circle. (Present participle modifying *jacket.*)

You act like a trapped animal. (Past participle modifying *animal.*)

See also *gerund.*

participle phrase. Phrase (also called *participial phrase*) containing a participle and functioning as an adjective.

The painting hanging on the south wall has won first prize. (Participle phrase *hanging on the south wall,* modifying *painting.*)

I will not take seriously anything said by him. (Participle phrase *said by him*, modifying *anything*.)

See also *phrase*.

passive voice. See *active voice, passive voice*.

person. Form of a pronoun or verb that indicates whether a person or other subject is speaking (first person), spoken to (second person), or spoken about (third person).

I am content. We walk slowly. (First person.)

You are mistaken. (Second person.)

He finds her difficult? She does not care. They are friends. The lion roars to show its anger. It quickly follows its prey. (Third person.)

See also *agreement*.

personal pronoun. Pronoun indicating people: *I, you, he, she,* and so forth.

phrase. Group of words lacking subject and verb and used to perform a single function within a sentence. See *adjective phrase; gerund phrase; infinitive phrase; noun phrase; participle phrase; prepositional phrase*.

possessive adjective. Adjective indicating possession: *my, your, its, her,* and the like.

My hat was ruined in the rain. (*My* modifies *hat*.)

Their concert brought a great deal of money to the charity. (*Their* modifies *concert*.)

possessive case (also called *genitive case*). Form of a noun or pronoun that shows possession. Pronouns in the possessive case resemble possessive adjectives but do not modify. Possessive adjectives modify.

Mine withstood the rain well. (Possessive pronoun functioning as subject of verb *withstood*.)

Jane's gave me no protection. (Possessive noun functioning as subject of verb *gave*.)

See also *possessive adjective*.

predicate. Full verb plus all its modifiers and objects or complements.

My daughter has completed three years of medical school. (The verb in this sentence is *has completed*. The predicate is *has completed three years of medical school*.)

She feels well in the morning. (The verb in this sentence is *feels*. The predicate is *feels well in the morning*.)

predicate adjective. See *complement*.

predicate noun. See *complement*.

preposition. Word or words that show the relation of a noun or pronoun to another word. Prepositions carry meanings of direction, position, time, or other abstractions. Some common prepositions are *toward*, *in*, *of*, and *during*.

They went quickly toward the burning building.

We will put the bicycles in the building.

We drive home in record time during vacations.

prepositional phrase. Phrase introduced by a preposition and functioning as a modifier.

Our friends want to leave after dinner. (After dinner modifies *leave*.)

A book without a cover will not last long. (Without a cover modifies *book*.)

principal clause. See *clause*.

principal parts of a verb. Infinitive, past tense, and past participle: *lift, lifted, lifted; see, saw, seen; ride, rode, ridden;* and the like. All tenses of a verb are formed from its principal parts. See also *progressive tenses; tense*.

progressive tenses. Verb tenses that express continuing action or state of being.

I am studying French. (Present progressive, active voice.)

Music is being played today. (Present progressive, passive voice.)

She will be singing tonight. (Future progressive, active voice.)

Frieda was paying close attention. (Past progressive, active voice.)

Money was being spent needlessly. (Past progressive, passive voice.)

You have been annoying Dolores. (Present perfect progressive, active voice.)

I will have been sitting here long enough by then. (Future perfect progressive, active voice.)

She had been phoning regularly until she lost her job. (Past perfect progressive, active voice.)

See also *active voice, passive voice; tense*.

pronominal adjective. Adjective that has the form of a pronoun but functions as a modifier, such as *my, our,* and *whose.* See also *relative adjective.*

pronoun. Word that takes the place of a noun. See also *demonstrative pronoun; indefinite pronoun; intensive pronoun; interrogative pronoun; personal pronoun; reciprocal pronoun; relative pronoun.*

proper adjective. Adjective formed from a proper noun.

Chinese cooking; French cuisine; English food.

proper noun. See *common noun, proper noun.*

reciprocal pronoun. Pronoun such as *one another* or *each other,* used as the direct object of a verb, indirect object, or object of a preposition.

We helped one another in every way. (Direct object of *helped.*)

They gave one another much encouragement. (Indirect object receiving the direct object *encouragement.*)

Emma and Dick spoke to one another frequently. (Object of preposition *to.*)

regular verb (also called *weak verb*). Verb that forms past tense and past participle by adding *-ed, -d,* or *-t.*

stayed; heard; slept.

relative adjective. Adjective that has the form of a pronoun and serves to introduce a dependent clause (also known as a *relative clause*) that functions as an adjective clause.

A mother whose children are grown can devote herself to her career. (The relative adjective *whose* introduces the relative clause *whose children are grown.* The relative clause modifies *mother.*)

See also *relative pronoun; clause; pronominal adjective.*

relative pronoun.   Pronoun introducing a dependent clause.

Some children who hate school succeed nevertheless. (The relative pronoun *who* introduces the dependent clause *who hate school* and serves as subject of the verb *hate.*)

restrictive modifier.   Modifier that limits or restricts a word or group of words and is therefore essential to the sentence. Omission of a restrictive modifier can substantially change the meaning of a sentence.

Your hat is soiled. (Without the word *Your*, the reader does not understand this sentence.)

The house I used to live in has burned to the ground. (Without the clause *I used to live in*, the reader does not understand the writer's intent in this sentence.)

The year before last was the best of my life. (Without the phrase *before last*, the reader does not know which year the writer has in mind.)

See also *nonrestrictive modifier.*

sentence.   Group of words normally including a subject and verb and expressing an assertion, command, exclamation, question, or wish. See also *complex sentence; compound sentence; compound-complex sentence; sentence fragment; simple sentence.*

sentence fragment. Sentence lacking a subject or verb or both. Sentence fragments can be used with success by skilled writers.

simple sentence. Sentence consisting of a single independent clause.

> *Telephones give us rapid communication.*

> *The oldest man here has just celebrated his hundredth birthday.*

strong verb. See *irregular verb*.

subject. Element of a sentence performing the action indicated by an active verb; element receiving the action of a passive verb.

> *Norma works crossword puzzles easily.* (*Norma* is subject of active verb *works*.)

> *The disclaimer was received this morning.* (*Disclaimer* is subject of passive verb *was received*.)

Intransitive verbs and linking verbs also have subjects.

> *The army marched all night.* (*Army* is subject of intransitive verb *marched*.)

> *Many were cooks in civilian life.* (*Many* is subject of linking verb *were*.)

Infinitives may also have subjects.

> *Hugh asked Tony to help him.* (*Tony* is subject of infinitive *to help*.)

See also *active verb, passive verb*.

subjective case (also called *nominative case*). Form of a pronoun showing that the pronoun is the subject of a verb.

She soon will find a job. (*She* is subject of *will find.*)

The pronoun *who* is in the subjective case. (The objective case of *who* is *whom.*)

Who stole my soap? (Subject of *stole.*)

I want a teacher who will not overload me with work. (Subject of *will overload.*)

subjunctive mood. Verb form used to express doubts, desires, conditions contrary to fact, and possibilities.

I wonder whether you want to learn. (Doubt.)

If he were still in charge, things would be worse. (Condition contrary to fact: he is, in fact, not in charge.)

I wish that she were here. (She is not.)

See also *mood.*

subordinate clause. See *clause.*

subordinating conjunction. See *conjunction.*

substantive. Word or group of words that functions as a noun. *When he awoke* was impossible to say.

superlative. See *comparison.*

tense. Change in verb form to show when an action is, was, or will be performed. The tenses are present, past, future, present perfect, past perfect, and future perfect.

I take. (Present.)

I took. (Past.)

I will take. (Future.)

I have taken. (Present perfect.)

I had taken. (Past perfect.)

I will have taken. (Future perfect.)

See also *progressive tenses.*

transitive verb.   Verb that takes an object or is passive.

> *The finch fed its young.* (The noun *young* is the object of the transitive verb *fed.*)

> *The fledglings were fed by our neighbor.* (The verb *were fed* is passive.)

See also *linking verb; intransitive verb.*

verb.   Word or words that express action or state of being of a subject.

> *Reservoirs* supply *drinking water to city residents.*

> *They no longer* are paying *their church dues.*

> *We* have been studying *Japanese for many years.*

See also *auxiliary verb; linking verb; intransitive verb; irregular verb; transitive verb; mood; tense.*

verbal.   Word derived from a verb but performing the function of a noun or modifier. See also *gerund; infinitive; participle.*

verb phrase.   Group of words forming a verb.

> *The helicopter* has been *fully* developed *in the United States.*

> *We* would have called *you if we* had known *you were sick.* (Of the three verbs in this sentence, the first two are verb phrases.)

voice.   Characteristic of a verb that indicates whether the subject is performing or receiving the action of the verb. See *active voice, passive voice.*

weak verb.   See *regular verb.*

Index

EUGENE EHRLICH

Eugene Ehrlich is Senior Lecturer in the Department of English and Comparative Literature at Columbia University. He is chief editor of the OXFORD AMERICAN DICTIONARY, co-author with Gorton Carruth of THE OXFORD ILLUSTRATED LITERARY GUIDE TO THE UNITED STATES, author of AMO, AMAS, AMAT AND MORE, co-author with Daniel Murphy of WRITING AND RESEARCHING TERM PAPERS AND REPORTS, and author of many other books.

Bantam Guides to Better English Usage

☐ 25552 THE BANTAM CONCISE
HANDBOOK OF ENGLISH $3.95
An inexpensive handbook to better English usage with more, easy-to-use advice on how to write clearly and effectively. The Bantam Handbook includes complete information on technical and business writing.

☐ 23933 THE BANTAM INSTANT SPELLING
HANDBOOK $3.95
The Bantam Instant Spelling Handbook provides a comprehensive, easy-to-use list of over 20,000 words. It also offers special sections on basic spelling rules, a list of commonly misspelled words, a list of commonly confused words with their definitions, and memory games to help you remember easily words with difficult spellings.

Bantam has a complete reference library to fill your needs:

☐ 24145 THE BANTAM BOOK OF CORRECT
LETTER WRITING $3.95
☐ 14344 BUSINESS WRITING HANDBOOK $3.95
☐ 24108 WRITER'S SURVIVAL MANUAL $3.95
☐ 26079 WRITING & RESEARCHING TERM
PAPERS $3.50
☐ 22695 WRITING IN GENERAL/THE SHORT
STORY IN PARTICULAR $2.95